BLETCHLEY

AN INMATE'S STORY

by

JAMES THIRSK

B
M & M BALDWIN
Cleobury Mortimer, Shropshire
2012

By the same author
A Beverley Child's Great War
Boyhood in Beverley: a mosaic of the 1920s

*This book was originally published by
Galago Publishing Ltd in 2008.
This new edition is published by*
M & M BALDWIN
24 High Street, Cleobury Mortimer
Kidderminster DY14 8BY

© James Wood Thirsk, 2008, 2012

ISBN 978-0-947712-47-1

All rights reserved.
No part of this publication may be reproduced or
transmitted in any form, or by any means,
electronic, optical or mechanical, including photocopy,
recording or any information storage system,
without the prior written permission
of the copyright owner.

Printed and bound by
MPG Biddles Ltd
24 Rollesby Road
Hardwick Industrial Estate
King's Lynn   PE30 4LS

Contents

Foreword by Professor Helen S. Wallace
      CMG, PhD, FBA (Lady Wallace of Saltaire)   5

Acknowledgements   7

Introduction   9

Abbreviations   11

CHAPTER
1. Soldiering before Bletchley   13
2. Interviews in London   17
3. On the way to BP   19
4. The Park   23
5. Recruiting   27
6. Civilian Billets   39
7. The Listeners   41
8. A Log-reader's Tale   47
9. The Fusion Room   51
10. Careless Talk   55
11. The Three Js   57
12. The Geese and Others who Cackled   61
13. The Poets of Bletchley Park   69
14. Shenley Road Military Camp   77
15. The Lucy Ring   83
16. War's End   89

OLLA PODRIDA   93

BIOGRAPHIES - A-Z   113

Bletchley Park Traffic Flow Diagram   188

Index   189

Now in his 99th year, Jimmy Thirsk lives with his wife Joan in part of the remains of Hadlow Castle, a neo-Gothic building in the Weald of Kent. After infantry training in the King's Own Royal Regiment, and a spell with the Royal Artillery Maritime Regiment, Jimmy served at Bletchley Park, in the Intelligence Corps, from 1942 until the end of the war with Germany. In a department known as SIXTA he was a traffic analyst, or log reader, examining the logs arriving from the intercept stations, that recorded every scrap of radio traffic other than the encrypted messages. By this means a picture of German units emerged, with their positions located by Direction-Finding techniques. His future wife, Joan Watkins, an ATS subaltern fluent in German, worked across the corridor in the 'Fusion Room', examining in great detail the contents of messages that had been decrypted by Hut 6. The fusion of Intelligence provided by Jimmy and his fellow log readers, with the Intelligence gleaned from the messages by Joan and her colleagues, provided an almost complete picture of the activities of the German army and air force. Gordon Welchman, a former Head of Hut 6, claimed in his book *The Hut Six Story* that we had a 'more detailed knowledge of the entire communication system that handled Enigma traffic, than anyone in Germany'.

Already a librarian when he joined the army in 1940, Jimmy had worked in seven different libraries by the time he retired in 1974 from the post of District Librarian, Acton Library, London Borough of Ealing.

Foreword

It is hard to overestimate the part played during the second world war by Bletchley Park (BP to its residents), yet somehow it remains a challenge to convey just what BP involved and just what the contributions were of the many people who worked there, clothed in secrecy. The increasingly well-documented story of BP is about the role of gifted cryptographers, linguists and military analysts in cracking many of the German military codes in ways that hugely helped the allies in pursuing the war against Nazi Germany. What is also well known is that the people who served there (with very few exceptions) kept the secret of what they were doing, not only at the time, but for decades afterwards. Yet what is rather less known is who those people were and what life was like for them during their period of service there. This splendid volume opens our eyes to the people as human beings who, often by quirks of chance, found themselves catapulted into this very esoteric version of intense and intensive service. Jimmy Thirsk has drawn together his own recollections and those of many of his close friends and colleagues, as well as those of his wife whom he met while working at BP. These recollections provide a vivid and poignant portrait of this very special experience of wartime collaboration in the best sense of close working together in a common cause yet under the cloak of secrecy.

It is a particular pleasure for me to write these few words of foreword. I am a child of Bletchley, born just after the war of parents, both linguists, who had worked together in the Fusion Room, described in Chapter 9. As small children my sister and I were told by our parents that they had 'painted spots on rocking horses' during the war. They spoke German to each other when they did not want us to understand something, although it was only much later that I realised just what strange German they spoke, peppered with both military vocabulary and those odd inventions of Nazi purists determined to rid their language of *Fremdwörter*. Our childhood was also marked by the arrival of friends of our parents who had also painted spots on rocking horses, always showing the warmth of very special friends who had shared very special experiences.

It was not until the mid-1970s that the rocking horses were transformed into code-breaking and analysis, and then we began to hear more substantial reminiscences. Sadly, our father Edward Rushworth, died in 1975, soon after the secrets of BP became generally known, through the publication in 1974 of Winterbotham's book, *The Ultra Secret*. I gathered enough to know that my father's passion for maps and his great gift for lateral thinking (shared by many colleagues at BP), stood him in good stead in figuring out, from one or other military unit, what some of the critical troop movements meant.

Our mother, Joyce Robinson, was one of a group of talented women working in the Fusion Room, one of the 'Three Js' of Chapter 11. Most of them were the first generation of women from their families to have had the chance to go to university (in some cases deferred until after the war was over), although Margaret Pope, later Phillips, stands out in my memory for having gone to the same degree-awarding ceremony as her mother and grandmother when the University of Cambridge eventually decided that women could indeed become graduates. Those talented women enjoyed a special opportunity to be professionally adept in what seems to have been a remarkably egalitarian working environment – splendid role models for their daughters. Yet it was easier for the women to disguise what they did at the time – our mother used to explain plausibly that she was a telephonist doing shift work.

As Jimmy Thirsk's select biographies in this volume record, the BP people went on to do many very different things in their subsequent professional and personal lives. A few remained in military or intelligence service, but most of them picked up their lives again in civvy street and firmly put away into closed boxes in their heads their recollections and their experiences. Some sixty years later some of those boxes have been opened to a wider audience. They make fascinating reading both as an insight into that special experience at BP and as an example of the skill that can be demonstrated in composing a multi-disciplinary and talented team for achieving what the Germans believed impossible – the cracking of the Enigma and Fish ciphers.

HELEN WALLACE

Acknowledgements

I wish to thank many people for their help, information and encouragement, some of whom read chapters of my book:-

My wife Joan, who was at Bletchley Park from 1942-1945, read all my book, corrected my grammatical errors and curbed my wilder fantasies; my daughter Jane Robinson; my cousin Valerie Trueblood; Lisa Hunt; Ralph Erskine; Michael Smith; Alfred Sugar (a fellow-worker at BP); Jean Wallwork, née Davies (one of the three Js mentioned in chapter 11); the late Joyce Rushworth (née Robinson, another J); Geoff Gardner and Allan Goodlet, former library colleagues; Rowland Grimes; Ann Baer, Peter Calvocoressi; John Gallehawk; Jonathan Bush; Janey Goddard; George Peters; Joyce Hewitt (née Peasegood); Hester Robinson; Janet Tourniere; Neil Webster's widow Elizabeth; Betty Webb (née Vine-Stevens); my sisters Betty Thirsk and Jean Blackburn, both of whom read most of my book, making helpful comments; and Mrs Morfudd Rees-Clark (Morfudd Rhys at BP). My son Martin showed great patience when solving computer problems, often put to him at short notice, by telephone. He also prepared the photographs ready for printing. I give special thanks to Jean Hyons (née Seabury), probably the youngest person to have worked at Bletchley Park during the war. I thank Mrs Margaret Sale for allowing me to copy the photograph of Colossus. Mrs Jean Sugar gladly let me use the photograph of her husband, Alfred, age 100

Thanks also to those who generously allowed me to include passages from their books: Aileen Clayton (née Morris), the WAAF author of *The Enemy is Listening* (Hutchinson, 1980); Iris M. Owen, author of *So Many Lives* (Toronto, 2000) ; and Len Moore, author of *Z17* (1966); and the Editor of *The Oxford Dictionary of National Biography* (ODNB). Thanks also to Sgt M.C Knowles who wrote the witty poem about Shenley Road Military Camp. I thank warmly Liz Hall for her work on my manuscript, and Tony Stiff, the publisher.

Finally, my thanks to Professor Helen Wallace for her foreword.

Introduction

Although, as I show in chapter 12 of this book, some of the secrets of Bletchley Park were revealed before 1974, it was not until the publication in that year of Group-Captain Winterbotham's book, *The Ultra Secret*, that it became widely known that Bletchley Park, a country house in Buckinghamshire, about fifty miles north of London, was the British cryptographic centre where many enemy ciphers were broken throughout World War II.

Looking back, and more than sixty years have gone by since I left BP, as we inmates used to call it, I often thought of comparing the activities of the thousands who worked there with those in a beehive. But although the honey produced there was excellent and became more and more appreciated by the commanders in the field, there are two serious objections to this comparison: there was no Queen-bee in charge, only two elderly naval officers in succession, Commanders Denniston and Travis. Also, although we were busy in our hives, we did, unlike the bees, enjoy days off duty.

What is remarkable is that very few of the thousands of inmates revealed their secrets before 1974. Some of them died without even telling their spouses and children what they had been doing at BP. Since Winterbotham's revelations there have been many books about the intelligence gleaned from decrypted enemy messages, how it was used by allied commanders and how it affected the outcome of battles. Other books have concentrated on the technical aspects of decryption including the early successes of the Polish, French and British mathematicians who penetrated the complicated German Enigma cipher machine. But apart from chapters by former inmates in such books as *Codebreakers, the inside story of Bletchley Park*, edited by Harry Hinsley and Alan Stripp (OUP, 1994) and *Action this Day*, edited by Ralph Erskine and Michael Smith (Bantam Press, 2001), few books by men and women who worked at BP during the war have been published. Michael Smith, in his book *Station X: the Codebreakers of Bletchley Park* (Channel 4 Books, 1998), did include interesting personal memories by many different people. So here is my story, that of an inmate who was a small bee in the Bletchley hive.

Although memories fade, I hope that I have captured in this book something of the atmosphere of BP, and brought back memories to those of my fellow inmates who have survived. Alas! Most of them have died and those who remain are in their eighties and nineties. One of my fellow log-readers, Alfred Sugar, died in his 101st year in 2007.

How remarkable it was that, from small beginnings, Bletchley Park grew to be a massive and successful intelligence service, run without rigid rules or formal structure. How admirable it was that here were thousands of men and women working side by side, with a common goal, in a democratic community, completely without the traditional discipline that was usual in the three services.

JIMMY THIRSK

Abbreviations

ATS	Auxiliary Territorial Service (the British Women's army), later renamed The Women's Royal Army Corps. Pronounced ats as in hats
BP	Bletchley Park, always referred to by inmates by the two letters
'C'	The head of the British secret service
CSM	Company Sergeant-Major
DF	Direction finding, used to locate enemy radio communications
DNB	The Dictionary of National Biography
GAF	The German Air Force (Luftwaffe)
GC&CS	The Government Code & Cipher School
GCHQ	Government Communications Headquarters, the later name for GC&CS
MI5	The security service dealing with operations within Great Britain
MI6	The British Secret Intelligence Service which gathered Intelligence abroad
MI8	Military intelligence dealing with signals and Communications
NCO	Non-commissioned Officer
ODNB	The Oxford Dictionary of National Biography
OKH	Oberkommando des Heeres (The German army High Command)
OKL	Oberkommando der Luftwaffe (High command of the German air force)
OKM	Oberkommando der Kriegsmarine (High command of the German navy)
OKW	Oberkommando der Wehrmacht (The German supreme command of the army, the navy and the air force).

RAF	The Royal Air Force
RN	The Royal Navy
RSM	Regimental Sergeant-Major
SIGINT	Signals intelligence, covering interception, decryption and interpretation
SIXTA	The traffic analysis section, attached to Hut 6
SLU	Special Liaison Unit
SOE	Special Operations Executive
TA	Traffic analysis, a method of deriving information about the enemy by studying his networks, callsigns, frequencies and chit-chat
V1	German flying bomb, popularly known as the doodle-bug
V2	German long-range rocket. The German name for V1 and V2 was Vergeltungswaffe (reprisal weapons)
WAAF	The women's auxiliary air force, which after the war became the Women's Royal Air Force. WAAF, whether referring to the service or to an individual was pronounced with the short 'a' as in d<u>a</u>ffodil
W/T	Wireless telegraphy
WRNS	The Women's Royal Naval Service. A woman in this service was referred to as a Wren
WVS	Women's Voluntary Service which later became the Women's Royal Voluntary Service
YMCA	Young Men's Christian Association

1

SOLDIERING BEFORE BLETCHLEY

Unlike those who came to Bletchley Park direct from university or school, my journey there was tortuous. When I was called up into the army in September 1940 I was a 26 year-old librarian at Great Harwood, in charge of a branch of the Lancashire County Libraries. Three months of infantry training in *The King's Own Royal Regiment,* at a camp on the outskirts of Birmingham, was hell for those who, like me, were not used to hard physical exercise. 'Wait till you get to Libya' was the only comfort our tough platoon sergeant could offer. But the army had other plans. At the beginning of the war all British merchant ships were armed with mounted guns mainly suitable for firing at low-flying enemy aircraft. At first, men from the Royal Navy manned these guns, but when Winston Churchill was told in 1940 that not enough naval men were available, he ordered men from the infantry to be trained in naval gunnery and transferred to *The Royal Artillery (Maritime Regiment).*

Having completed our infantry training, a random collection of about thirty of us was dispatched, without any choice in the matter, to a naval gunnery school at Hull, my native city. One month later, having celebrated the end of the course by firing a six-inch gun out to sea from Kilnsea, a desolate place on the East Yorkshire coast, we moved to Liverpool as qualified port-gunners. Six soldiers were placed on each of the many ships in port, but only four had to be present on board to man the gun. Two of us could go ashore for twenty-four hours in turn. When the sirens warned of approaching bombers we went to the gun deck to set out the shells close to hand. There we sat, sometimes all night, hoping that the Germans would not unload their bombs on our dock. We listened to exploding bombs and sometimes we could hear the hiss of hot shrapnel as it hit the water in the dock. Only the captain of the ship could give orders to fire the gun; this he never did, for our gun was only suitable for firing at low-flying aircraft. Our shells would probably have landed on houses near the docks. On shore, the much more powerful anti-aircraft guns of the Royal Artillery attempted to destroy raiding German bombers, while we sat helpless on the gun-deck, waiting for the sirens to sound the all-clear.

Life was pleasant on the ships in which I served, except for the sleepless nights during raids. Sometimes we were on board for a fortnight or three weeks, with no bombardiers or sergeants ordering us about; we were just four gunners enjoying watching the ever-changing dockland activities – the unloading of cargoes, followed by the loading of goods or armaments for export. We appreciated the meals provided by the ships' cooks, most of whom could work miracles with the army rations delivered daily by truck. It was a life any soldier would have envied. One ship we were on was unloading hundreds of sacks of shelled peanuts from India, destined we imagined for the margarine factories. We had our fill of them, for some of the sacks tore open as they unloaded them. One morning the truck driver brought our mail. For me there was a parcel from home. Mother had enclosed a Mars bar and a small packet of peanuts.

One day when the truck driver arrived with our rations he said he had been told to take Gunner Thirsk back to the battery office, which was housed in a building in a street off the London Road. I was mystified and somewhat alarmed. But all was well. Captain Hall had been told that I was a librarian. 'Just the man', he said, 'to take charge of this card index of hundreds of soldiers manning the guns on merchant ships all over the world. You can start work immediately', he added, pointing to a trestle-table on which stood a large card-index box and a file of papers waiting attention. The index provided an up-to-date record of the whereabouts of all gunners in our battery, serving on merchant ships. For example, the major would ask 'Where is Gunner David Jones at present?' The index would reveal that he was at present serving on the *MV Gascony* which had arrived at Rio de Janeiro on the 4th of January, 1941. Or perhaps his ship had been torpedoed and he and his shipmates had been rescued by the Royal Navy. Lists of ships and their location came to us every day from the Admiralty, which included the names of our gunners. The lists were locked up in a safe every evening when we finished work, for they contained secret information on the whereabouts of ships.

After the May 1941 blitz on Liverpool, with German bombers overhead night after night for more than a week, it was decided that we should move to Southport, a pleasant town on the coast above Liverpool. The battery office moved into the Bold Hotel in bomb-free Lord Street. It was a non-industrial town unlikely to be a target for the Luftwaffe. The saloon bar was open to the public, but the whole of the upstairs of the hotel was taken over for offices and sleeping quarters for our staff. Major Stephenson commanded the Battery and Captain Corrin was his adjutant. Both of them had served as young officers in the army in the Great War. The battery-sergeant-major, whose name I cannot remember, was hated by everybody. He was known to all the troops as 'Fishface'.

One day in the autumn of 1941 I was reading the printed *Army Council Instructions*, which came weekly from the War Office, when I saw this notice:

INTELLIGENCE CORPS

Men with suitable qualifications required
for transfer to the Intelligence Corps.

No further details were offered. I was tempted. A romantic at heart, I began to imagine all kinds of clandestine operations in which I might be involved. But what qualifications were required? Languages? I had taken some French lessons since schooldays, but I could not say I was fluent. Examinations? I had passed some of the library examinations just before the war, which meant that I was now an Associate of the Library Association. I decided to take the plunge, ignoring the advice of all the old soldiers I had met. 'Never volunteer', they said. I confided my plan to Captain Corrin, who, after some discussion, agreed to speak to the major. During a long talk, Major Stephenson questioned me about my job as a librarian and agreed to support my application for transfer. Thinking that I might be questioned at an interview about my knowledge of intelligence work, I spent some of my time off duty reading appropriate articles in the *Encyclopaedia Britannica,* in the reference room at Southport public library.

Several weeks later a request came from the War Office that I should go for an interview at Trafalgar House, in London, a building at the north end of Whitehall. Captain Corrin, deciding that I would impress the interviewing board if I arrived with one stripe on my arm, promoted me from Gunner to the imposing-sounding rank of Lance-Bombardier.

2

INTERVIEWS IN LONDON

London was not entirely new to me, for I had taken a holiday there several years before the war; also I had passed through a couple of times on the way to France on holiday in 1938 and 1939. But wartime London, with mountains of sandbags outside buildings, was different. I travelled down the day before the interview, staying the night in a private hotel in Kensington, next door to where my sister was in digs.

Arriving at Trafalgar House in the morning, expecting to be interviewed by several officers, I was surprised to be taken to a room occupied only by a captain in the Intelligence Corps. He invited me to sit in a chair on the other side of the table, and it was all very friendly and informal. He began by questioning me closely about my job as a librarian and also about the work I was doing in the battery office at Southport. 'Do you ride a motorbike?' 'No, sir.' 'Have you ever done any revolver shooting?' 'No, sir.' He seemed disappointed. 'At present', he said, 'we are looking mainly for men suitable for field security work.' He explained that in a field security section, you moved around mostly on motorbikes with the rest of your colleagues, usually ten or twelve men and one officer. Your job involved interrogating prisoners, seizing enemy documents and testing the security of our own forces. 'It's a pretty tough course', he added, 'and you don't appear to me to have the physique for the job'. At that time I was about five feet and seven inches tall.

He passed across the table a copy of the free French newspaper published over here during the war. 'Please read the paragraph I have marked'. I stumbled through the news item, which contained many large numbers such as 'two and a half million rounds of ammunition'. 'Your French is not very fluent', said the captain. 'I didn't claim that it was', I replied. 'True', he said, glancing at my application. 'At least you are better than some who claim to be fluent and can barely say *La plume de ma tante.*' He paused a moment, scanning my application form. 'And you don't have any German.' My prospects began to look poor. Suddenly, however, he brightened up. 'There's another branch of intelligence you might be more suited for. I can't tell you about it, but I'll send your name in and you may hear from them. In the meantime, thanks for coming.'

I went back to Southport, doubting whether I would hear any more. But Captain Corrin, our wise old adjutant was more hopeful than I. Occasionally, if I met him in the corridor, he would raise a forefinger to his lips, as one invoking secrecy. Several weeks later a telegram came from the War Office summoning me for interview at Devonshire House in Piccadilly, London. When I arrived I found that it was a large motor showroom. A separate side door, led upstairs to many offices. Could this, I wondered, be the headquarters of British Intelligence, cleverly disguised? There were ten of us waiting for interview, eight soldiers, one ATS girl and one male civilian. For two hours I waited, as the candidates went in alphabetically for their interviews, which usually lasted ten minutes or a quarter-of-an-hour. I was the last to go in, and was surprised to see a group of about seven officers seated behind a long desk, all wearing the red tabs which showed that they were staff-officers.

Questions were fired at me. What was my job before the war? What was I doing in the army at present? Did I do crosswords? Was I a chess player? It was a much more intimidating interview than that with the Intelligence Corps captain at Trafalgar House. The chairman of the panel, a colonel, thanked me for attending. 'Return to your unit', he said, 'we will write to your commanding officer.' No hint was given of success or failure.

I returned to my index and to the pleasant life in Southport, where I had good friends in the battery office, and where the people of that happy Lancashire town were so hospitable. Weeks went by and I had given up hope of hearing any more. Anyway, I thought, I had enjoyed two visits to London, with all expenses paid. But one day, about six weeks after the interview, Captain Corrin came towards me smiling and waving a telegram in his hand. 'Better start packing, Thirsk', he said.

3

ON THE WAY TO BP

I had only one more day in Southport before travelling again to the motor showroom in Piccadilly. Part of me wanted to stay with friends I knew and with my colleagues in the battery, some of whom I had known since infantry training days at Birmingham in 1940; but the siren voices won the battle, and the other part of me was keen to plunge into the unknown world of intelligence.

One more evening remained for celebration in the saloon bar of the Bold Hotel where we had spent so many happy hours. The following morning I said goodbye to Major Stephenson and Captain Corrin, who both wished me good luck. Loaded with kitbag, gas mask, steel helmet, large and small packs and a small suitcase full of books, which I hadn't had time to send home to Beverley, I asked our unfriendly battery-sergeant-major if a driver could take me to Southport railway station in one of the trucks. 'No, you can find your own way', he said. But unknown to him, one of our odd-job soldiers, Gunner Springate, came to my rescue, shouldering my kitbag as we walked down Lord Street. I thanked him warmly as he helped me on to the Liverpool train.

The train from Liverpool reached London in the afternoon. I couldn't face trundling all my luggage down into the Underground, so I took a taxi to the offices in Piccadilly where I had been interviewed, and where I expected I would be working. But a corporal in the office told me that my destination was Beaumanor, a country house in Leicestershire. 'It's too late to go this evening. You'll have to stay the night in an Army transit camp. Catch the train to Quorn in the morning from Marylebone station. Here's a travel warrant, and here's a chit for one night at the transit camp near the station. It's the old Grand Central Hotel, taken over'. In room 320 by myself in a luxury hotel, now stripped of all furniture and fittings, I was wakened the next morning by the sound of *Reveille*. The bugler went from floor to floor, his bugle-call echoing in the empty carpetless corridors.

By lunchtime I was near journey's end. As the train steamed into Quorn and Woodhouse, the nearest station to Beaumanor, I began wondering again if I had been wise to leave the comfortable Southport life and move into unknown territory. There was no turning back now. Outside the station an Auxiliary Territorial Service (ATS) girl was waiting for me in a 'flivver', a small utility truck in common use before the coming of the jeep. 'Beaumanor is less than a mile from the station', she said, as I threw all my luggage into the back of the truck. After a short journey on the road we turned off, passing through an imposing gateway, winding our way down a long drive bordered by ancient trees. As the old house came into view I wondered whether, at last, I was arriving at the secret headquarters of British intelligence.

In the entrance hall of this large Victorian mansion, built in the Elizabethan style, I was welcomed by Lieutenant Rodney Bax. We sat on a long sofa on the landing, half way up the main staircase. 'Do you know the difference between a code and a cipher?' was his first question. He seemed pleased that I knew the answer. Afterwards I thought it was an odd question, because we were not concerned directly with codes and ciphers. 'I expect you're wondering what you've let yourself in for, Bombardier Thirsk', he said. Then, after a few enquiries about my civilian job as a librarian in the Lancashire County Library service, and about the various jobs I had done in the army, he explained that the unit I had joined was a branch of MI8, known as the Central Party; the staff were known as log-readers and their job was to analyse German and other wireless signals or 'traffic'. He explained that in many places all over Great Britain, hundreds of men and women, trained in the Morse code, listened and wrote down on pads of paper everything they heard on different frequencies. 'These records are called logs,' he said, 'and our job is to study this traffic, hoping to construct pictures of German air force and army formations'.

When he told me that the intercepted messages were all in cipher, I asked whether the ciphers were being broken. To this he replied that some simple ciphers had been decrypted, but that we were not concerned with cryptography. He was a good liar. It was not until nearly ten months later that we log-readers were told that messages transmitted on the 'impregnable' German *Enigma* machine cipher were being decrypted regularly. Lieutenant Bax told me that one of the largest intercept stations was at Beaumanor itself, buried in huts and buildings in the extensive grounds. Some logs came from other intercept stations by despatch rider.

At Beaumanor we received no training in the art of log-reading. 'I'm afraid that we have to throw you in at the deep end', said Lieutenant Bax. 'But for a few days you will be working alongside Corporal Newte'. Arriving at Beaumanor a few hours before me, Lance-Corporal Eric Plant, another recruit, was already under the wing of Corporal Newte. I joined them under the other wing. For the first few days Eric and I were mystified. Several times as we listened to Corporal Newte's explanations, I caught Eric's eye, realising from his expression that he was as baffled as I was. The trouble was that Newte, although a gentle, erudite scholar, who had left his job as a college lecturer, was not good at explaining the mysteries of traffic analysis. But we survived, and before many days had passed we were both reasonably proficient log-readers.

Before the end of the first month we heard rumours that we were about to move to a place called Bletchley. Eric and two others went there the day before the main party and were described as 'the Advance Party'. What their duties were was never made clear. But they were lucky, for Eric and his pals missed the backbreaking jobs the rest of us had loading all the furniture on to army trucks, together with masses of read and unread logs and other equipment. We piled into the trucks along with the furniture for the journey to Bletchley Park. Awaiting our arrival at the gate was the Advance Party. Eric, with beaming smile, rubbed his hands with glee. 'The food in the cafeteria here is fantastic', he exclaimed.

4

THE PARK

Eric was right. The food in the cafeteria, compared with some of the crude army fare that most of us had experienced, was fantastic. No more gristly grey slabs of tinned liver and no more to be greeted at breakfast with the stench of boiled fish. Instead we were offered interesting salads and dishes we had never seen in the army. 'It is almost like arriving in heaven', one soldier said. All were treated equally, and it was an interesting sight to see a colonel or some other high ranking officer standing in a queue with a humble private next to him.

As we started unloading desks and chairs from our army truck and carrying them into one of the wooden huts, the window of a neighbouring hut opened. A young civilian woman called out: 'Hello, Jim! What are you doing here?' 'Hello, Bunty', I replied, 'you're not supposed to ask!' It was one of my sister Betty's best school friends from Beverley in Yorkshire. I knew that she had graduated from Westfield College, University of London, with first class honours in mathematics and had gone into a teaching job which she hated. But I had no idea that she had been recruited to Bletchley.

After being allocated a billet, provided with meal-tickets for the cafeteria, and a pass without which we could not enter the Park, we soon settled down to the new routine. Curiously, I never realised how extensive the grounds were at BP until fifty years later on visiting the place again. During the war there was no ban on walking in the grounds anywhere, but most of us were content to confine ourselves to the area near the mansion and the lake. The large expanses of land where later the numerous blocks were built had no interest for me or my fellow workers. After lunch, when on the day shift, we lingered by the lake if the weather was good, reading or talking with friends; in bad weather we went into the main building - the mansion we called it - where coffee was served.

The huts in which we worked were uncomfortable in both summer and winter. When the sun shone we roasted inside, even with all windows open. On the evening or the night shifts, with blackout curtains drawn, we sweltered in the heat of a hut which had stored the heat during the day. In cold weather, in the winter, with windows tightly closed we were warm enough, but were poisoned by the stench of the coke stoves, or the smoke from oil-stoves. What a relief it was to step outside to gulp in deep lungfuls of keen frosty air! Relief came when we moved into the newly-built blocks, first into Block D and later to Block G. There it was cooler in the summer in the large airy rooms and warmer in the winter, with central heating which few of us had experienced in peace-time.

At the time, I don't think any of us gave much thought to the staff who organized the transport system with such efficiency. What a task it must have been to keep the buses going, many of them ancient, of all shapes and sizes! They were available at all times throughout the day and night, If you were billeted away from BP, you walked to an agreed picking up point to catch your bus, which carried you to BP to start work at 9am, 4pm, or midnight according to the shift you were on. The return journey to your billet began a quarter of an hour after these times. After midnight, in the dark, lit only by the feeble headlights of the buses, you found your bus with difficulty, the drivers with their hand torches calling out the names of the villages or destinations. On the buses you met and began to know many fellow-workers - army, air force and civilians - but you had no idea where they worked or what they did. Entering the Park, the bus was always boarded by one of the guards, who inspected everybody's pass before letting the bus through. There was no check of names on boarding a bus and you could always take a bus to any destination if you fancied a trip to that place on one of your days off duty.

Many extra mural activities thrived at BP, some of these provided by those in charge and others promoted by enthusiastic staff. A drama group remained active throughout the war. A miniature rifle-range was provided in a hut, which could be used by service men and women and civilians alike. Strict discipline was enforced on the range. The tennis courts were popular in the summer. I remember at least one winter when the ice on the lake was thick enough for safe skating. Although not a skater, I remember watching with envy a young American soldier skating with the careless abandon shown by Charlie Chaplin in *The Rink*. A putting green was popular in summer.

I have read of rounders being played on the lawn in front of the mansion, but that was in the early days when GC&CS first came to BP in 1939. When the Americans began to arrive in 1943 you might have thought that they would have introduced baseball, a game not unlike rounders. Perhaps there was not enough space, for by the time they arrived most of the blocks had been built.

Having been a keen cinemagoer from early youth I and a group of enthusiasts obtained permission to start a film club. Several of us formed a committee, sharing the job of borrowing films from the British Film Institute, hiring projection equipment and arranging shows. I remember writing to the famous *Observer* critic, Miss C.A. Lejeune, for advice and receiving an encouraging letter from her. One of the films we showed was *Night Mail,* the Post Office documentary, with Auden's poem on the sound-track.

With several other librarians whom I knew, we helped to organize a recreational library open to anybody working at BP. We obtained stocks of books from a central body in London, which encouraged the public to give their unwanted books for the benefit of the forces by dropping them into a sack in any post office. We took turns manning the library, mainly at lunch times, helped by some civilian women. Our library operated in a room in the mansion.

With all these activities within BP I wonder nowadays why so many of us were not content to stay there on our days off. But for some of us the lure of London, with its theatres, cinemas and restaurants, was overpowering. Others, like me, always spending part of our free time haunting the second-hand bookshops, sometimes took days off in Oxford or Cambridge, both easy to reach by train at that time.

Some, perhaps mostly those still in their 'teens during the war, have spoken of BP being like a university campus. But the overwhelming impression I had was that I was living in a community where almost everybody was dedicated to the job in hand, where talk and argument was incessant, but always reasonable. It was also a place where few people lost their tempers, where people fell in love and out of it. In short, we were a civilized and friendly community, where talk was leavened with good humour and wit; where, contrary to a view which has become popular in recent days, the mad eccentric ones at BP were few in number and certainly not more numerous than in the general community.

5

RECRUITING

The period from the beginning of World War II to the German onslaught in May 1940 was known as the phoney war or the Sitzkrieg. Neither the Germans nor the French and British forces seemed to wish to make the first move. During this stalemate, jokes about the army abounded. Typical was a cartoon portraying two retired colonels. 'During the Great War', one of them is saying, 'there were too many square pegs in round holes in the army.' 'Yes, but things are going to be different in this war', says the other colonel, 'we are going to do just the opposite!'

Yet the same old mistakes were made, with apparently no attempt to put conscripts where they would be most useful. When you were called up, you had first to present yourself for a medical examination in which you were passed from doctor to doctor, one checking the heart, another the lungs, and so on. At the end of the line, having dressed, you were interviewed by one man who asked if you had any preference to serve in the Army, the Royal Air Force or the Royal Navy. Methods of interviewing may have varied at different call-up centres, but I doubt whether there were serious attempts anywhere to find out special aptitudes which might recommend recruitment to a particular branch of a service. In my case, having been told I was medically graded A1, I was only asked which service I wished to serve in. When I replied: 'The army, preferably the Royal Artillery,' that was the end of the interview. A few weeks later my call-up papers came, requesting me to report to an infantry/pioneer training centre, to join a recruit company of *The King's Own Royal Regiment*.

When the Government Code and Cypher School (GC&CS) moved from London to Bletchley just before World War II, the organisation was small, as it had been all through the inter-war years. Now recruits were needed urgently; at first they were found largely through recommendation by serving officers or foreign office staff in other departments. As the demand for yet more recruits grew, the net was spread wider. Universities were approached, and schools were asked to suggest names of school leavers who had achieved distinction in mathematics and languages, especially in German. In spite of these diligent searches more recruits were needed. Yet there, buried among the thousands of men and women in the armed forces, were many square pegs in round holes who, but for chance, might have ended their army days in jobs for which they were unsuited.

A Potato-peeler Mathematician

One such soldier was Neil Webster, who was recruited in what must have been one of the most bizarre ways. In the army your fate was ultimately in the hands of the gods, although for all present purposes it was your platoon sergeant who organised your life. Sometimes your future was determined in the most unexpected places. In the case of Neil, the moment of destiny came in the cookhouse of a unit of *The London Scottish Regiment* while he was peeling potatoes.

Born in 1908 at Cheltenham, Neil went to school at Cheltenham College as a day boy, moving afterwards to Corpus Christi College at Oxford, to read Classics. He should really have been reading mathematics, for he excelled in that subject at school, achieving distinction. But as Neil's brain found no difficulty in coping with problems in mathematics, and believing that further study in that direction would be unprofitable, he turned to classical studies. Having graduated and thinking that this alone would not be a good qualification for work in the outer world, he then moved to Cambridge where, at another Corpus Christi College, he achieved a second degree, in business studies. By this time the Great Depression of the 1920s and 1930s had spread from the USA to Europe. Neil, unsure of a congenial future, went to America to seek his fortune, an unlikely plan of action in view of the grim state of the economy there.

Returning to England after a couple of years, he tried several jobs, none of which appealed to him. Before the war came in September 1939, he decided to volunteer for the Army, choosing *The London Scottish Regiment* because he had some Scottish blood in his veins. He survived gunnery anti-aircraft training in North Wales, in spite of his less than medium height and a body unused to the robust exercise endured by all recruits to the Army.

Posted to the 3rd battalion (anti-aircraft) in the London area, Gunner Neil Webster and his comrades worked hard during the London blitz, attempting to shoot down enemy aircraft. One day a mathematical problem had arisen in connection with the alignment of the gun. Neil, overhearing discussions about this between the officers and senior non-commissioned officers (NCOs), ventured a solution, which proved accurate and was immediately adopted with great success.

One morning Neil was in the cookhouse, with several others, peeling a mountain of potatoes required for the midday meal. On that particular day, a visiting brigadier was on a tour of inspection of their unit. Pausing in the cookhouse, the brigadier looked at Neil and asked his name. 'Gunner Webster, sir', replied Neil. 'You don't seem to be making a very good job of peeling those potatoes, Webster', said the brigadier. Neil, finding difficulty paring off thin slices of skin, was removing also large chunks of potato, and agreed with him. 'No, sir', he replied. The battery-sergeant-major, who was escorting the inspection party, intervened. 'But Gunner Webster is brilliant at mathematics, sir', he said. 'He's a very clever man. He helped to solve a problem with the gun.' The brigadier took Neil aside later, questioning him about his education and civilian job. 'I would like you to go to see a friend of mine, because I think he may have a more suitable job for you. I'll be in touch with your commanding officer'. The next day, a telegram came to the unit, ordering Gunner Webster to proceed to the Ritz Hotel in Piccadilly the following day, to meet Squadron-Leader Hector Bolitho at 1800 hours.

Bolitho, a New Zealander who had made his way to England in the nineteen-twenties, was a prolific author of travel books, biographies and history, and was now working in a new section of Air Ministry Intelligence, headed by Brigadier-General P.R.C. Groves, a former Royal Flying Corps pilot in the Great War. Hector greeted Neil warmly, and over a champagne cocktail he decided that Neil would be an excellent recruit for MI8. However, he could not tell him the nature of the work. 'You'll be working for the intelligence services and it's the sort of work I think you will like', he said.

So it came about that the potato peeler of The London Scottish Regiment arrived at a branch of MI8, known as the Central Party. From its offices in London this unit moved to Beaumanor in Leicestershire and afterwards to Bletchley Park. Neil, who became Major Webster, worked in the Fusion room there and had close liaison with the cryptologists in Hut 6 and with the top people in Hut 3 who examined the decrypted enemy messages.

Neil did not have to move into the Shenley Road Military Camp, for he had rented a house in nearby Fenny Stratford, where he lived with his wife Elizabeth and their two children. Neil worked for many years after the war at the Central Office of Information. He died in 1990, leaving his wife, two sons and one daughter, twelve grandchildren and six great-grandchildren. Elizabeth Webster is the author of many novels.

At Bletchley Neil had the reputation of being absent-minded. There was still a lot of his childhood lingering within, and at times, although having a friendly and outgoing manner, he appeared to be living in a dream. All those who worked with him had a warm affection for Neil. One night in Hut 6, when there had been a power failure, Neil was the one who arrived bearing candles. A wag, seeing him, called out: 'Here comes Wee Willie Winkie!' The name stuck and to many of us thereafter he was always affectionately known as Willie Webster.

Wee Willie Winkie runs through the town
Upstairs and downstairs in his night-gown,
Rapping at the window, crying through the lock,
Are the children all in bed, for now it's 8 o'clock?

Barging into the War Office

Of all the routes by which men and women came to Bletchley during the war, that taken by Freddie Edwards was probably unique. Frederick William Edwards, born in London 1916, attended the Merchant Taylors' School, in Northwood, Middlesex, leaving in 1933 at the age of 17. At the memorial address at his funeral in 1993, a school-fellow, Arthur Foss, recalled Freddie's short-sightedness which was a great handicap during games. 'Freddie liked to tell the story how in an important school rugby match he found himself, as a second row forward, suddenly, with the ball in his hands; whereupon he ran the length of the field, brilliantly handing off those trying to tackle him, only to find that he had scored a try behind his own line'. Foss also recalled that 'his mental intelligence and agility were such that he excelled at such pursuits as bridge, chess and crosswords'. Most of his companions went on to university, but Freddie, not having enough money to follow them, because his father had died unexpectedly, went to work in the legal department of the Prudential Assurance company. It was during this period that he studied for the bar and was called to the Middle Temple in April 1940.

On the outbreak of war in 1939, he volunteered for the services, but was rejected because of his short sight. Conscripted with his age group into the Pioneer Corps in May 1940, he was, according to his CV, 'transferred to intelligence duties after ten days'. The legend circulating among us at Bletchley was that Private Edwards of the Pioneer Corps, walking past the War Office on his first day off duty, went inside and asked whether they had any suitable jobs. Whoever it was who interviewed him must have been impressed with his abilities, for he was quickly removed from the Pioneer Corps and transferred to the Intelligence Corps at Bletchley, arriving there with the rank of Private.

What is beyond legend is that, by early 1941, he was commissioned as a First Lieutenant, became a Captain the same year and a Major in 1943. Freddie worked mainly in the Fusion room attached to Hut 6. There, the intelligence gained from the decrypted Enigma messages was fused with material gleaned from traffic analysis. Subaltern Joan Watkins of the ATS, also in the Fusion room, remembers that Freddie 'often disappeared to London for days on end. When he came back, he would be armed with many probing questions to which he required accurate answers. He always seemed to have a complete grasp of the organisation of the German armed forces'.

Neil Webster's widow remembers their friendship with Freddie during the war and the wonderful arguments they had with him at their house in Fenny Stratford. Neil told her how Freddie coped with his poor eyesight 'by holding any document at arms' length, at right angles and glancing at it sideways. He also managed to memorise the whole page, as he had a remarkable photographic memory'.

Towards the end of the war he worked overseas as Commanding Officer of an intelligence unit, with headquarters in Palestine and sections in various places ranging from Gibraltar in the West to Habbanuja in the East.

After the war Freddie returned to the Prudential Assurance Company, but soon found other employment with Butterworths, a legal publisher. Freddie was responsible for the editing and publication of *Halsbury's Statutory Instruments*, a work of twenty-five volumes. Subsequent jobs included work with companies in Egypt, until, at the time of the Suez war, he was deported from Egypt, with all his money and goods sequestrated. Back in England, he worked for several firms, including Guest, Keen and Nettlefold, for whom he travelled widely in the Near and Middle East as an export director. His knowledge of languages, for he knew several, including Arabic, was useful at this time.

At the end of his career he left the business world, going into partnership with the owners of the Aldeburgh bookshop. Freddie died in 1993, aged 77. His wartime marriage had ended in divorce. His second wife, Jean, died a few days after Freddie. They had no children.

A Balliol Man

As the activities at Bletchley Park expanded, more and more recruits were needed. One of the most active recruiting agents was Lieutenant-Colonel John Tiltman (later Brigadier), a veteran of the Great War, who had served in the 1920s as a cryptologist in India and later in London at the GC&CS.

One summer day in 1942, Colonel Tiltman, in civilian dress, accompanied by an Intelligence Corps officer, visited Oxford on a recruiting mission. He turned up at Balliol College, where, doubtless, the Master, A.D.Lindsay, had been warned to assemble suitable undergraduates for interview as possible candidates to attend the training courses at Bedford which Tiltman himself supervised. One young man of twenty years, chosen for interview, was George Peters, then in his second year at Balliol, reading Classics.

The interviews were brief and at the end George was little wiser about the job he was being recruited for, than he was at the beginning. 'All we can tell you is that you will be studying languages and doing work of national importance,' said Colonel Tiltman. George was asked if he did crosswords or played chess. They also asked him to tell them about his present studies. That was all.

Within a few weeks, George was installed in a civilian billet at Bedford and was enduring an intensive course on the Japanese language, with thirty or so other recruits, including one woman and a WAAF, who had lived in Japan as a missionary. The course included some training in signals intelligence.

Six months later George moved to Bletchley Park to work in a hut devoted to Japanese naval affairs. Translation and interpretation of decrypted Japanese messages occupied most of his days, evenings and nights. He was one of a motley crew, composed of civilians, naval and army personnel. Before long he became head of a small section of five people, among them a midshipman, two navy lieutenants and an RAF sergeant. George himself was by this time in the Intelligence Corps with the rank of captain, but he did not wear uniform.

One of his colleagues, Lieutenant Frank Taylor, was in peacetime a librarian at the John Rylands Library in Manchester. Peter Laslett, another older colleague, had graduated from Cambridge several years before the war, with a double first in history. He had served in the ranks in the navy until spotted as a likely candidate for transfer to BP. Laslett became a distinguished historian at Cambridge after the war.

George returned to Balliol after the war to finish his degree. Now a grandfather, in his eighties he looks back on a lifetime of teaching modern languages in secondary schools, a career vastly different from the wartime years in the Japanese naval section at Bletchley Park.

Field Security Rejects

The branch of the Intelligence Corps known as FSP (Field Security Personnel) collected information about the enemy in the field, either by interrogating prisoners of war, or by capturing enemy documents. An additional duty was the testing of the security of our own forces. The FSP consisted of hundreds of sections stationed in many countries, each section made up of an officer, usually of the rank of captain or lieutenant, a company-sergeant-major and up to ten or twelve non-commissioned officers; these latter were usually lance/corporals with the temporary rank of sergeant, to give them a little more authority when dealing with British forces. All ranks in these sections were trained motorcyclists; they carried revolvers and had fluency in at least one language other than their own.

The training of men for FSP duties was carried out at the main depot of the Intelligence Corps at King Alfred's College, Winchester. Here were gathered soldiers from many different units of the British Army. Some were volunteers; others were singled out when, for example, it was discovered that they were fluent in languages, especially in German, Italian and Arabic. Great emphasis was put on smartness of appearance. To this end, all the drill instructors at Winchester were non-commissioned officers from the Grenadier Guards, whose ministrations made a lasting impression on all those who passed through the rigorous training programme. The commanding officer at Winchester was also a stickler for smartness. *Bluenose*, as he was cruelly named, insisted on the use of a special dark-green blanco on all belts, webbing and large packs. All soldiers on arriving had to buy a tin of this revolting blanco and set to work on their equipment before their first parade. Bluenose would not tolerate any other hue.

Unfortunately, not all recruits to Winchester proved suitable for the rigours of a career in the FSP. The chief difficulty for most of them was mastery of the motorbike, followed closely by incompetence in revolver shooting. Men either take to motor-biking like ducks to water, or fail completely to be at one with the machine. Many were the comical tales of minor disasters during escorted processions on the country roads around Winchester. I never heard of anybody being shot during revolver practice, but I imagine the instructors had many anxious moments.

My friend Alfred Sugar, a fellow log-reader at BP, who was one hundred years old in 2006, still remembered his days at Winchester vividly:

The Guards instructors were sometimes sadistic. I remember one gentle private in particular, who spent his spare time in the college library, reading Dante in Italian. Like so many of the academic studious types he had failed motor-cycling and had injured his leg and knee in the process. On the day he was passed fit for duty we went on a route march in full FSMO (field service marching order), which meant that you had to carry most of your possessions in a large pack on your back. It was a hot day in July and we found it tough. The NCOs found it amusing to make the meek private a platoon runner, frequently sending him to run at the double from the rear platoon to the front one!

After failing motor-cycling a second time, Sugar, along with others, had to parade with full kit early one morning. With them went the unexpired portion of the day's ration, which usually consisted of a cardboard carton full of thick cheese sandwiches

Escorted by the Guards NCOs we were marched to the station, put on a train with no idea where we were going, met with a lorry at Waterloo station in London which took us to Liverpool Street station. Another train eventually deposited us at Cambridge where we were marched to a large Victorian house in Bateman Street and told to assemble immediately at the college opposite. That was the last we saw of our Guards escorts. We assembled in the college hall. A lieutenant-colonel came to a rostrum and said: *Gentlemen be seated.* From that moment we were still in the army, but it was an army in which we were valued for our brains and minds rather than for our ability with weapons and machines.

What could be done with these misfits? Bletchley was crying out for more hands, and so it was that a number of them arrived at BP. Some of them came direct; but later in the war many first attended a course at Bedford, which included some instruction in signals intelligence and lessons on the composition of the German armed forces. Most of these failed motorcyclists joined us log-readers in SIXTA (Hut 6, traffic analysis).

Miss Peasegood of the Foreign Office

During the war women were subject to compulsory national service unless they were married and looking after young children or working in a reserved occupation. Most of them elected to join the women's army (the ATS) but sometimes their choice was restricted. This was the case when Joyce Peasegood of Pontefract attended for interview.

Born in Hull in 1924, Joyce was still at school when the war broke out in September 1939. When the Luftwaffe began to bomb Hull, Joyce's father and mother decided to move with the family to Pontefract, in the West Riding of Yorkshire. On leaving school there, Joyce found a job in a furniture manufacturing firm in nearby Castleford. For some strange reason which she never understood, her post in the firm was regarded as a reserved occupation. Despite that, in 1943, she received her call-up papers and had to attend a local centre for medical examination. Joyce fancied joining the women's Navy (the Wrens), but to her astonishment she was told, after passing A1 at the medical, that women's recruitment to the armed forces was temporarily suspended. 'There are vacancies in the Land Army, in munitions or on the railways', said the woman interviewing her. Joyce couldn't believe it, and while she was desperately trying to think which was the least unattractive job of the three, the woman broke in : 'There's a job in the Foreign Office, if that would interest you.' Joyce jumped at the suggestion.

There followed an intense one month course in typing and the Morse code, at Bedford. Joyce was proud that she picked up these two subjects so quickly. At the end of the course she was transferred to Bletchley Park as a civilian. She was soon immersed in a job which lasted the remainder of war. The work entailed a lot of typing of five-letter jumbles of letters. Working three shifts, Joyce and her fellow-workers, about fifty in number, were never told whether their work was successful. She told herself that somebody somewhere must be breaking the German ciphers they were typing. But she never knew for certain.

At first Joyce was billeted in the town of Bedford, from where she travelled to Bletchley on one of the dozens of buses of every shape and size which ferried the BP inmates to their billets. She and a female friend with whom she was billeted attempted one evening to attend a dance at Bedford Town Hall. At first they were refused entry because the dance was organised for the Forces only; but after some argument, they persuaded the doorman that, as 'Temporary women clerks, grade 2, Foreign Office' they were as eligible as those in uniform. When they entered they found it was not a dance, but a concert by Glenn Miller and his band, with Vera Lynn also singing.

Joyce's pay, on arrival at Bletchley was £2-8s-6d a week, plus war bonus. She was one of the small cogs of the vast machine at Bletchley Park, without whose work, success would never have been achieved.

Towards the end of the war Joyce volunteered to serve in India. This would involve a short training course in uniform as a member of the Fanys (First Aid Nursing Yeomanry), a British Corps of military nurses. But in the middle of the course the war ended.

One of her abiding memories is of two of them rowing the little boat on the lake at Bletchley Park, in the middle of the night, on their way back to Block E, after a meal in the canteen.

Joyce Hewitt (nee Peasegood) returned to Yorkshire after the war. Married to an ex-soldier who had been badly injured driving a tank, Joyce had two children, a boy and a girl. Now a widow and an octogenarian, she lives alone, but sees her children and grandchildren.

The Youngest Recruit

Probably the oldest of all those who worked at Bletchley Park during the war was Commander Alexander Denniston, the person in charge until 1942. He was born in 1881, and had served as a cryptographer in the Royal Navy under Admiral 'Blinker' Hall in the Great War, in the famous Room 40 OB at the Admiralty. But who was the youngest?

About the time Denniston left Bletchley, a young girl began working at BP at the age of fifteen, who may well have been the youngest recruit ever. I never heard of Jean Seabury until she was seventy-eight. It was then that she told me that she was only twelve years old, at school in West Wickham in Kent, when the war started. She was the only child in the family. Her mother had become almost blind by 1939, with glaucoma; her father, much older than her mother, who had served in the Great War, was away from home doing demolition work. Together Jean and her mother were evacuated to New Bradwell, near Wolverton, a small town several miles north of Bletchley. When Jean reached the age of fifteen, her former headmaster, Mr Kidwell, of West Wickham school, supported her application for a job at nearby Bletchley Park.

She had no idea what sort of work she would be doing, but having signed the Official Secrets document, she soon found herself too busy to wonder what it was all about. BP provided plenty of variety. She was trained to operate the telephone switchboard, but her main job was that of messenger girl and runner, skipping from hut to hut and from block to block. At first she was working and living at Shenley Brook End, a disused school owned by BP, with other girls of about her age. But soon she was billeted in a house at New Bradwell, very near Wolverton, travelling to Bletchley like the rest of us on the BP buses. Jean did shift work and it was a new experience to be working all night, with a meal at the cafeteria half way through the shift. She loved the rice puddings and was always allowed a second helping.

Life was hectic, for after work she had to help her nearly-blind mother at home. Later she worked in the main building with other girls, under Commander Bradshaw, who was in charge of personnel. Jean remembers little of the work there. It was mainly general office work under Dudley Smith and she had no more running here and there with messages. Once when on duty at the main telephone switchboard she managed to cut off the main electricity supply, but does not remember being reprimanded. Jean was carefree and young enough not to worry too much about the war. She remembers little about BP, but she recalls rowing on the lake with one of her pals in a leaky boat. She also remembers people dancing on the flat roof of one of the blocks on VE day.

Towards the end of the war a chance meeting with a young sailor was to turn her world upside down. Signalman James Hyrons, known on the lower deck as a 'bunting tosser', only two years older than Jean, had already had hazardous voyages in the Royal Navy. 'Did he have a rough time?', I asked. 'Not really', she replied. 'He was on the Arctic convoys going to Russia, and he helped to tow Mulberry Harbour across the Channel on D-Day'. She added: 'Jim was at Tokyo on his ship when the Japanese surrendered.' After Mulberry, Jim was given a well-deserved leave, for he and his shipmates had been battling with the waves for nearly a week, with little sleep. All he wanted was to have a long, long sleep in a bed. But on reaching home in the London area he found that the V1 doodlebugs were arriving overhead regularly, preceded by the wailing sirens. In desperation he decided to spend the rest of his leave at his sister's house at Wolverton, well beyond the range of the V1s. Having recovered quickly from his strenuous activities in the Channel, Jim smartened himself up one evening to attend a dance that was to be held in the Science & Arts Institute building at Wolverton. It was there that he met seventeen-year-old Jean Seabury, his future wife. Jean never told Jim about her activities at Bletchley until many years later when all the secrets of BP were revealed. By then she was running a school of dancing.

So there were many ways to Bletchley Park. Every recruit had a story to tell and no doubt, more than sixty years after the war ended, there are still survivors of BP who could tell even stranger tales.

6

CIVILIAN BILLETS

When I arrived at Bletchley Park with the other log-readers in May 1942, we were each given the name and address of a householder with whom we would be billeted. The population of Bletchley Park at that time had not reached the point where all newcomers were billeted miles away from the Park; some of us were in the town, quite close. My billet was only a few hundred yards away in a terraced house occupied by Mr and Mrs B. Mr B. was a railway engine driver and during the few months I was there I saw little of him. Mrs B. provided no meals and at that time received six shillings a week for providing a bed. And what a bed! It was enormous, with a feather mattress which almost buried me. After some of the hard beds I had endured in the army so far, it took some getting used to. All meals, including breakfast, I ate at the large cafeteria near the entrance just inside BP; we were issued with a week's supply of meal-tickets at a time.

Mrs B. had no children and I did not see much of her. If I was on duty until midnight she was asleep when I returned and if I was on the night-shift I slept all day and saw her only briefly. Trouble came when she complained that I was consuming too much electricity when reading in bed. I pointed out to her that the 40-watt bulb in the bedside lamp consumed very little electricity, but she continued to grumble and I continued reading after midnight. One night, plunged into darkness in mid-sentence, I realised that Mrs B. had turned off the main switch in the meter cupboard.

The next morning I saw the billeting officer as soon as the office opened. By this time billets near Bletchley Park were scarce and I was offered one in New Bradwell, a largish village near the railway town, Wolverton. This suited me well, for several of my friends were billeted there or nearby and the bus service provided by BP at all hours was excellent.

It was dark when, a few days later, I took the bus to New Bradwell to my new billet and I had difficulty finding number 28 Spencer Street in the black-out. I knocked on the door. It opened and I heard a woman's voice cry out in a broad Welsh accent: 'Come in now, boy, and make yourself at home'. In this small terrace house Mr and Mrs Jones lived with their four children. Mrs Jones could easily have refused to have anybody, but the billeting officer had persuaded her to take one person, by offering to provide a single bed that could be erected in the front parlour. Mrs Jones provided all meals except those that I had in the cafeteria during the day or in the middle of the night. For meals and accommodation she was paid just over £1 (twenty-one shillings a week). What meals they were! With a husband and four children Mrs Jones had six ration books. She also had mine. For nearly fifteen months I lived on the fat of the land. Sometimes, when Mr Jones had gone to work and the children to school, I enjoyed a large breakfast of egg, bacon and mushrooms (which one of the boys had collected in the fields not far from the house), followed by bread, butter and marmalade. If I arrived home at 0045 after an evening shift, a light snack would be waiting for me, which I ate quietly, with all the family asleep upstairs.

In the early 1920s, Mr and Mrs Jones had emigrated from Wales to England, bringing up their four children in New Bradwell. Mrs Jones had worked in a munitions factory when a girl during the Great War; Mr Jones had worked in the mines. Now he worked at the railway engineering works in Wolverton. His oldest boy of sixteen followed him there on leaving school. The other children, two boys and a little girl of six, Marina, were all still at school.

The house was a typical terrace house of its period. There was no bathroom and the water-closet was outside in the backyard. My front parlour was comfortable, especially on winter days, when Mrs Jones would light a coal fire for me.

It was sad to leave such a warm and hospitable billet, where I had enjoyed living with such a happy family. In January 1944 all army personnel had to move to the newly built army camp adjacent to Bletchley Park. Our billets were to be taken over by the ever increasing number of civilians who were flooding into the Park.

7

THE LISTENERS

Switch on any short-wave radio set and you will hear the babble of Morse code signals. Some of these are messages passing between merchant ships; more will be in cipher from the naval, army, and air forces of the world. In World War II this traffic increased so much that it was impossible to monitor all of it.

The branch of British Signals Intelligence (SIGINT), responsible for intercepting or monitoring all such traffic, whether enemy or neutral, was known as the Y service. It was also responsible for direction finding (D/F), which made it possible to locate the place from which any signal was being broadcast. All over the world men and women, most of them in the services, were engaged on interception. At first office staff from the post office telegraphic department, who were trained in Morse code, were recruited to enlarge the small force which was employed on this work in peacetime. But, as many more were needed to cope with increased traffic, hundreds and later thousands of men and women from among those called up for military service, were trained to become intercept operators. Women in the WAAF (the women's section of the Royal Air Force) and the ATS (the women's army) outnumbered the male recruits. Some civilians were also employed

Although a number of books on the subject have been published since the war, the unglamorous interception service has never attracted as much attention as the cryptographic work. Yet without this continuous flow of raw material, neither the cryptanalysts nor the traffic analysts would have had anything to do. Aileen Clayton, a young woman in the WAAF, whose book: *The Enemy is Listening* was published in 1988, contains a tribute to her and her colleagues from Air Chief Marshal Sir Frederick Rosie :

There was no publicity and no glamour, but they were engaged in a shadowy, secret war. Without this gifted band of men and women, the direction of events in the Second World War, and the ending, might have been different.

The intercept operator's job was arduous and only those who had survived a gruelling training were employed. Working round the clock on a three or four-shift timetable, they sat for hour after hour with headphones attached, transcribing the Morse signals as they arrived. Often atmospheric conditions were poor, signals faded, stations drifted from their frequencies and overlapping transmissions confused the sound. Iris M. Owen, in her book *My Many Lives* (Toronto, Colombo company, 2000), spoke of the difference between training and real interception

> Until now the signals we had been sent in the classroom were clear, if not always loud. Now we had to deal with listening to Morse signals that were underneath or mixed up with all kinds of other traffic, from commercial, entertainment, or from other military units. We discovered that although theoretically each station had its own wave-length, because of the vast range of our sets, we were picking up all sorts of traffic from far away or near…it was similar to being at a noisy cocktail party and attempting to listen to the private conversation of a couple at the other end of the room.

Len Moore was another intercept operator who wrote, in his book *Z17*, published in 1996, of the stress endured by him and his colleagues. Some of his fellow-workers chain-smoked through the watch and often were utterly bored by long periods of silence which might change suddenly to furious activity. He was stationed at Beaumanor, a large Victorian house in the Elizabethan style in Leicestershire, in the grounds of which had been built a number of camouflaged huts, one of them disguised to look like a cricket pavilion. Len's hut looked like two semi-detached cottages. Beaumanor was one of the largest intercept stations, employing more than a thousand operators towards the end of the war. Spread around the grounds were the wireless masts bearing the aerials. Len described the scene in his hut:

> There must have been about fifty operators for each watch on duty. We sat in pairs at tables butting against the two long side walls of the building and each table bore two wireless sets side by side, complete with 'cans' (headphones). We all faced towards one end of the hut where there sat a supervisor in charge of the watch, He directed us where to sit each time and which stations/frequencies to cover – or to go on general search - as we took over from the outgoing watch. It was quite a scramble at such times.

Great concentration and patience were essential, Len added, and recalled the hours of boredom, writing down a jumble of letters and figures which meant nothing.

> We didn't know the worth of our efforts and assumed they were of some value.

Sometimes the intercept operators became so familiar with the 'fist' of a German transmitting in the Morse code that they would make a note on the log that the German operator today was the same man who had used a different callsign the day before. One listener added a note: 'Italian operator', having recognised a Latin rhythm in the transmission. Such information proved very useful to us log-readers engaged on traffic analysis, when the Germans began encoding their callsigns. Hitherto we had been able to recognize German stations because we knew what callsign each station would be adopting each day.

The intercept operators had on their desks two pads of paper, one on which they wrote messages in cipher; on the other they recorded all the chit-chat between German operators, which they used in order to keep in contact with their colleagues. The messages in cipher were dispatched to Bletchley Park by teleprinter to enable the cryptanalysts of Hut 6 to attempt to decrypt them as soon as possible. The chit-chat, written on printed forms known as logs, came directly to Bletchley by road. Motorcycle dispatch riders arrived throughout the day and night bringing batches of logs from Beaumanor, Chicksands in Bedfordshire and other intercept stations, for analysis by us log readers at BP. In my mind's eye I can still see an army motor-bike dispatch rider, arriving one dark winter night at Bletchley Park from an intercept station. Covered from head to foot with snow, he dumped on the floor two large pannier bags full of logs. These were then sorted by frequency and allocated to the log-reader who was responsible for the particular German air force or army network to which that frequency belonged.

The Germans, of course, also had intercept stations and were monitoring British and American traffic. However, it is believed that they were successfully deceived by an elaborate operation codenamed *Fortitude South*, mounted by the British in 1944 in south-east and eastern England, whose object was to persuade Hitler and his generals, partly by an unusual weight of signals traffic, that the Allied invasion was going to be launched in the Pas de Calais in the middle of July. The Allied Command hoped that the Germans would think that the D-Day landing which took place on the Normandy coast in June was only a feint to persuade them to transfer troops from the Pas de Calais to Normandy. Hitler and his advisers firmly believed that the main attack would be in the Calais region.

To achieve this deception an enormous phantom army of allied troops was stationed in Kent and the south-east. In fact, it consisted of about fifteen hundred men. Dummy landing craft were placed in harbours and estuaries and inflatable tanks were lined up in fields. Above all, radio traffic was broadcast in cipher all over the region from mobile signal trucks, simulating the traffic which would have been generated by an army of two million. The Germans were also led to believe that the general in charge of this army was the flamboyant American General Patten. The German log-readers were completely deceived by the spurious traffic recorded by their intercept operators. By these means the German High Command was persuaded to keep the main body of their forces in the Pas de Calais region.

Even with information gleaned from Enigma decrypts, it was not always possible to say with certainty where a particular unit of the German Air Force or the German army was stationed. This is where direction-finding (popularly referred to as D/F) enabled us to locate any German transmitter with reasonable accuracy.

At Bletchley Park, all that I and my fellow log-readers had to do if we wished to know the location of a German unit which we were studying, was to consult Major Firnberg and his staff. Armed with the callsign and the radio frequency of the German station I wished to locate, I would go to the D/F room in our building and ask them to locate the transmitter. Firnberg's staff firstly passed the request to the intercept station at Beaumanor in Leicestershire. There they had a department which controlled the D/F stations in Britain, in such disparate places as Land's End, the Shetlands and Northern Ireland. These outstations then established the direction from which the radio signal was coming. The line bearings taken by two or preferably three stations were then plotted on a map at Beaumanor. Where the bearings coincided gave a fairly accurate position of the German transmitter. The result would be passed back to Major Firnberg's department. If requests were not too numerous, and, bear in mind, there were hundreds of requests daily, then, if interception of radio signals was clear, his staff could produce an answer within an hour or two.

In addition to bearings obtained from D/F stations within Britain, invaluable bearings were regularly supplied by army, RAF and naval stations in the Middle East, North Africa and later in Italy. Extra bearings from such sources helped considerably when German units had penetrated deep into the USSR.

The work of the D/F section at BP grew as the war continued. At the end of the German war Major Firnberg's staff had increased from himself and two non-commissioned officers to himself and fourteen others. After D-Day, when many German units were being moved to different positions, the work of the D/F department increased again enormously

The interception of messages enciphered by conventional hand ciphers or by the Enigma machine was straightforward if the Morse signals were clear and the intercept operator skilful. Far more difficult were the messages produced by another German cipher machine, the Geheimschreiber, a kind of teleprinter which, instead of using the Morse code, produced electrical impulses which enciphered and transmitted messages which, when received by another machine, were automatically turned into German words. Known to the British as *Fish*, the Geheimschreiber was not a portable machine to be used in the field like Enigma. It was used only by Hitler, the top ranks of the German army, navy and air force, and by the government.

Eventually, by the use of Colossus, the massive forerunner of the modern computer, the *Fish* ciphers were regularly decrypted. However, the interception of these non-Morse transmissions was only achieved by skilful operators. One of these, Iris M. Owen in her book *My Many Lives*, writes of her experience with *Fish*. Iris, becoming bored with her job in the Civil Service, volunteered for service in the ATS, without waiting for her call-up. After the discomforts of initial army training she was chosen with a small group for training in the Morse code. At first they thought they were going to work in the Royal Signals but after more than nine months training, most of it on the Isle of Man, they were told they were being trained to be intercept operators, listening to enemy radio traffic. She and her classmates became so proficient

...that every noise we heard was translated into Morse code ...even now, fifty years later, when I hear a bird whistle, I immediately translate it into Morse.

Later in the war Iris intercepted the *Fish*, or Geheimschreiber traffic.

Messages were passing between high commands at Berlin, Vienna and the Russian front itself. Some of this material also originated from Hitler's own personal headquarters ... we had an intercept set built to take this traffic... the sets were fitted with large rolls of tape, and a message of some considerable length would be sent in a few seconds. As one was intercepting over such a long distance the problem for us was tuning out all the background flak and interference. If this was not done properly, all one got was a lot of meaningless scribble. I was found quite good at operating this machine, and it was given to me as an assignment for quite a period of time.

Close liaison was maintained between Hut 6 and the intercept stations, whose cryptographers sent daily requests to them asking for coverage of certain networks. They also went by cable to overseas intercept stations such as the one at Cairo, asking them to concentrate on particular networks which were difficult to cover in this country.

Apart from the regular interception service, manned by thousands of young men and women in the forces and by some civilians, another group of interceptors existed, known as the Radio Security Service (RSS), or MI8 (c). Their history began in the summer of 1939, before the beginning of World War II, when Lord Sandhurst of MI5 approached Arthur Watts, then President of the Radio Society of Great Britain, asking his advice about enlisting enthusiastic radio 'hams' to help the woefully undermanned interception services. Kenneth Morton Evans, an officer in the Territorial Army, who had for some years experimented with amateur radio communications, was an ideal recruit for the new service, which eventually employed fifteen hundred volunteer interceptors.

At first they were asked to track down enemy agents operating within the United Kingdom; but when it became clear that there were no more, they moved to other traffic. Their first headquarters was at Wormwood Scrubs prison in west London, but when this was bombed, they moved to Arkley View, near Barnet, in north London. These amateurs, who had become experts in peacetime in recording faint short-wave transmissions from 'hams' all over the world, proved to be excellent recorders of German and other enemy traffic.

In 1941, Brigadier Richard Gambier-Parry, the communications head of MI6, asked Kenneth Evans to become deputy controller of the Arkley View headquarters. Kenneth, who was promoted to the rank of lieutenant-colonel, may never have visited Bletchley Park. But, without his unit's work and that of the intercept stations all over the country and abroad, the successes of the BP cryptanalysts would never have been possible.

8

A LOG-READER'S TALE

Our job as log readers was to analyse the contents of the logs, with the object of building up a picture of an enemy army or air force unit. We did not deal with intercepted naval material. We never called ourselves traffic analysts, preferring the simple designation log readers. What was there to read on those thousands of logs? They poured in daily from Beaumanor, Chicksands and other intercept stations, carried by despatch riders on motor-bikes or by other transport, unlike enciphered messages, which usually came to BP by teleprinter.

To a newcomer what appeared on the logs was gibberish. Everything a British intercept operator heard through his or her headphones was written down. It was all heard in Morse code, but could appear on a log occasionally in clear German language. This was strictly against orders; but who could blame a German operator if he broke off transmitting to go to the toilet? 'Pissen Moment' appeared more than once on logs. Anything other than the odd German word consisted of (a) rows of letter K (dash,dot,dash) which the German operators used to keep in touch with their outstations and (b) 3-letter Q-Code words.

The Q-Code, a long list of 3-letter words of which the first letter was **Q,** devised by the British before the Great War, was universally used in war and peacetime by wireless operators of all countries. The Germans used it, not only with the accepted meanings, but with special meanings which they had added to the international list. QSA, followed by a question mark meant 'What is my signal strength?' The answer usually came back with a number added. QSA 5 meant that the signal strength was very good. QSA 1 meant it was hardly audible.

Each of us was allocated a particular network, or perhaps several networks, used by units of the German army or airforce. The most common type of operational group was in the form of a star (*Stern* in German), which was used by a headquarters (Control) with two or three outstations. In some cases outstations were allowed to contact each other direct. Another type of network was in the form of a circle (*Kreis*). Here two or three stations, usually of equal status, communicated with one another. To make things clear, we log-readers would make a diagram on a pro forma sheet, drawing lines between the various outstations and their headquarters, or between stations in the case of a *Kreis*. By placing arrows on the lines, using coloured pencils, we could indicate each message and the direction it was travelling. We did not see the enciphered messages themselves, which the intercept operators wrote on a separate pad. But we knew when a message was about to be sent. In short, the purpose of all this 'chat' on the logs was to make sure that when a message was ready to send, the recipient was alert and ready to receive it.

The cryptanalysts asked us to watch out for regular reports, often situation reports sent at specified times, which often had standard opening phrases, like *Morgenmeldung* (morning report). The RAF was asked on some occasions to provoke a standard German report, by sending a lone aircraft near a German outstation, for example, in Brittany, hoping that a report using standard phrases would be forthcoming. Such a message could sometimes help the cryptanalysts by providing a 'crib'.

Under our diagrams we wrote notes, in pencil, about the activities of our stations during the past twenty-four hours. We also noted any unusual flows of traffic and any changes from normal procedure. Once a week we compiled a report about the networks we were studying. These were passed to a room we log-readers were not allowed to enter. There the intelligence gathered from decrypted Enigma messages was married with the information in our reports, to give a complete picture of the activities of any German group. In those early days the log-readers had not been told that German Enigma messages were being decrypted.

Each separate unit in the German army or air force used an identifying label, known as a call-sign, when sending or receiving traffic. Each call-sign consisted of three jumbled letters; for example, LTU, or BFK. To make the job more difficult the Germans changed all their call signs daily at midnight, according to a fixed programme. During World II the German army and air forces used five printed callsign books which they named the B,C, D, E and F books . Each one contained thousands of callsigns, arranged in columns and rows, so that a station, knowing the column which had been allocated to it, could select its correct callsign for the day. Known to the log-readers as the 'bird book', book B was used by the German Air Force from the beginning of the war until 1st April, 1944 when it was superseded by book F (Fox).

Before the Central party moved to Beaumanor several members had, during the years 1940 and 1941, largely reconstructed the bird book by studying the callsigns over a whole year. We used a well-thumbed copy every day to identify stations. It was always missing from the central table in the room and the familiar cry would be heard again and again: 'Has anyone got the bird book?' A German copy was captured in Libya in December 1941. The other callsign books C, D, E, and F were not used so frequently by the Germans. When the German army began to encipher callsigns in November 1944 we were unable to identify networks by predicting changes of callsigns at midnight. That lasted until March 1945, when a copy of the German instructions for enciphering callsigns was captured. That information was also invaluable to the intercept stations, enabling them again to identify networks even if they had changed frequencies.

Before the Central party left Beaumanor and came to Bletchley entirely, we log readers numbered about fifty men, mostly non-commissioned officers in the army and only a handful of women of the ATS. But by the end of the war the log readers numbered nearly one hundred, with more women, mostly ATS, than men, and with a handful of WAAFs. There were no WRENS serving with us. Ranks ranged from the lowly lance-corporals to the highest non-commissioned rank of RSM. Among my fellow log readers were barristers, teachers, solicitors, librarians, accountants, journalists, and bank clerks. Among those too young to have had jobs before the war, were undergraduates and graduates, male and female, who had recently completed their degrees or who had been called up before finishing at university.

As the war went on we were all promoted regularly. I suspect that this was partly to bring our army pay to the level of the salaries paid to the civilians, who were on Foreign Office scales. We were all doing the same kind of work and the ranks meant nothing. To those of us who had earlier experience of the crudities of army life it was good to be working with men and women in a friendly atmosphere with no need for heavy discipline. For the most part we were on friendly terms with everybody. Indeed, some others became lifelong friends.

Several couples married. I fell in love with Joan Watkins, a young sergeant in the ATS who worked in the Fusion room and later we were married. In the days before our marriage this led to no problems within Bletchley Park, where ranks meant nothing. But when all military personnel were moved from civilian billets and housed in a newly-built army camp adjacent to BP, liaison between an ATS subaltern, (for Joan had now been commissioned), and a company-sergeant-major was frowned upon. We were not permitted to meet in the officers' mess or in the sergeants' mess. But the cafeteria inside BP was more democratic, being a place where a colonel could sit at the same table as a private. Even after the move into the army camp, where Joan and I ate in separate messes, we still ate in the cafeteria when on night duty. More democratic also was the Garden Café and the force's canteen in the railway station. Occasionally we would have a fine dinner at the more expensive Fountain Hotel on the road to Stony Stratford and within walking distance of BP.

We all knew that we were a long way from the real war and far from bombs, unless we chose to go to London on days off. The perils of the 8th army slogging it out in Italy, the Soviet forces slowly overpowering the mighty German forces, the nightly departure of Allied bombers, some flying to their deaths, at times knowledge of these events made log reading seem a bizarre occupation. Yet although we were only small cogs in an enormous intelligence machine, the combined efforts of all those thousands of men and women who worked at BP, together with the work of many others working in the intelligence services all over the world, were helping to win the war.

9

THE FUSION ROOM

What went on in this secret room to which we log-readers were denied access? When we were finally let into the secret that the cryptanalysts of Hut 6 were regularly decrypting Enigma messages, all became clear. The officers who worked in the Fusion Room at BP, composed of men and women, some in the army and others civilians, were comparing decrypted German messages obtained from Hut 6, with the corresponding data which we log readers had extracted from the daily radio traffic between enemy stations. In this way they were able to build up a W/T picture of the networks of the German air force (GAF) or army which had originated the messages and traffic.

Like many departments at BP, the Fusion Room grew and grew from a small beginning. It began life as a one-man band in 1940, which, by the end of the war in 1945 consisted of perhaps two dozen men and women, including a handful of American army officers who had arrived in 1943. In July, 1940, after the fall of France, Captain Edward Crankshaw of MI8, a literary man turned soldier, was working on Enigma decrypts from BP at a building in Caxton Street, Westminster, London. He was attempting to construct a picture of the GAF communications systems in France, using information gleaned from call-signs, addresses and frequencies. On another floor below him a newly-formed group was reading logs supplied by the intercept stations and constructing diagrams showing the routeing of messages flowing between GAF units in France. One day that summer Crankshaw visited the log reading party, which became known as the Central Party, and borrowed some of their diagrams. By fusing the information from the logs with the information he had from the Enigma decrypts, he was able to construct much clearer pictures of German networks in France.

The work increased and more staff were recruited to the work of fusion, the aim being to continue the work Crankshaw had begun and produce as complete as possible a picture of the W/T networks in any area where the GAF was operating. From France, studies expanded to cover the activities of the GAF in the Low countries, the Balkans and Africa.

In October, 1940, the Central Party, moved first to Harpenden and then in July, 1941, to Beaumanor, a large pseudo-Elizabethan house near Quorn in Leicestershire, where the largest British intercept station was already installed. It was then that the Fusion Room was first so-named. At first we log readers were not allowed to enter the rooms occupied by the Fusion Room staff because we had not been told that the Enigma ciphers were being decrypted at BP and sent to Beaumanor. But after the Central Party moved to Bletchley on 3 May 1942, it was decided, after much argument, that the log readers should be let into the secret. Gordon Welchman, the Cambridge mathematician who was in charge of Hut 6 at that time, was in favour of revealing the secret, which would make the work of fusion so much easier. It was he who gathered together about forty of us log readers on 23 January, 1943 to tell us the good news. The following day we moved into the new Block D, after more than eight months in two different crowded wooden huts.

As the war progressed, the Central Party from Beaumanor became an integral part of Hut 6, mainly assisting the cryptanalysts with information about German networks. There was considerable overlapping of effort because a special liaison party, attached to Hut 3 which had enjoyed a close relationship with the Central Party when we were at Beaumanor, was still operating. Now, with both units at BP, there was talk of amalgamation. This was not achieved, however, until November, 1943, when we moved yet again to new quarters in Block G. It was at this point in our history that the new enlarged unit became known as SIXTA.

The Fusion Room became the central part of SIXTA. By collecting information from the logs provided by the intercept stations, it was able to construct the complete W/T picture of the enemy order of battle. It supplied information which enabled Major Morrison to build up his famous wall-map which revealed the up to date picture of the disposition of German forces. Hut 3 intelligence officers frequently consulted the Fusion Room on intelligence matters. It was also able to help the cryptanalysts of Hut 6, by providing information about call-signs and frequencies and repeats of messages. A weekly publication, the SIXTA SUMMARY was circulated to sections of Huts 3 and 6.

The men and women of the Fusion Room all had a good knowledge of the German language, many of them having been recruited as undergraduates or graduate students of that language. By 1944 the number of staff in the Fusion Room had risen to about twenty-four. Many more had worked in the department and had moved on to other intelligence departments.

Working in senior positions in the Fusion room were three men whose jobs included close liaison with the cryptanalysts of Hut 6 and the interpreters of intelligence in Hut 3. The phrase 'lateral thinking' only came into the language in about 1966 when Dr Edward de Bono wrote of two methods of thought – vertical and lateral. The latter may be described as a method of seeking solutions of difficult problems by ignoring the orthodox logical approach and arriving at solutions from different angles. These three men who practised such methods all held the rank of army major. They were Freddie Edwards and Neil Webster ('Willy'), whose changed fortunes I wrote about in Chapter 5, on RECRUITMENT. The third, Edward Rushworth, appears in the Biography section at the end of this book.

10

CARELESS TALK

On any night when the moon was full the Luftwaffe could not have failed to find Bletchley Park if they had known of its existence. The main railway line from Euston station in London passed through Bletchley, where it was intersected by lines east and west to Cambridge and Oxford. With the moonlight gleaming on the railway lines German bombers would easily have found the target. Early in the war a lone German bomber dropped several bombs over Bletchley, only one of which landed in the Park, doing little damage. It was thought the pilot had lost his way or that he was trying to find the big railway repair building at nearby Wolverton. Fortunately, the Germans did not appear to have known the whereabouts of GC&CS, which, during the inter-war years, had been in London and had moved to Bletchley Park at the beginning of World War II. There were no air raid shelters at BP. If bombs had fallen the safest places would have been in the wooden huts, except in the case of a direct hit. There would have been a greater chance of survival in a hut than if one had been buried in the ruins of a two-storied block or the Mansion.

Many of the thousands of people in Bletchley Town and in the surrounding villages, who provided billets for the hordes of civilians, army, air force and naval personnel, must have guessed that BP was some kind of intelligence centre. Some may even have guessed that wireless communication was involved. Mrs Jones, at whose home I was billeted for more than a year, overhead careless talk one day when she was returning from a shopping trip to Oxford. As her train steamed into Bletchley, a man in her compartment of the carriage had spoken openly about the 'wireless goings-on' in the Park. Mrs Jones told me about this, knowing like everybody else the slogans that appeared on posters: 'Careless talk costs lives', 'Walls have ears', and the infamous 'Be like Dad, keep Mum'. I reported Mrs Jones's story to a security officer at BP who called at the house and questioned her; but although she was able to describe the man, she did not know him. We heard nothing more.

Visiting my sister Jean, a farmer's wife in Yorkshire, on a week-end leave, I was startled when Arthur, my brother-in-law, suddenly, as we ate our evening meal, said, 'Don't you sometimes get tired, Jim, reading all those codes?'. Although I was not working on codes and ciphers, it was a shrewd guess. Taken by surprise I mumbled 'What do you mean, Arthur?'

Towards the end of the war it was decreed by the War Office that shoulder flashes should be worn on all army battle dress. In most cases this meant the name of the regiment. In our case the prominent words INTELLIGENCE CORPS appeared in white on a green background. Long-distance train travellers from the north must have been puzzled to see ten or twenty Intelligence Corps soldiers boarding the train at Bletchley station when it stopped there on the way to London.

Few of the thousands working at BP on minor ciphers and on clerical and machine duties knew anything about Enigma. Even senior officers at the front other than generals were not aware that the intelligence fed to them was derived from German ciphers. The information sent to them was always disguised to make it appear that it came from spies or from captured documents. Only a few knew about the German Enigma cipher machine and that its messages were being regularly decrypted. Those of us at BP who did know about it were all aware how important it was that this information should never reach the Germans. Mr Churchill's well-known remark about the code-breakers, that 'These were my geese who laid the golden eggs and never cackled', may have been apocryphal. However, it was fortunate that the only cackling that occurred was of help to the Russians, our allies, and not to the Germans.

John Cairncross and Anthony Blunt, believing that we were not giving enough intelligence to the Russians through the British Military Mission in Moscow, both passed on some intelligence derived from Enigma messages. Cairncross, who had worked at BP, claimed that it was the information about the German order of battle which he gave the Russians that enabled them to win the important battle of Kursk. Although some intelligence was shared with the Soviet Union, through the British Military Mission, great care was taken to hide the sources. It was feared that if the Russians knew that we had decrypted Enigma they might inadvertently reveal the secret to the Germans. In fact they did learn of our success from Cairncross, Blunt and probably Philby, and they obviously guarded the information securely. It is still not known whether the Russian cryptographic experts had also broken the Enigma cipher.

I do not remember seeing any armed soldiers patrolling BP. The huts and brick buildings could be freely entered but nobody wandered in to other departments or wished to do so. There was, of course, tight security at the main gate, with admittance only to those with a pass. The guards would enter all buses arriving, flashing their torches as we held up our passes.

11

THE THREE Js

Who were the three Js? They were three of the thousands of women recruited to Bletchley Park to serve as civilians, or members of the three services. Jean, Joan and Joyce were in the Auxiliary Territorial Service (ATS), which was the women's army. They arrived together at BP one day in October 1942.

Jean, the youngest, was not quite sixteen years old when World War II started. Jean Faraday Davies, still at school in Wales, had a Welsh father and an English mother. She had decided to specialise in modern languages and, after taking the necessary exams at school, went to Manchester University to read French and German. After one year she left, deciding that reading modern languages was pointless in time of war. Wishing to do a useful job in the war she applied to join the Forestry Corps. Before commencing work however, she happened to meet her old headmistress, who was horrified to hear of her decision. The headmistress must have mentioned Jean's abilities in German to someone on high, for a few days later a telegram arrived, summoning her to an interview in London. This took place in an office above Rootes' motor show room in Piccadilly and included a German test. Shortly afterwards Jean received a notice asking her to report to Talavera training centre in Northampton, where she arrived on the same day as the second J.

A little older than Jean, Joan Watkins, a Londoner, was seventeen when the war began. With the surname Watkins, her father's ancestors must have come from Wales. Her mother had a French grandfather who had emigrated from Le Havre to Soho in London about the time of the French Revolution. Joan was also a student of modern languages, at Camden School in London, where she was specialising in German. She had won a language scholarship from the London County Council to enable her to improve her fluency by living with a family in Switzerland. In normal times students would spend months with families in Germany before going to university, but, because of the tense international situation it was considered wiser to go to Switzerland. The war came when Joan was living with a family in Berne. She could not communicate with her parents in London. Mobilisation was at its peak in France, which meant that most of the trains were occupied by French soldiers. After some delays Joan joined a group of British people crossing France by train. They eventually reached the coast, where they found a ship to carry them in the dark across the English Channel. Joan arrived home to find her parents overjoyed to see her, having been uneasy and worried, not knowing whether she might be marooned in Switzerland for the duration of the war.

Most of the London schools had been evacuated at the beginning of the war, because of the expected massive bombing by the Luftwaffe. Joan joined her school friends at Camden School, which by this time had been evacuated to Uppingham in Rutland. The school moved later to Grantham in Lincolnshire, but when bombs fell there, it finally came to rest in Stamford. Two years went by. Joan passed her exams and won a scholarship to Westfield, one of the women's colleges of the University of London. This was not the end of her travels, for Westfield had also been evacuated from London. Leaving its Hampstead home, the college had gone to Oxford, where it occupied the building of St Peter's Hall (later to become St Peter's College) in New Inn Hall Street. It was an interesting world. Joan joined the University Labour Club, meeting young men and women, some of whom would in later life become well-known authors. Among them were Iris Murdoch, the novelist and philosopher, Philip Larkin, the poet, Kingsley Amis, the novelist, John Terraine, the military historian and Jim Holt, who became Professor of Medieval History at Cambridge.

After one year at Oxford Joan had to choose whether she would complete her course and become a teacher , or do some kind of national service. Not wishing to become a schoolteacher, she chose the latter. Like Jean she was called for interview at the same offices in Piccadilly, and finally arrived at the Talavera training centre in Northampton.

Joyce Robinson, the third J, was a Yorkshire girl, the youngest of five children. Only seven years old when her father died suddenly, Joyce, her mother and the family, had tough times making ends meet in the 1930s. Joyce was a bright scholar, and, through the generosity of her older brothers was the only one in the family to go to university. She had decided to read French and German at King's College, University of London. When a schoolgirl she had spent a happy summer holiday in France with a French family. In 1939 she was again staying with this family and hoping later to spend a year at the Sorbonne. When the war started in September, Joyce hurried to the Gare du Nord in Paris, where in the confusion she nearly boarded the wrong train, which was taking French poilus to the Front. She arrived safely home without further mishaps. Having completed her degree in 1941, Joyce started looking for war work. Appointed to a post in a regional office of the Ministry of Home Security in Birmingham, Joyce soon became bored and applied to join the Army, the Navy or the Royal Air Force. After interview she also came to Talavera camp in Northampton .

The three Js had to endure a couple of weeks of square-bashing, learning how to salute and how to tell your left foot from your right. Kitted out and dressed in khaki they were sent to Beaumanor in Leicestershire, for a month-long course in the rudiments of radio signals and communications. After that they were ready to enter the unknown world at Bletchley Park, where their knowledge of German was soon put to the test.

Before the end of the war all three of the Js became commissioned officers. Later in the war Joyce married Major Edward Rushworth ('Rush') who worked in the Fusion room. Joan married me, Jimmy Thirsk, in September, 1945; at that time I was a Company-Sergeant-Major, reading logs in SIXTA, attached to Hut 6. Jean married an ex-soldier who had served in the Royal Engineers. The friendship of the Js during the three years they worked together at BP continued after the war. All three had satisfying jobs in later life. Jean completed her degree at Manchester and later, taught English, and later, linguistics at the university in Nairobi, Kenya. Her husband, Gordon Wallwork, was a railway engineer in Kenya. When they had to leave Kenya Jean taught at Furzedown Teacher Training College. Joyce taught French at different schools, firstly at a night school, then at two secondary schools in Leicester. Joan completed her degree at Westfield College, but changed horses in midstream by reading History instead of German and French. University posts at the London School of Economics and Leicester University led to her final job as Reader in Economic History at Oxford. Joyce died in 2002 at the age of eighty-three. The other two Js are close neighbours in Kent. Joyce had two daughters, Helen (who wrote the foreword to this book) and Diana. Jean has a son and a daughter, Helen and Hugh. My wife Joan and I have a son and a daughter, Martin and Jane. The three Js and their husbands all rejoiced in their grandchildren. Jean and Joan and their husbands still do.

12

THE GEESE AND OTHERS WHO CACKLED

'These were my geese who laid the golden eggs and never cackled'

It is unlikely that these words were ever spoken by Churchill in public, for he died in 1965, long before the secrets of Bletchley Park became generally known. When Group-Captain Frederick W. Winterbotham's book *The Ultra Secret* was published in 1974, it aroused great public interest by its revelation that the British had been regularly decrypting messages transmitted by the German cipher machine known as Enigma. Winterbotham (1897-1990), head of the Royal Air Force section of MI6 from 1930 to 1945, had an important job, for he was responsible for the distribution of intelligence, derived from Enigma decrypts, to Winston Churchill, the Prime Minister, to the Joint Intelligence Committee, to the chiefs of staff and to commanders in the field. After the publication of *The Ultra Secret* some of his old colleagues deplored the revelations in it; but in fact the text was vetted by the authorities before publication.

However, the fact that we were decrypting Enigma during the war had already been revealed a number of times after the war ended in September 1945. Some of these revelations must have come to the notice of the authorities; yet no prosecutions under the Officials Secrets Act were made. Presumably the government did not wish to promote the widespread publicity which would have followed any court proceedings.

As long ago as 1947, when I was working in the Information Department of the now defunct National Central Library, I found, under the subject-heading 'ciphers', in the American *Readers' Guide to Periodical Literature*, two articles which were probably the first to deal with wartime cryptography. They were in the popular and widely-circulated American magazines *Life* (26 November 1945) and *Time* (17 December 1945), published less than four months after World War II had ended. They revealed to the general public that the Americans and British had been decrypting Japanese and German enciphered messages during the war. The *Time* article reported the hearings in December 1945 of the United States Senate Joint Committee on the investigation into the attack on Pearl Harbour in 1941. The Committee insisted on officially recording two letters dated September 1944 from General Marshall, then in supreme command of the United States forces, which he had written to Governor Dewey, a candidate for the Presidency, after the death of Roosevelt in 1945.

The war against Germany and Japan had ended and Marshall had heard that Dewey might refer during his campaign to the breaking of Japanese machine ciphers. In one of the letters he warned Dewey of serious consequences if such secret information were made public. He added that

> a further source of embarrassment is the fact that the British government is involved concerning its most secret sources of information, regarding which only the Prime Minister, the chiefs of staff, and a very limited number of other officials have knowledge.

Time quoted General Marshall, writing in one of the letters 'that the U.S. with the help of the British, had decoded German as well as Japanese messages.' *Time* pointed out that the publication of these two letters 'thus gave the Germans their first knowledge that their code had been broken,' and added, 'It was also a breach of diplomatic confidence with the British, who had let the U.S. in on the secret on the understanding that it would be kept.' Governor Dewey agreed not to mention these matters during his campaign. But in December 1945, after the war had ended, the Committee ignored General Marshall's plea that the letters should not be published. If the *Time* and *Life* articles did come to the notice of the Japanese and German intelligence services, it must have been a bitter blow for their organisations to realise that their machine ciphers, which they thought impregnable, had been broken.

In Chapter 3 ('Magic') of Roberta Wohlstetter's book *Pearl Harbor, Warning and Decision (*Stanford U.P., 1962*)* appeared more revelations about the breaking of Japanese and German ciphers. The principal American cryptologist, Colonel William F. Friedman, and his wife and colleagues had constructed replicas of the Japanese cipher machine known as *Purple*. In 1941, one of the replicas 'had been sent to Great Britain in return for the keys and machines necessary to decode German codes and ciphers.'

There were in fact many more occasions after this that the successes of the American and British cryptologists were revealed in books and newspapers. Seven years before the publication of Winterbotham's book, Malcolm Muggeridge, journalist and former MI6 officer, also revealed that the British broke German ciphers during World War II. In a long review of the English translation of the book: *The Lucy Ring (La Guerre a été gagnée en Suisse)* by P.Accoce and P.Quet, in *The Observer* (8 January 1967), Muggeridge wrote:

> I had occasion while serving as an intelligence officer, to visit the establishment in which, if my supposition is correct, the Lucy pabulum was being produced. It was a country house where the cipher-breakers —for the most part dons, chess-players and violinists, as far as I

could gather--lived together. In the lunch interval there was a game of rounders on the lawn, in which I joined.

In another passage in his review, Muggeridge spoke of a country house, without naming it :

Here the Intelligence department concerned with code-breaking, greatly expanded and enriched by an infusion of amateurs during the war, had succeeded in cracking the German military ciphers -- a terrific and, for security reasons, little known feat, never before, to the best of my knowledge, pulled off on anything like the same scale. It meant that, thanks to radio interception, a British general could look to have his German opposite number's orders of the day on his breakfast table, along with the morning paper -- a great help in winning battles.

A little over five years later, Muggeridge, reviewing two books in the *Observer* (2 April, 1972)) again spoke of the cipher-breakers playing rounders 'to refresh themselves for their arduous labours.' In this review he mentions that the country house was at Bletchley.

Hugh Trevor-Roper (later Lord Dacre), Regius Professor of History in the University of Oxford wrote of the decrypting of Enigma. In his book *The Philby Affair*, published in 1968, he mentioned GC&CS, in a chapter entitled 'An imperfect organisation.' Although he did not reveal that it was at Bletchley Park, he wrote that it 'produced invaluable results which were supplied direct to the intelligence departments of all the services.' He also referred to 'C', (Sir Stewart Menzies), the head of the Secret Intelligence Services (SIS) 'who every day conveyed a somewhat arbitrary selection of these most secret sources to the Prime Minister.' Later in the same chapter he wrote of 'the breaking of the Enigma machine', describing it as 'the great intelligence triumph of the war.'

Winterbotham himself had also already written about Enigma before the publication of *The Ultra Secret* in 1974. In his book *Secret and Personal*, which appeared in 1969, he mentioned cryptography during World War II. Pointing out that intelligence depends on pipelines laid in peacetime, he added:

It was in 1940 that one such pipeline provided us with evidence that there would be possibilities of considerable, if intermittent, success against the German cipher machine Enigma.

Winterbotham also mentioned that he became Sir Stewart Menzies's personal liaison officer with the principal allied commanders. He was also responsible for sending important items to the Prime Minister, who asked 'that I should give him a short note of explanation in such circumstances'. Winterbotham was also in charge of the Special Liaison Units which were stationed with the commanders in the field and so was responsible for passing Ultra material to them. He also wrote of his memories 'of the role played by our most valuable and reliable source of intelligence in a few of the vital turning points of the war.'

Also in 1969, Richard Deacon's book *A History of the British Secret Service* was published. Richard Deacon was the pseudonym of Donald McCormick who was at one time editor of *The Sunday Times*. A prolific author, he also wrote books on the secret services of China, Russia, Israel and Japan. Many other books were published under his pseudonym, mostly but not all about intelligence matters. In a chapter of his *A History of the British Secret Service* about the Lucy Ring, he wrote that 'British Intelligence succeeded quite early on in cracking German military codes and ciphers.' He also told of 'a team of cipher experts closeted away at a country house near Bletchley.' He added that the Germans had developed a machine cipher and continued: 'Soon it was possible to speed up the process of deciphering German messages so as to prepare a day-to-day analysis of German intelligence.'

Not one of Churchill's geese, but a voluminous writer on the history of intelligence and on military history, was the next person who revealed some of the secrets of BP. Ladislas Farago, was born in Hungary in 1906. Working in America in the middle of the 20th century, he had for ten years been gathering material for a book about the Abwehr, the German secret service, whose head was Admiral Wilhelm Canaris. In 1967 he came across a hitherto unknown box of microfilms in the National Archives at Washington DC, which covered the work of the Abwehr during the period 1920-1945. Farago's book entitled *The Game of the Foxes*, based on these records, was published in the USA in 1971 and in Britain by Hodder and Stoughton in 1972. Its subtitle was: 'British and German intelligence operations and personalities which changed the course of the second world war'. In one of his chapters in this book he revealed the whereabouts of the Government Code and Cipher School:

In 1941, a major breakthrough enabled MI 5 to gain direct access to all Abwehr messages that went on the air. The brilliant cryptologist Dillwyn Knox, working at the Government Code and Cipher School at the Bletchley centre of British code-cracking, solved the keying of the Abwehr's Enigma machine.

In another chapter he mentioned that the British had obtained a working model of the Enigma machine from the Poles:

The Polish-Swedish ring represented an indispensable link in Britain's overall coverage of German activities. It was the first to alert the British to the impending German invasion of the Soviet Union in 1941. And thanks to its efforts, the British obtained a working model of the Enigma machine, which the Germans used to encipher their top secret messages.

In a footnote Farago mentioned the Enigma machine again, explaining that:

During World War II, the battery-powered, typewriter-sized device (which required three men to operate) was the Wehrmacht's top system.

Kim Philby, one of the five Cambridge undergaduates who became Soviet agents before World War II, had also during the war joined the British secret service, working in a variety of departments, but never I believe at Bletchley. He had, however, access to Ultra material. In his autobiography *My Silent War*, first published in 1968, Kim Philby mentioned GC&CS many times. When he worked as a journalist on *The Times* while awaiting call-up in 1940, he had an unsuccessful interview 'arranged by a mutual friend, with Frank Birch, a leading light in the GC&CS, a cryptoanalytical establishment which cracked enemy (and friendly) codes.'

He wrote of interception and cryptographic matters often in his autobiography.

By interception of wireless signals, it is possible to obtain huge quantities of secret intelligence without breaking any national or international law. Before wireless messages can be read, they must be decyphered. This was done in wartime Britain by the so-called GC&CS at Bletchley. Much of their work was brilliantly successful. By early 1942, the trickle of intercepted Abwehr telegrams had become a flood. This was largely the work of Dilly Knox, who had succeeded in penetrating the secrets of the cypher machine used by the Abwehr.

Another book published about six years before Winterbotham's *The Ultra Secret* was *The Codebreakers* (Weidenfeld and Nicolson, 1968*),* which had already appeared in America. David Kahn, the indefatigable American author of this truly monumental book of 1164 pages, is one of the leading world experts in the field of cryptography. His book, subtitled 'The story of secret writing', goes back to the earliest times. In his preface Kahn pointed out that the book is not exhaustive:

for a foolish secrecy still clothes much of World War II cryptology – though I believe the outlines of the achievements are known – and to tell just that story in full would require a book the size of this.

Kahn was clearly aware that the British had cracked the German Enigma cipher at Bletchley.

In 1939, the Foreign Office moved what it euphemistically called its Department of Communications to Bletchley Park, an estate and mansion in Bletchley, a town in Buckinghamshire about fifty miles northwest of London.

Kahn also knew that:

the Foreign Office, finding this mansion too small, added many buildings, including a cafeteria and a large hall. ... Eventually, seven thousand worked and trained here, including members of the armed services.

In this veritable *olla podrida* of a book were also many references to 'Purple', the Japanese cipher, so named by the Americans. Kahn describes the solution of this machine cipher by William Friedman, his wife and staff, as: 'the greatest feat of cryptanalysis the world had yet known'.

One of the first books entirely about the German Enigma cipher was published in Paris in 1973, the year before Winterbotham's book appeared. It was *Enigma, ou la plus grande énigme de la guerre 1939-1945*. The author, Brigadier-General Gustave Bertrand, head of the French cryptographic services, had been closely connected with the breaking of the ciphers produced by the early versions of the Enigma machine, for he had collaborated with the Polish cryptographers in the 1930s. In his book he told of bringing over to England in August 1939, one of the two replicas of the machine, constructed by the Poles, a present to their colleagues in France and England.

As a captain in the French army, Bertrand, working in the cryptographic department, first became aware that the Germans had started using an electrical cipher machine, in the 1920s. Michel Garder, in his book *La Guerre secrète*...(1967) claimed that the French had also constructed a replica of the Enigma machine and had some success until the Germans introduced more refinements.

Bertrand's book has never been translated into English; it received little publicity in this country and is unknown to the general public, although well-known in intelligence circles.

There are no doubt many other revelations about Bletchley Park which were published before Winterbotham's book that I have not seen; but the few about which I have written above make it clear that his book did not come as a surprise to the intelligence services, or to those members of the general public who were interested in the subject and who read books and articles about intelligence matters.

The most important example of a goose who cackled secretly while the war was still on, was that of John Cairncross. In his case, however, although he has often been called a traitor, he was passing Bletchley intelligence to our ally, the Soviet Union, not to Germany. Many people who did not live through the war do not realise the warm feelings most of the British had for the people and soldiers of the Soviet Union. They realised that, just as we were fighting for our lives, so were they. Their contribution to the defeat of Germany was appreciated by the British people, and it was clear that had the Nazis won the war against the Soviet Union, the whole might of the German army would have been turned on to their western front. Could the British, the Americans and our other allies have withstood such an onslaught?

John Cairncross (1913-1995), was a Scot who had graduated from Glasgow University before the war with a degree in French and German, followed by study at the Sorbonne; at Cambridge, his next place of study, he attended Communist Party meetings. In later years he claimed that he was never a party member, describing himself as a fellow traveller. He then sat for the civil service examinations, and, having achieved the highest marks that year, began work at the Foreign Office in 1936. Soon afterwards he was recruited to work as an agent of the Soviet Union. After working as private secretary to Lord Hankey, in which role he was able to pass cabinet and foreign office papers to his Soviet controller, Cairncross was called up in 1942, serving briefly in the Royal Armoured Corps. From there, because of his excellent knowledge of German, he was transferred to Hut 3 at Bletchley Park. During more than a year there as an army captain, he regularly went home to his flat in London, passing on to his Soviet controller masses of documents, including raw, decrypted, but untranslated German messages. His next move, at his own request, was to the Secret Intelligence Service (SIS), where he worked in a section devoted to counter-espionage abroad. He continued supplying intelligence to the Soviet Union, and after the war when he was employed at the Treasury. His name did not come to the attention of the press until after Thatcher, the Prime Minister, had denounced Anthony Blunt in 1979. Cairncross was not prosecuted, although interrogated on numerous occasions.

Cairncross held the view that, although Britain was supplying the Soviet Union with some intelligence, disguised in the case of Ultra material, we were not giving them all the information which would help them to win the fierce battles they were waging against the Nazi invaders. It is true that the British Military Mission in Moscow passed much intelligence to the Russians; they even presented them with a captured Enigma machine, complete with instructions, but with no instructions how to decrypt messages. The British were fearful that the Russians might inadvertently give away our secret which might lead the Germans to improve their methods, rendering our decrypting methods useless. In fact, the Russians must have known, from material supplied by Cairncoss, Blunt and others that we were decrypting Enigma. If the Russians cackled, the Germans failed to hear them; for they remained convinced that their Enigma and other machine ciphers were secure.

Some have described Cairncross as a traitor. But those who do so must answer this question: Did the information he passed on to the Soviet Union help them to win the battles against the German forces? If the answer is yes, it follows that it was to our advantage also that Germany was being defeated. To quote his own words:

The Soviet Union was fighting a life or death struggle against the Germans and the military information was crucial. I was providing information at the time to help Britain's allies – the Russians –to win.

Cairncross was one of the five Cambridge undergraduates who, in the 1930s had espoused the Communist cause. The others were Anthony Blunt, Guy Burgess, Donald Maclean and Harold "Kim" Philby, all of whom became agents of the Soviet Union. All of these, except probably Maclean, had access to Bletchley material, although Cairncross was the only one who had worked at Bletchley. Maclean, who had been third secretary at the British Embassy in Paris before the war, moved to the Foreign Office. Towards the end of the war he transferred to the British Embassy in Washington,DC, becoming first secretary. There he was closely in touch with the post-war development of the atomic bomb, information about which was eagerly received by the Soviet Union. In 1951, knowing he was under suspicion, he fled to the Soviet Union with Guy Burgess.

Philby worked in SIS from 1940, later joining section 5 (counter-intelligence) in 1941. By 1944 he was head of section 9 which was concerned with the collection and interpretation of information about communist espionage and subversion. After serving in Turkey after the war and later in Washington DC, he finally became a journalist in Beirut. In 1963 he was offered immunity from prosecution if he returned to London and made a full confession. Turning this offer down, he fled to Russia in 1963 and later became a Soviet citizen.

Anthony Blunt also handled Ultra material from Bletchley which he passed on to his Soviet controller when he was working at MI 5. It is said that he passed on more than a thousand documents. Blunt, a distinguished authority on art from his undergraduate days, was later appointed Surveyor of the King's pictures (later the Queen's); he also became Director of the Courtauld Institute of Art and a Professor of the History of Art in the University of London. When his wartime activities became known in 1964, MI5, who had had him under suspicion for years, offered him immunity from prosecution if he made a full confession. No prosecution followed, but Blunt was stripped of his knighthood.

All the five Cambridge undergraduates and other agents had codenames by which they were known to the Soviet intelligence services. Long after the war, when the American codebreakers began decrypting old Soviet messages to many countries, some of these codenames were revealed for the first time. Most of them were equated with known agents, but there was one person with the code-name BARON, who had apparently worked at Bletchley Park during the war. This goose (or gander?) may never be identified, unless more records are released here or in Russia.

13

THE POETS OF BLETCHLEY PARK

Many of my fellow log-readers were devoted to literature, ancient and modern. A few of them wrote short stories and poems in their leisure hours. There were I am sure many amateur poets among the thousands of men and women at BP. For most of us were young then and although we were not living in a very heaven, it was certainly bliss to be alive. Perhaps some of their poems still exist in penny notebooks or on scraps of paper?

Some wrote satirical verse and here is one delightful poem that has survived :

BP (Bumph Palace)

I think that I shall never see
A sight so curious as BP.
This place called up at war's behest
And peopled by the strangely dressed;
Yet what they do they cannot say
Nor ever will till Judgement Day.

For six long years we have been there
Subject to local scorn and stare.
We came by transport and by train,
The dull and brilliantly insane.
What shall we do, where shall we be
When God at last redunds BP?

The Air Force types who never fly,
Soldiers who neither do nor die,
Landlubber Navy, beards complete,
Civilians slim, long-haired, effete;
Yet what they did they never knew,
And if they told it wasn't true.

If I should die think only this of me
I served my country at BP
And should my son ask 'What did you

In the atomic World War II ?'
God only knows - and He won't tell,
For after all – BP was Hell!

Ena Mary "Bobby" Osborn (later Lady Hooper)

There were, however, at least four poets at BP who had published poetry either in journals or in volumes of poetry before the war. At the time I only knew that two were working there: Vernon Watkins, and F.L.Lucas. The others were Henry Reed and Frank T. Prince. There may have been more poets at BP, if so, I am sure that I shall be told about them by somebody who reads this page.

Vernon Watkins, a Welshman, was born in 1906. Although his parents were Welsh speakers, he never learned to speak the language, although he could read it with a dictionary by his side. Yet his widow Gwen, who was also at Bletchley, said later that 'The rhythm of that noble and ancient tongue beat in his blood'. She also wrote that he called himself 'A Welsh poet writing in English'. Watkins was interested in poetry at the age of five and was already writing verse by the time he was eight. His father worked at Lloyd's Bank all his life, and Vernon was eventually to follow him into banking. But first he was sent to a public school at Repton in England; then on to Magdalene College, Cambridge to read German and French. After one year he resigned, telling the Master of the College, A.C. Benson, the essayist, that he was only interested in writing poetry and did not want to see it 'criticised out of him'. Benson told him that he would live to curse the day he was born, to which Vernon replied 'I have already done so'.

At twenty-two, according to Gwen, his eyes were opened to the nature of time and eternity. 'His themes' she said, 'were constant and recurrent, but they were the themes of the bards in all ages: Birth and Death, Love and Forgiveness'. His first volume of poems was published in 1941 with the title *Ballad of the Mari Lwyd*. A second volume *The Lamp and the Veil* appeared towards the end of the war, in 1945. *Selected Poems, 1930-1960,* was published in 1967, the year of his death.

There is no doubt that the influence of Welsh mythology was powerful; but he had translated into verse poems by a number of the German and French writers who had also influenced his work. The poetry of W.B. Yeats was a constant inspiration to him, and one of his poems commemorates Vernon's visit to Yeats in his old age. Kathleen Raine, the poet, described him as 'the greatest lyric poet of my generation.'

When the war came Vernon served in the Home Guard. Later, when he was called up in December 1941, his job was in the RAF Police. This proved to be a clear case of 'A square peg in a round hole', and he was transferred to RAF Intelligence, eventually coming to BP with the rank of flight-sergeant. I do not know what he did at Bletchley, but presumably his knowledge of German was useful. At BP a fellow-worker, Gwendolin Mary Davies and he were married on the 2nd of October, 1944. His friend, the poet Dylan Thomas, was to have been his best man, but he failed to turn up at the wedding, later confessing that he could not face a crowd of strange people. Vernon and Gwen lived at Stony Stratford after they were married.

For a man who had once cursed the day he was born, Vernon was not unhappy at BP. Writing to a friend, the poet Michael Hamburger, he refers to being demobbed early in 1946 and 'lucky to have a pleasant environment during the last three years'. To the same friend he wrote in 1952 on the subject of critics:

You know what I think generally about critics in this country, with perhaps two or three exceptions. I also believe that there can be no great criticism without love and that the very nature and habits of most critics makes them incapable of an act of love.

Here is the first stanza of his poem *Peace in the Welsh Hills:*

> *Calm is the landscape when the storm has passed,*
> *Brighter the fields, and fresh with fallen rain.*
> *Where gales beat out new colour from the hills*
> *Rivers fly faster and upon their banks*
> *Birds preen their wings, and irises revive.*
> *Not so the cities burnt alive with fire*
> *Of man's destruction: when their smoke is spent,*
> *No phoenix rises from the ruined walls.*

In 1967 he went with his wife to Seattle by invitation from the University of Washington to be Visiting Professor. Vernon had a heart problem and he died soon after arriving there, after playing the winning stroke in a long men's foursome game of tennis. He was only sixty-one years old. Vernon had many friends who were poets. After his death, a book was published in 1970, edited by Leslie Norris, in which Gwen and twenty friends, mostly poets, recalled his life and works, some writing in verse, others in prose.

Another poet friend was Philip Larkin. Joan, my future wife, was a sergeant in the ATS at BP; her name was also Watkins, but she was not related to Vernon. One day a telegram from Philip Larkin arrived on her desk addressed 'Sgt Watkins'. Joan had met Larkin at Oxford when he was a fellow member of the Labour Club, but, realising that the telegram was not for her, she found Sgt Vernon Watkins's telephone extension number and passed on the message, which was an arrangement to travel from Oxford to meet Vernon near Bletchley.

I did not know that Henry Reed was at BP until long after the war when I read in an obituary notice that, after military training, he was seconded to naval intelligence at BP in 1942, the year that I arrived there. Like me, Reed was a 1914 baby and like me he was called up into the army. It was his initial training which inspired the writing of his best-known poem, *Naming of Parts*. Some of us in the army knew this poem, having first seen it when it appeared in *The New Statesman* in 1942. The poem recalls the harsh days of infantry training when platoon sergeants barked their way through three long months. Nobody who endured this training can ever forget it. In 1940, in the months after Dunkirk, there was a great shortage of arms. The rifle I was given was a Lee-Enfield dated 1917, which must have been mothballed in the inter-war years. In Reed's poem the Sergeant is instructing his platoon in the mysteries of the rifle. To be heard to best effect the poem should be partly read in the barking voice of the Sergeant, followed in each verse by the soft voice of the poet, whose attention has drifted to other subjects.

NAMING OF PARTS

To-day we have naming of parts. Yesterday,
We had daily cleaning. And to-morrow morning,
We shall have what to do after firing. But to-day,
To-day we have naming of parts. Japonica
Glistens like coral in all the neighbouring gardens,
And to-day we have naming of parts.

This is the lower sling swivel. And this
Is the upper sling swivel, whose use you will see,
When you are given your slings. And this is the piling swivel,
Which in your case you have not got. The branches
Hold in the gardens their silent, eloquent gestures,
Which in our case we have not got.

This is the safety-catch, which is always released
With an easy flick of the thumb. And please do not let me
See anyone using his finger. You can do it quite easy
If you have any strength in your thumb. The blossoms
Are fragile and motionless, never letting anyone see
Any of them using their finger.

And this you can see is the bolt. The purpose of this
Is to open the breech, as you see. We can slide it
Rapidly backwards and forwards: we call this
Easing the spring. And rapidly backwards and forwards
The early bees are assaulting and fumbling the flowers:
They call it easing the Spring.

*They call it easing the Spring: it is perfectly easy
If you have any strength in your thumb: like the bolt,
And the breech, and the cocking-piece, and the point of balance,
Which in our case we have not got; and the almond-blossom
Silent in all of the gardens and the bees going
backwards and forwards,
For to-day we have naming of parts.*

After the war, this poem was included in Reed's first volume of poem: *A Map of Verona* (1946). It has been reprinted in many anthologies. It would have been good to have met Henry Reed at BP, but we knew nothing of people who worked in other sections. After initial training in the Royal Army Ordnance Corps, Reed caught pneumonia. Following convalescence he came to BP, firstly in the Italian section, and then in the Japanese, having had a crash course in the language. In later years he wrote radio plays. Translating and book reviewing kept him busy and there were a few more poems. His *Collected Poems* was published in 1991, five years after his death at the age of seventy-two in 1986.

I did not find out that Frank Templeton Prince was at BP until many years after the war. Frank was born in Kimberley, Cape Province, South Africa, in 1912, the son of a Jewish diamond merchant of Dutch ancestry. His mother, Margaret Hetherington was a schoolteacher of Scottish descent. After studying architecture at the University of Witwatersrand, Frank came to Balliol College, Oxford, to read English. After graduation he attended Princeton University in the USA as a visiting Fellow.

He had started writing poems in the early 1930s and had been in correspondence with T.S. Eliot, who had published several of his poems in *The Criterion*, the periodical of which Eliot was editor. His first book, *Poems*, was published in 1938, by Faber & Faber. Frank was then twenty-six years old. After working from 1937 to 1940 at the Royal Institute of International Affairs, at Chatham House, in the Study Groups department, Frank volunteered for the army. Soon, after infantry training, he was transferred to the Intelligence Corps. At Bletchley he worked on Italian codes and ciphers under Major Peter Alexander. There, in March 1943, he married Elizabeth Bush, who also worked at BP. Soon after they were married, Frank was sent to Egypt, only to find when he got there that the war with Italy had ended in September 1943. Back at Bletchley a year later, he stayed there with Elizabeth until the end of the war. Before demobilisation, in the Spring of 1946, Frank was sent to an Italian prisoner of war camp in Wales, as an interpreter.

Soon after leaving the army, Frank obtained a post at Southampton University as a lecturer in the English department. He remained at Southampton, as a Professor of English Literature from 1957 until his retirement in 1974. But Frank never really retired, for thereafter he taught overseas as visiting professor at the University of the West Indies, Jamaica, at Brandeis University, at Washington University, at Amherst College, Massachusetts and at Sana'a University, North Yemen.

Frank became interested in poetry at a very early age, when his mother introduced him to English literature and particularly to English and Scottish poetry. In an interview long after his retirement he confessed that 'although my poetry seems quite literary… I cannot write anything which doesn't grow out of some experience.' Curiously, he told the same interviewer that his best-known poem *Soldiers Bathing*, much anthologised, contradicted this statement. 'My best known poem, *Soldiers Bathing*, is a reflective poem, rather than being directly about the war. It's not a good poem to my mind. It's not a poem of direct experience at all.'

Roy Macnab reminds us that whereas Frank's

native South Africa, in its physical beauty of flower and fauna …provided him with the themes of his early poems …the broad tradition of European civilisation and in particular Renaissance Italy exerted a later and more profound influence on his writing, not only as a poet but as critic and university teacher.

Macnab also wrote that:

what really makes Prince's work memorable is his own humanity and compassion, a sombre note, amounting almost to melancholy, marking much of what he writes.

Here are a few lines from his poem *Handfast Point:*

> *Pale cliffs and sky*
> *Grow dim, and dimmer;*
> *The headlands die,*
> *And scarcely glimmer.*
> *Night climbs, and in a breeze*
> *Touches the trees.*
> *And one star glows*
> *In the peach-pale west,*
> *And nothing shows*
> *On the bay's dark breast,*
> *And ghostly whispers pass*
> *Through the dry grass.*

Frank died in 2003, leaving his wife, Elizabeth and two daughters. I telephoned him earlier that year to tell him about this chapter on the poets at BP and to ask if I might include him. He readily agreed.

My fourth Bletchley poet is F.L.Lucas, a Cambridge don better known for his literary criticism, his work on classical literature and his translations. Originally a classical scholar, he turned to English literature, on which he lectured at Cambridge through the inter-war years. Born at Hipperholme in Yorkshire in 1894, the son of the headmaster of an ancient Grammar school there, Lucas was of that generation of men who served in both world wars. Commissioned as a very young officer in 1914 at the beginning of the Great War, he survived being wounded in 1916 and gassed in 1917. After these ordeals he was transferred to the Intelligence Corps towards the end of that war.

Lucas was a man of tremendous energy who, between the wars, wrote poems, his first volume *Time and Memory,* appearing in 1929. There followed novels, including a semi-autobiographical one; plays, of which two reached the London stage; many books of literary criticism, and a definitive edition in four volumes of the plays of John Webster. Lucas's seven volumes of poetry were mostly published before World War II, but *Messene Redeemed* appeared in 1940 and *From Many Times and Lands* (1953) was one of the largest of his volumes of verse.

No doubt, his experience of intelligence work in the Great War led to his call to Bletchley. In an essay *Of Books*, Lucas tells how he was summoned to war work at BP in September 1939, leaving behind twenty years of literature and books. His work at BP was not with the cryptanalysts of Hut 6 but in a senior position in Hut 3, having earlier served in the 'Watch' who examined and translated the contents of the decrypted German messages. He was a civilian at BP and one often saw him, striding swiftly through the grounds as if he had not a moment to spare. On one occasion he gave a lecture to us log-readers about the value of the intelligence derived from the Enigma messages. We were all impressed by his grasp of the subject and how well he explained it.

In the essay *Of Books* which appeared in the volume of essays *The Greatest Problem*, Lucas does not mention Bletchley Park, for it was published in 1960, long before the secrets of BP were generally known; he does however, write about his years in Buckinghamshire. Remembering the war, he says:

And yet - though it seems almost disgusting - never was I happier. For, firstly, there was work to be done both fascinating and vital. Secondly, I have never had better colleagues to work with...However long I live, I shall always remember with nostalgia the quiet

Buckinghamshire villages, there at the very heart of England, and of English nature and of English good nature; the sunlight in hours off duty, among the fir woods above Woburn Sands; the blaze of bluebells in Duncombe Wood by Great Brickhill, that no terrors oversea or overhead turned pale in their Spring glory; the brave thunder, as we worked through the small hours, of the night-expresses for Holyhead and Carlisle which not all Hitler's bombardments could keep from their indomitable course. Books with a purpose may often suffer; but life rammed with purpose is surely the best. I shudder at the thought of such time's return; but I would surely not have missed it.

F.L.Lucas died in 1967 at the age of seventy-three. Here is part of a moving poem which Lucas dedicated to his two young children Jenifer and Oliver ('O best of all my works!') They too must follow soon the 'tracks of this rough world':

> *Ah to have left for you a happier one!*
> *We dreamed to build. But on our walls begun*
> *Twice roared the waters of another Flood,*
> *Leaving earth heaped with ruins and bones and mud*
> *Upon our wreckage, yours to build again.*
> *Where we could but defend, may you attain!*
> *Yours be a world, not perfect, yet at peace*
> *A kindlier earth, where slave and tyrant cease.*
> *We leave you our courage (may you need it not!)*
> *Our hope; at the least, our love - when we too lie forgot.*

14

SHENLEY ROAD MILITARY CAMP

Most of the men and women who lived at Shenley Road Military Camp from January 1944 until the end of the war could tell you amusing and often hilarious stories of life in the camp. But it would require the pen of Jaroslav Hasek, the Czech author of *The Good Soldier Schweik,* to tell the story of the strange adventures of Colonel Fillingham of the *Durham Light Infantry* and his underlings, whose attempts to impose order and discipline on the men and women of Bletchley Park proved impossible. The ghost of Schweik certainly stalked the muddy tracks in the camp.

How did the camp come to be built? The number of civilian billets in Bletchley and in the towns and villages in the region was rapidly dwindling as the population of BP increased. Buses ran day and night all over the countryside bringing us in to work, then taking us home again; finally it became impossible to find any more billets. It was then that the decision was taken to withdraw army men and women of all ranks from their civilian billets and transfer them to an army camp. To this end, unknown to us who knew nothing of the plan, builders, carpenters, plumbers and electricians had been hard at work during 1943, building an army camp, adjacent to BP, but outside the perimeter.

This Shenley Road camp was declared ready for occupation in January 1944, when all the BP men and women, army officers and other ranks, had to leave their billets, where most of them had been comfortably lodged. The first few days were appalling. The huts they had built were surrounded by muddy tracks; not all the electricity was working, and the army type coke-stoves, with chimneys up through the roofs of the huts, were unlit. 'Palliasses' a notice read, 'should be collected from the Quartermaster's store and filled with straw from the building next door.' The canny ones, with previous experience of straw mattresses, made sure that their palliasses were stuffed until they would hold no more; the inexperienced ones soon found that their mattresses became like pancakes after a couple of months.

Staff-Sergeant Betty Vine-Stevens, who worked in the Japanese section, remembers that:

… the ATS had three square palliasses for each bed. In order to reduce the risk of falling into the gaps as they slithered and slipped during the night, we sacrificed a blanket in which to parcel the palliasses. That helped! Although the huts were designed to sleep 16 to 18, there were, in fact, 32 in some of them. We arranged our beds head to toe down each side and got up in rotation so that we had room to dress. Each of us had a shelf and a barrack-box to house our personal belongings. Because the huts were built of breeze-blocks the extremes of temperature were at times difficult to bear. In the heat of summer when we could not sleep, some of us went out of the back of the huts into the fields beyond to cool off. In the worst of winter, our face-flannels froze overnight. A hectic game of table tennis in the mess just before bedtime would keep us warm for a while. For all that: happy days! I am glad to have been there and to have met so many people from such varied backgrounds.

Another suffering ATS girl was inspired to compose a poem commemorating the move to the camp:

OUR CAMP

What means this commotion, as loud as the ocean
Resounding through Beds, Herts and Bucks?
Oh! Bletchley's fair daughters are moving their quarters
And splashing through puddles like ducks.
We're laden with bags and our energy flags,
And the paths are a bit of a mess;
Sing ho! for the mud, the rain and the flood,
Sing hey! for the ATS

We're used to hard knocks, and a shelf and a box
As furniture suits us the best.
(The honours we pass to a privileged class
With a table, two chairs and a chest).
Our 'biscuits' are tough, but we find them enough;
To weakness let nobody pander;
Sing ho! for the lumps, the creases and bumps,
Sing hey! for the Senior Commander.

We'd all give our souls for the little tin bowls
We use to perform our ablutions.
We go off our heads for our nice wooden beds
A comfort to frail constitutions.
Our joy may be dashed by the mud that is splashed
On tunics just cleaned (chez Sketchley)
But ho! For the camp, the dirt and the damp
And hey! For the Belles of Bletchley!

Sgt M. C. Knowles -*ATS*

An unusual feature of the camp was that the rank of private was unknown except among Colonel Fillingham's own men. Because we BP workers in the army would have received low pay in the lower ranks, we were promoted regularly in the case of non-commissioned officers to the better paid ranks of corporal, sergeant, staff-sergeant, company-sergeant-major and regimental-sergeant-major. By this means our pay kept pace with the pay of civilian workers at BP.

The regimental-sergeant-major in the army is a man of great importance, feared by all the other ranks and even by junior officers. Yet here at the camp there were a dozen or more of them, plus many company-sergeant-majors, innumerable staff-sergeants and sergeants. It was not surprising that Colonel Fillingham and his staff were bewildered when they saw non-commissioned officers of all ranks strolling through the camp. We never found out why the colonel had been chosen to take charge of the camp. Fortunes of war! Perhaps the *Durham Light Infantry* decided to get rid of all loose cannons before going into battle.

Colonel Fillingham was a formidable figure. Not tall, but with an awe-inspiring aspect. One of his eyes pierced you like a gimlet at close quarters; the other remained tranquil, with almost a benign look. He never wore battle dress and was impeccably turned out, with gleaming Sam Browne belt and walking-stick in hand. He was a stickler for saluting. One day, as a fellow sergeant and I were walking through the camp on the way to work, the colonel, at least fifty yards away, started waving his stick and bellowing: 'Sergeants!' We had seen him but had thought that he was too far distant to salute. 'Let the dog see the rabbits', said he as we arrived in front of him, piercing us with his gimlet eye. Then, asking us our names, he pointed out that we were not saluting him, but the King's Commission. On a later occasion the colonel stopped me, pointing out that my hair would benefit from a session with the barber. 'What is your name, sergeant-major?' When I told him that my name was Thirsk, 'Oh', he said, 'I suppose your father is Lord Thirsk of Thirsk?' I could have replied that my father was of humbler origin, had served in France thoughout the Great War, and at present was a Captain in the Home Guard in Beverley; but I did not wish to shatter his belief that we were mostly of aristocratic families who had cleverly found ourselves cushy jobs.

Colonel Fillingham had brought with him from the *Durham Light Infantry* a retinue, including the adjutant, Lieutenant Bickerstaffe. None of them was allowed to enter Bletchley Park and they knew nothing of the work we were doing. Understandably, they were puzzled and frustrated.

One day, when I did not think he had seen me, the Colonel caught me trying to leave the camp without saluting him. I was very close to his office in a hut near the camp entrance. Escorting me inside, he demanded the salute which I had failed to give. I produced a salute which my old platoon sergeant in the *King's Own Royal Regiment* would have been proud of. 'That didn't cost you half a crown, sergeant-major?' 'No, sir', I replied. 'Not a florin?' 'No, Sir'. I waited patiently until he had reached sixpence. 'No, Sir'. 'You see, sergeant-major, it didn't cost you anything'. I agreed. 'A little politeness and a salute doesn't cost anything.' I agreed again. He now began to trace lines on the floor with his walking-stick. 'Do you know what I'm doing, sergeant-major?,' I could see that he was pretending to look for buried mines with a hand-held mine detector. But like the good soldier Schweik in similar situations, I knew that he dearly wished to act out his little play. So I replied 'No, Sir'. He made another search for the buried mines. 'I'm looking for mines', he said. 'You might at this moment be in the African desert looking for real mines', he added. I couldn't disagree with that; after all, my old sergeant in 1940 frequently told the platoon that we would all be in Libya before long. 'Yes, Sir', I said. He concluded the interview with a short homily on how lucky I and my fellow-workers were to have safe jobs at BP and how necessary it was to salute. I agreed with him, saluted, turned smartly and marched out of the office.

To his credit Colonel Fillingham introduced a number of amenities. There was a library well stocked with books, which I and several fellow-librarians helped to run; in it were armchairs for those wishing to spend leisure hours reading, studying or even sleeping. The huts where we slept at night or in the daytime if you were on the night-shift, had about sixteen beds into two rows. They were bleak and uncomfortable places and the library was a haven of peace compared with the sergeants' mess. There the beer flowed and the shouts of those at the dartboard or playing table tennis drowned all conversation. When free cheese sandwiches were served in the evenings there was a mad stampede to the counter.

One evening, Colonel Fillingham called in at the camp library. Seeing a young Intelligence Corps corporal, he inquired what he was reading. *'The Way of all Flesh'*, Sir, replied the corporal. The Colonel gave a knowing smile. 'But Sir', said the youth, 'it is a famous classic novel, by Samuel Butler.' 'Ah, my boy', said Fillingham, 'you don't need to make excuses, I was young myself once!'

Physical training (PT) before breakfast was ordained for all other ranks under the age of thirty. This was a great hardship for those who had led inactive physical lives for several years. I was twenty-nine years old, but by good fortune the office staff who compiled the under-thirties list had omitted my name. My friend Eric Plant, a couple of years younger than I, slept in the same hut. He groaned every morning as he donned his PT kit, and was always threatening as he ran out of the hut that he would tell them in the office that I was not yet thirty. I stayed in bed until breakfast time.

Sergeant Stuart Eborall Rigold, known to all his fellow log-readers as 'Riggy', was a talented caricaturist. Riggy never seemed quite at home in battle-dress. With his untidy appearance he had crossed swords several times with the colonel. Inspired by such encounters, he drew a brilliant cartoon featuring two long-haired languid sergeants shambling across the small parade ground in front of the colonel's hut. Leaning out of his window, Colonel Fillingham, with apoplectic face, brandished his walking-stick. Turning to his adjutant, Lieutenant Bickerstaffe, who stood behind him, poised like a setter-dog, the colonel was shouting: 'After them, Bickerstaffe!' I hope that somebody somewhere treasures that cartoon, which delighted all of us. Riggy died in 1980, within a year of his retirement as Principal Inspector of Ancient Monuments and Public Buildings at the Department of the Environment. One winter, several years after the war, I saw him in London at a lecture about medieval deserted villages. He was still wearing his old army greatcoat, which he had dyed blue, probably using woad, that amazing plant with which it is said the ancient Britons painted their bodies.

In the end, life became tolerable in the camp and there was much mirth about the activities of Colonel Fillingham and his henchmen.

I had left BP so I did not witness the closing of Shenley Road Military Camp. Fifteen years after the war my wife Joan and I were motoring to the north from London with our two-year-old son Martin asleep on the back seat. Taking a detour, we drove to Bletchley to see what remained. As the car stopped outside the entrance to BP, Martin woke up and, gazing around, said 'Lordy-Lordy.' The main building was still untouched and all the huts, although neglected, still stood. But of the camp nearby nothing remained but a few blocks of concrete. The huts had all gone and the scene was one of desolation.

As for Colonel Fillingham, he has long gone to that Valhalla where all old colonels rest. About ten years after the war I was a librarian at the Westminster Central Reference library near Leicester Square. When on duty at the enquiry desk one day I saw Colonel Fillingham advancing towards me. Dressed in a civilian suit he looked strangely innocuous; it was almost as if the uniform, the stick and the Sam Browne belt had been responsible for his former menacing aspect. But the gimlet eye still gleamed. I produced some government publication that he wished to consult, saying, as I handed it to him: 'This is the one you require, Colonel Fillingham.' 'How do you know my name?', he almost barked. 'I was at Bletchley Park during the war', I replied, nearly adding 'Sir'. We spoke for a minute or two, remembering the past. I watched him leave the library, a sad figure compared with the bristling warrior of former days. How are the mighty fallen!

15

THE LUCY RING

La Guerre a été gagnée en Suisse. (The War was won in Switzerland). With this dramatic title a book was published in France, in 1966, by Pierre Accoce and Pierre Quet. Their book told the story of an anti-Nazi German, Rudolf Roessler, who during World War II regularly supplied the Soviet Union with vital information about the disposition of the German forces on the Eastern front, through the agency of the Lucy Ring, a Soviet spy network in Switzerland. The authors' contention was that this intelligence, continuing for several years of the war, helped the Soviet Union to win many battles, including the great tank battle at Kursk, and led to the defeat of the Germans in 1945.

Where did Roessler (whose codename was Lucy because he lived in Lucerne) obtain for several years such detailed information about the battle plans and disposition of the German armed forces? The view expressed in the book by Accoce and Quet, translated into English in 1967, with the title *The Lucy Ring*, is that Roessler was in regular contact with a number of anti-Nazi German generals, friends of his from pre-war days, who were intent on the defeat of Hitler and his regime. Many have agreed with this explanation of the sources of Roessler's intelligence.

Rudolf Roessler, born in Germany in 1897, was only a youth when he was a soldier in the Kaiser's army during the Great War. On demobilisation he worked on newspapers and later became secretary of the *Buehnenvolksbund*, an actors' society. In 1933 he left Germany, moving to Lucerne, where he founded the publishing house *Vita Nova Verlag*. Roessler was an ardent and dedicated opponent of National Socialism. He was not a communist or a member of the Soviet spy ring, which had been established before the war in Switzerland. The director of the ring, which the Germans named *Die Rote Drei,* was Sandor Rado (codenamed Dora). Radolfi (his full name) was a Hungarian Communist, a map specialist who had set up a shop in Zürich. Among his agents, a motley crew of different nationalities, was Alexander Foote, an English Communist sympathiser who had fought in Spain with the International Brigade. Recruited into *Die Rote Drei,* better known now as The Lucy Ring, Foote was the chief radio transmitter of enciphered intelligence to the Soviet Union.

At first the Soviet intelligence centre in Russia was sceptical about the Lucy intelligence supplied to them by Rado. They constantly asked him to give them information about Lucy and his sources, but Roessler only released his material on the condition that its source was not revealed to anybody. Gradually, the accuracy of the information was appreciated by the Russians, who came to depend heavily upon it. At times they transmitted urgent requests to Rado for information about particular German movements and plans, and Roessler was usually able to reply within a day or two. Alexander Foote laboriously enciphered the intelligence using an elaborate hand cipher, often working well into the night in his flat in Lausanne, transmitting to the Soviet Union.

Another theory about the origin of Roessler's extraordinary intelligence about the disposition of German forces was put forward by Malcolm Muggeridge, the journalist, in *The Observer* on 8 January 1967. Reviewing the English translation of the book *The Lucy Ring* by Accoce and Quet, Muggeridge, who had served in the Intelligence Corps during the war and had briefly visited Bletchley, suggested that the intelligence Roessler passed on to the Russians was derived from German messages decrypted by the British at 'the country house where the cipher-breakers, for the most part dons, chess-players and violinists, as far as I could gather, lived'. This review by Muggeridge appeared seven years before the secret was first revealed to the general public by Winterbotham in his book *The Ultra Secret (1974)* that the German Enigma cipher was being regularly broken. Muggeridge believed that the British were feeding this intelligence through the Lucy ring to Russia. The problem, as he saw it, was how to pass intelligence:

...relating to operations on the Eastern Front to Russian Commanders without either jeopardising the source ... or risking the incredulity and suspicion with which Stalin normally greeted intelligence passed to him by his loyal allies.

Muggeridge knew Alexander Foote, who had returned to England after the war and who, after writing a book *Handbook for Spies (1949)*, worked at the Ministry of Agriculture and Fisheries.

We several times discussed the mystery of Lucy's sources, wrote Muggeridge ... A knowing flicker of Foote's left eye left me in no doubt that he for one, as an experienced radio operator, did not for a moment take seriously the possibility that Roessler received his information in a steady and undetected flow from the German High Command.

When Muggeridge put to Foote his theory about the origin of the intelligence sent to Russia, 'Foote', he wrote in his *Observer* review, 'looked faintly startled and then abruptly changed the subject'. However, in his book *The Infernal Grove* (1973), volume 2 of *Chronicles of Wasted Time*, Muggeridge claimed that Foote confirmed his theory.

Incidentally I learnt from Alexander Foote ... that, in fact, Stalin was getting the requisite Bletchley material. It was being sent to him by the Lucy Ring; purportedly from sources in the OKW (the German High Command).

When I wrote to Mr Muggeridge in 1989 asking whether Foote had definitely stated that the intelligence came from Bletchley Park, he could not confirm this, explaining that 'unfortunately now I am 86, my memory is not as perfect as I would like it to be'.

In the official history: *British Intelligence in the Second World War,* edited by Professor F.H. Hinsley and others, Hinsley baldly and briefly states that:

There is no truth in the much-publicised claim that the British authorities made use of the 'Lucy' ring, a Soviet espionage organisation which operated from Switzerland, to forward intelligence to Moscow.

One wonders why Hinsley was so emphatic. Surely as a careful historian he should have said 'I found no evidence to support the much-publicised claim ...'

But against this official view there have been a number of writers who have believed that Bletchley material *was* fed through the Lucy Ring by Roessler. A whole book supporting this theory by Anthony Reed and David Fisher, *Operation Lucy*, was published in 1981. Moreover, in both of his books *The Swiss Corridor (*1981) and *Intercept*: *the Enigma War(1979),* the Polish historian Jozef Garlinski was of the same opinion; as also was Constantine Fitzgibbon, who had worked at Bletchley Park, whose book *Secret Intelligence in the Twentieth Century* (1976) has pages on the Lucy Ring. Richard Deacon also held the same view in his *History of the British Secret Service* (1969).

One other British writer who accepted the views of Anthony Read and David Fisher was Edward Crankshaw. Reviewing their book *Operation Lucy* in *The Observer (*12th October 1980), he described it as 'a genuine contribution to the history of World War II.' Major Edward Crankshaw was at Bletchley Park where he was for a short period in charge of SIXTA, the traffic analysis section attached to Hut 6, in which I worked. He had also been in Moscow earlier in the war, with the British Military Mission, and had first-hand knowledge of the intelligence we were officially giving to the Russians through that mission.

Although two books by those operating within the Lucy Ring have been published, Alexander Foote's *Handbook for Spies (*1949) and Sandor Rado's *Code Name Dora (*1977), neither of them reveals the source of the intelligence they were relaying to the Soviet Union. Probably neither of them knew. Roessler, in spite of many questions put to him, remained silent, dying in Switzerland in 1958, without revealing the secret. Earlier it is claimed that he gave the names of four Germans who had been his sources. But these were never traced.

Unless more Bletchley Park documents are released by the British National Archives, or by the German, or indeed by the Swiss governments, further speculation on the source of Roessler's intelligence is unprofitable. However, there are certain aspects which I believe have not yet been explored. Alexander Foote was for several years transmitting from his flat thousands of enciphered messages to the intelligence centre in the Soviet Union. Were they intercepted by the Germans or the British? In either case, these hand ciphers, although elaborate, would probably have been decrypted without much trouble. If by the British, they would have been invaluable if Roessler's sources were from dissident German generals. If the intelligence came from Bletchley Park, the British would have monitored it to ensure that Foote was conveying correctly the intelligence which they had given to Roessler. Are the logs of any such messages in the National Archives?

It could be argued that, if Bletchley material was being given to Roessler through the British spy network in Switzerland, this would have been known to the intelligence people at BP who sent their findings, in disguised form, to commanders in the field. On the other hand, with or without Churchill's approval, such material may have been passed to Claude Dansey, our senior MI6 officer, who ran his own spy service in Switzerland. People at BP had little information about the ultimate destination of their intelligence after it had been despatched.

The true history of the sources of intelligence which reached Roessler may never be known. In the world of spies few documents are kept and most are destroyed. All the grist that came to his mill was carefully sorted by Roessler so that only the best was passed on to the Lucy Ring for onward transmission to Russia.

Neutral Switzerland, during World War II, as it had been in the Great War, was a hotbed in which spies of all the nations pursued their murky machinations. The Swiss, always fearful of a German invasion, strove to be on good terms with the Nazis. However, their intelligence chiefs and police made no attempt to thwart the transmission of Roessler's material to the Soviet Union, via Alexander Foote and the other wireless operators. It appears also that Roessler exchanged intelligence with the Swiss Captain Hans Hausamann, head of the semi-official Swiss intelligence organisation known as the *Bureau Ha*. At the same time, the Swiss leaders, always knowing that a German conquest of Europe and Russia would probably lead to an attack on Switzerland, more and more favoured an allied victory as the tide turned against Germany, particularly after their defeat at Stalingrad. Roessler was in touch, directly or indirectly with the French resistance, the Italian partisans and with British Intelligence. All the foreign embassies in Switzerland including that of the USA later in the war, had their intelligence agents attached.

But what of Roessler's contacts in Germany? He never revealed any names and there has been much speculation about who in Germany supplied him with intelligence and how it was conveyed. A book published in Zürich, Switzerland, by Schweizer Verlagshaus AG in 1973, supplies some of the answers. It is *Die Augen Moskaus: Fernschreibzentrale der Wehrmacht in Berlin, zwei Mädchen gegen Hitler.* The author was Bernd Ruland, a German journalist (1914-1976), who was employed as a Fernschreiboffizier (teleprint officer), at the headquarters of the OKW (the Oberkommando der Wehrmacht - The High Command of the German Armed Forces) and the OKH (Oberkommando des Heeres - The High Command of the German Army). Although in the army, he was permitted to wear civilian clothes at his place of work that was in the Bendlerstrasse in Berlin. From his description, here was a veritable ant-hill, employing thousands of people in many departments. Telephones, teleprinters, and radio transmitters in their hundreds were active twenty-four hours a day, transmitting messages to all commands. A vast card index enabled him and his colleagues to locate German units in all countries. There was little security and the staff, who were for the most part on friendly terms with each other, were free to consult documents of all kinds, or even to copy them. In this way the place resembled Bletchley, where there was no security check of baggage when leaving and only a brief inspection of a security card on entering. At the Bendlerstrasse and at Bletchley Park it would not have been difficult to take away documents if one had wished to do so.

Ruland himself was not involved in giving information to the enemies of Germany, but he was not a supporter of the Nazi regime, and, although he knew that some members of the staff were passing information to the enemy, he did not betray them. His book tells the story of two young women to whom he gives the pseudonyms Angelika von Parchim and Maria Kalussy, both ardent anti-Nazis, who regularly supplied secret information about the German forces and plans to an army officer at the Bendlerstrasse, named Werner Kemper, presumably also a pseudonym. Kemper took papers home, edited them and passed them on to Roessler in Switzerland, using mainly a courier service which went to that country via Milan. Ruland claims that, although he knew what Angelika was doing and had discussed matters with her, he did not know until after the war that her friend Maria was also involved. The two girls were very close friends who both hated the Nazis. Angelika, born in 1916 was a lively, intelligent, friendly girl whose father ('the best in the world') had been an officer in the German army. Released on health grounds in 1938, he was put in a concentration camp in 1944 for plotting against Hitler. Maria, born in 1918, worked at first in business. She was one of the first women employed in the teleprinter office. Her father, a communist, spent a year in a concentration camp in 1933, subsequently fleeing to the Soviet Union. He died in 1937, fighting in Spain with the International Brigade.

It was only after the war that both girls knew that their intelligence material went to the Russians. Their understanding was that their friend Werner Kemper was sending all their documents and information to Switzerland to help the western allies and the Swiss. They were both glad to learn that their intelligence had helped the Soviet Union, Maria knowing that her father would have approved. Angelika married an American army officer, living with him in the USA until his death in 1969. He was a colonel employed at the Pentagon. Maria also married, living with her husband in the Ruhr where he was a merchant. Werner Kemper, transferred to active service in 1944, was killed in April that year.

It is curious that Ruland's book has seldom been mentioned in the West. The Polish historian, Jozef Garlinski, in his book *The Swiss Corridor:Espionage Networks in Switzerland during World War II* (Dent, 1981), refers to Ruland's book, classing him among those authors 'publishing revelations appropriate to sensational novels' and describing *Die Augen Moskaus* as a 'classic tale of fiction'. But anybody who has carefully read this book, with its amazing amount of detail about the activities of the two girls at the Bendlerstrasse, must surely conclude that this is no work of fiction.

My own belief is that intelligence came to Roessler in Lucerne from many sources. Some of it from Angelika and Maria, and some may well have come from Bletchley through the hands of Lt-Colonel Claude Dansey; some also came from Swiss intelligence, some from German sources other than Werner Kemper and the girls. Roessler examined it all, selecting the good corn from the bad and, with the expert eye of an experienced miller, produced a flour of excellent quality that was transmitted to Russia by the Lucy Ring, and undoubtedly helped the Red Army to defeat the Nazi invaders.

But wars are not won by superior intelligence only. The dogged endurance of the soldiers of all the allies, facing formidable enemies, won the day. On Germany's eastern front, the Soviet soldiers, dying in their thousands, finally routed the Nazi forces. Had Stalingrad fallen, permitting the transfer of a large part of the German army to the western front, who knows how many more years would have passed before the remaining allies finally conquered Nazi Germany?

16

WAR'S END

In April, 1945, it became clear that the end of the war against Germany was near. Assailed from the east and the west, but still fighting desperately, Germany at last accepted the terms of unconditional surrender on the 7th of May. I missed any celebrations that were held at BP for I was at home on leave at the time. As I wandered through the market place at Beverley on VE Day (Victory in Europe), I thought of that day when, at the end of the Great War, I, then a small boy, had seen a procession through that same market place, headed by an effigy of Kaiser Bill, the German Emperor, borne on Mr Leighton's (the fruiterer's) horse and cart. It was on the way to a bonfire on the Westwood.

That morning I did not see much rejoicing in the streets of Beverley, for the war with the Japanese was still raging. Nor were those rejoicing who had lost husbands, sons, daughters and other relatives. I found Mr Pottage, the ironmonger, hanging bunting outside his shop. I gave him a hand, but his heart was not in the job, for his younger son, Brian, a fighter-pilot in the RAF, had been reported 'missing, believed killed' over the Mediterranean. His older son Markham, a friend of mine from schooldays, had survived when the Canadian pilot of a night-fighter plane told him to bale out when their engine failed. Markham landed by parachute in a garden on the south coast of England. His pilot died when the plane crashed into a cliff. My family also had suffered when my brother David, a Lancaster navigator, was killed over Milan in 1943, leaving a wife and two small daughters.

The German war had ended, yes. But all over Europe and the Soviet Union, in the USA, the Commonwealth and in other lands, families mourned their dead. The Germans had left a trail of bitterness and misery which brought despair to millions of people, many of whom still grieved for the dead of the Great War. However, almost everyone was glad that Hitler and the Nazis had been defeated. The older generation, having seen all this before, had no illusions about the future.

Returning to BP I found there were no logs to read. All the German transmitters were dead and we were without the material on which we depended. After a short lull more logs began to appear, this time recording French and Russian radio traffic. Some log readers, amazed to learn that allied wireless traffic was now being intercepted, refused to take part. We formed a group and protested. A senior officer, a captain whose name I cannot recall, attempted to justify the work. But we argued and told him that we would not read the logs of former allies under any circumstances. 'In that case', he said, 'you are redundant'.

This would have been fine if we could have gone home and returned to our jobs in civilian life – those that had them. But when you become redundant in the British army, release is more complicated. You return to depot. In most cases this meant a return to regimental headquarters, but in the Intelligence Corps, our HQ was at Wentworth Woodhouse, a fine old country seat near Rotherham in Yorkshire.

There were many weeks of waiting before we headed north. The Japanese sections worked on until the Japanese surrender later in the year. I spent as much time as I could revising for two examinations of the Library Association, one in the German language and the other in Bibliography. Some were employed writing the histories of their sections. Joan and I were married in September and she was released immediately under a special dispensation for students who held university scholarships. This allowed her to return to Westfield College, University of London, now back in London after wartime evacuation to Oxford. Originally a student of modern languages, and having already passed half her exams in German and French, Joan had changed her mind at Bletchley and had decided to read for a history degree.

In the end, it was not until October that a group of us dissenters left BP for good, travelling to Rotherham by train, via Bedford. My friend Eric Plant, a Manchester man who had arrived at Beaumanor on the same day as I in 1942, was one of our party. As the train sped northwards, fences and brick houses gave way to dry-stone walls and stone houses, and Eric became more and more exhilarated. *The North!,* he cried out, *The North!* From Wentworth Woodhouse a group of fifteen of us set out for Germany to join the occupying British forces. My days in the army ended on 12 March, 1946, having spent the last few months in a section of Field Security Personnel (FSP) at Cleves, checking barge traffic on the Rhine. But that is another story!

Looking back to my log reading days, I wondered sometimes what our job had contributed to the war effort. Some of us had doubts about its usefulness. So it was heartening many years later to read the view of Gordon Welchman, who was the head of Hut 6 during part of the war. In his book *The Hut 6 Story* (1982), he wrote:

I believe the Central Party that became part of the Hut 6 organisation at Bletchley Park had more detailed knowledge of the entire communication system that handled Enigma traffic than anyone in Germany. It followed the movements, changes in control, retransmissions, the handling of different keys, and of course the chit chat that appeared on the logs.

What was achieved can only truly be seen in the context of the whole Enigma story. The intercept operators supplied the raw material without which we would have been unemployed. Our study of this traffic, combined with intelligence from those who worked in the Fusion Room on the decrypted messages supplied by Hut 6, gave a detailed picture of German army and air force formations over the whole of Europe and North Africa. This was of great value to the military and air advisers in Hut 3, who prepared their intelligence reports. Those reports were the final fruits which proved decisive in guiding the decisions of British and American commanders in the field.

Only in recent times did I see a letter to all his staff from Sir Stewart Graham Menzies, who, as head of the Secret Intelligence Service, was the overall director of Bletchley Park. It was a letter that could not be published at the time and I have only seen it reproduced in one publication. Here it is:

MESSAGE FROM THE DIRECTOR GENERAL
The following message has been received from the Director General:

On this ever memorable day, I desire that all who are doing duty in this Organisation should be made aware of my unbounded admiration in the way in which they have carried out their allotted tasks.

Such have been the difficulties, such has been the endeavour, and such have been the constant triumphs that one senses that words of gratitude from one individual are perhaps out of place. The personal knowledge of the contribution made towards winning the War is surely the real measure of the thanks which so rightly belong to one and all in a great and inspired organisation which I have the privilege to direct.

This is your finest hour.

(signed) S.G.M.
8th May, 1945

OLLA PODRIDA

One memorable day a long time ago I enjoyed a meal with a Spanish family in Madrid. The mother of the family had prepared a *cocido madrileño*, a kind of stew cooked in a large clay pot, which contained a mixture of pieces of chicken, ham, beef, sausages, pigs trotters, with added chickpeas and other vegetables. I learned later that this dish was very like the Spanish *olla podrida*, a peasant meal of great antiquity, which was well-known to the hungry Sancho Panza, the squire of Don Quixote. On one occasion Sancho speaks of :

That great dish that stands fuming there before me, methinks 'tis an *olla podrida*; and by reason of the diversities of things it hath in it, I cannot but meet with something that will do me good.

(Translation by Thomas Shelton, who was a contemporary of Cervantes) *

When I started writing this book about Bletchley Park, certain subjects readily arranged themselves into separate chapters. But I could not find a place for dozens of memories which came to mind so easily. Other incidents, which were buried too deep in memory for recall, came to the surface again when I re-read entries in a diary I had written sporadically during the war years.

It was then, remembering the *olla podrida* that I had enjoyed in Madrid, that I began to jot down these snippets of memory, throwing them one by one into the pot. I hope that some of the old timers who worked at Bletchley Park will find a few pieces in my pot which will entertain them and bring back memories. Others will perhaps be surprised to learn that not everything that went on at Bletchley was concerned with codes and ciphers.

*Sancho Panza *: Aquel platonazo que está más adelante vahando me parece que es olla podrida, que por la diversidad de cosas que en las tales ollas podridas hay, no podré dejar de topar con alguna que me sea de gusto y de provecho.*

ABLUTIONS

'Lord, how the eighteenth century stinks!' was the cry of the actor Leslie Howard, playing the part of the young man transported back from the twentieth century to the 1780s in the play, *Berkeley Square*. The smell of London and its people appalled him. Perhaps, if we could return to Bletchley Park in the 1940s, our reaction would be similar. For baths and even bathrooms were rare in the houses in which we were billeted and it was difficult to find anywhere you could have a shower or bath. Bletchley town had no municipal baths, but at nearby towns such as Northampton, the local authority provided what were known as 'slipper' baths, attached to indoor swimming pools, where for a few pence, you could soak in a warm bath, with soap and flannel, rather than sponge, provided. Later in the war, I found that a shower room in the mansion at Bletchley Park could be used by anybody for a small charge. Not many seemed to know about it, for I do not remember any queues.

When all of the Bletchley Park army personnel, men and women, moved in January, 1944, into Shenley Road Military Camp, which was built next door to BP, but outside the perimeter, showers but not baths were provided for men. Staff-Sergeant Betty Vine-Stevens remembers the separate ablutions hut for the women:

..which had very bare concrete floors, with duck-boards to stand on, by the basins. Queuing for the rationed bath times was no fun either, there being nowhere to sit except on the floor while we waited our turn.

For the men there were no separate cubicles, just a number of overhead showers in a hut, with the water, not always very hot, cascading over the concrete floor. We didn't have to queue.

Lucky were those whose parents lived in places nearby or in London, where they could enjoy the comfort of a bath on their days off. There was one other alternative which I discovered. Next door to the Hotel Russell in Russell Square, London, was a luxurious underground Turkish bath, probably built in late Victorian or Edwardian times. There, in surroundings of oriental splendour, you could, for a modest charge, not only enjoy the pleasures of a hot shower and the steam or dry heat rooms at whatever temperature you could bear, but also a good night's sleep on a low divan bed, enveloped in a large fleecy white towel. In the morning, wakened with a cup of tea, you hurried to nearby Euston station to catch the Bletchley train. After breakfast in the forces' canteen on Bletchley station you walked into the park and sat down at your desk to read the day's logs.

THE AMERICANS

I don't suppose that many of my fellow log-readers had ever met an American, male or female, before the war. I had cousins in the States, but I had never seen them; for the truth was that Americans other than those on business were rare visitors. However, we knew what they sounded like, for we were all familiar with the many different accents in the early talkies (as we called the films or movies of the 1920s and 1930s).

When we heard during 1943 that several male American traffic-analysts (log-readers to us) were joining us, there was no dismay or resentment – just curiosity. Deep down we all knew that Britain alone could not win the war, and that with the Soviet Union and the USA as allies there was hope of victory in the end. Most of the Americans who joined us seemed to have had a variety of jobs before joining the forces, although still in their twenties, unlike most of us who for the most part stuck to one career. Cec (pronounced Cease) was an amiable Texan with a rich velvet Texan accent and a laid-back manner. Before military service he had been running a small radio station. Fluent and full of stories, he became everybody's friend and was a popular member of our happy band. T4 Kidder, a quiet American but just as friendly and well-liked as Cec, worked in public libraries in the USA. The T4 I believe was a technical rank.

Cec and T4 Kidder were non-commissioned officers. In addition, two young American lieutenants were allocated to the Fusion Room. One of these for a time took command of one of the log-reading sections. We soon realised that he was suffering from new-broomitis. Having surveyed the large room in Block G in which we worked, he decided that a more logical flow of work would make for increased efficiency. To this end he even organised the repositioning of some of our trestle-table desks. Fortunately, the disruption passed me by, for my position in the room apparently did not interfere with his plan. It was just as well, for my *Daily Telegraph* war map (which I still have) was fixed to the wall with drawing-pins (US thumb-tacks) along with a card inscribed with my favourite quotation from *The Good Soldier Schweik:*

There's a war on, said Schweik, and people are doing things they never dreamed about before.

In other departments at BP many more Americans worked, some in Hut 6 on cryptography, others in Hut 3 on intelligence derived from decrypted messages. There were also senior people like Telford Taylor, a lawyer in charge of all the Americans at BP. But of such people we knew nothing at the time. Their story has been well told in an entertaining book *The Ultra Americans,* by Thomas Parrish (N.Y.,Stein & Day, 1986).

Peter Calvocoressi, of Hut 3, told me a story about a young American lieutenant who had joined them. Talking one day to Peter and Jim Rose, who shared the same room, he was telling them of his great admiration for the Cambridge English don F.L.Lucas, who had written many plays, poems and essays. 'I must try to see him in Cambridge on my first day off duty', he said. Peter and Jim both laughed. 'You don't have to go to Cambridge, he's two doors down the corridor, on the left!'

We envied the smart uniforms the Americans wore. The fine cloth of their uniforms, the neat shirts and ties made us more than ever aware of the defects of our khaki battle dress with bum-freezer jackets and shapeless trousers. Eric Plant maintained that our battle-dresses were made out of old bean-sacks and referred to us as the 'beansack brotherhood'.

THE BLACKOUT AND THE STARS

It is just after midnight. Not a chink of light showing anywhere. No moon, no stars. We stumble in search of the buses lined up on the driveway, in the dark. The bus drivers are shouting: 'Leighton Buzzard, Wolverton, Stony Stratford, New Bradwell...' They have only just arrived, bringing in the night shift. As we of the evening shift find our buses we long for our beds in our billets and a long sleep before the next day's evening shift beginning at 4pm. Fortunately, the drivers know the country lanes and roads of Buckinghamshire well. They need to, having only partly-obscured headlights.

But on moonless, cloudless summer or winter nights the full beauty of the starlit sky is revealed. How pleasant it was to pause by the lake on the way back from a meal in the cafeteria in the middle of the night. We town-dwellers seldom saw the stars in peacetime.

THE BLETCHLEY CO-OP AND UNCLE JOE

The Co-op shop, a branch of the Co-operative Society, stood in the main shopping centre at Bletchley. I used to go there occasionally to buy tobacco, and once to have a repair job on my spare battle-dress jacket. Yes, they had a tailoring service. When you paid for anything, the girl at the counter asked you for your co-op dividend number so that, at the end of the year, you could receive a portion of the total profits. She would then operate a weird machine, pressing down a number of levers to coincide with the digits of your dividend number. In some marvellous way, the transaction would be recorded so that your total annual purchases determined the size of your dividend.

If, like me at that time, you were not a member of the Co-operative Society, you could, if you wished, give the number of the *Aid to Russia* fund, which was prominently displayed on the counter. 'Give it to Uncle Joe', people would tell the girl if they did not have a co-op number, or if they were feeling generous. In those days nobody had heard of the evil deeds of Stalin in the pre-war days. All we knew was that the people in those parts of the Soviet Union occupied by the Germans were being slaughtered or were suffering incredible hardships. We knew also about the siege of Leningrad and how the German forces had been held at Stalingrad. We rejoiced that they were now retreating under the fierce onslaught of the Red Army.

The Aid to Russia fund was endorsed by Winston Churchill, the Prime Minister, who knew how the Soviet people were suffering; he also knew that, towards the end of the war, in his own words: 'the guts of the German Army have been largely torn out by Russian valour and generalship'. Churchill's wife, Clementine, became President of the Red Cross Aid to Russia Fund in 1941. Not merely a titular head,

Jimmy Thirsk 1942

Tommy Evans, Jimmy Thirsk, Eric Plant, Benny Erends
SIXTA Log-Readers

SOME OF THE OFFICERS FOR HUT 3A in 1944
© Peter Calvocoressi from his book "Top Secret Ultra"

(Left to Right, back) : Peter Labertouche, Kenneth Brooke, Eric Faure, Brinley (Bryn) Newton-John, Charles Haskins (USA), Bragg, Ware, Frank Squire.

(Left to Right, front):- Wing-Commander Peter Calvocoressi, Langdon Van Norden (USA), Neville Harrow, Geoff Myers, Tadde Pilley, Peter Manners-Wood, Wing-Commander E.J.B. (Jim) Rose, Reginald Cunningham (Cully), William (Bill) Millward.

The Pink Hut and two others, many years later

MOSTLY MEMBERS OF HUT 6, CELEBRATING THE END OF THE WAR IN EUROPE

Standing (left-right) Sub Joan Watkins, Elizabeth B Granger, Sub Jean F Davies, Jane Morris, Pat Downing, R.A. (Bob) Roseveare, Sheila Rawson, Harold D Fletcher, Squadron Leader George T Davis, RSM Asa Briggs, Molly R Bruce, Pam Bevington, Jessie L Proctor, Sheila Dunlop, Jean E Proctor, Sub Joyce Robinson, Major J C Manisty, Miss Honour M Pass, Daisy A W Genge, Gwen E Thomas, Mrs H M Queening, Miss P Hope Wallace

Sitting or kneeling (left-right) Miss Iona Jay, Mrs Winifred Smith, Mrs Maureen Gentry-Kewley, Major Neill ('Willy') Webster, Peggy Rawlings-Smith, Paul H Coles, Major J C Monroe, Mary Groves, Major Edward Rushworth ('Rush'), Audrey Cocking

One of the old huts

MEMBERS OF HUT 6 CELEBRATING THE END OF THE WAR IN EUROPE

Standing (left-right) Stephen Michael A Banister, Lieut L Smadbeck, Mrs S M A Banister, Corp H Thielbar, A Coldwell, Arther H Read, Corporal J Fletcher, Miss H M R McCreath, Lieut A J Levenson ('Art'), Sgt G B Evans, Miss A G Pegg, Sgt A N Lewis, Sgt J Leahy, Douglas R R Nicholl, Betty M Morgan (hidden), Penelope C Storey, Daphne H Hinton, Mrs J Hyman, Sgt J Hyman, Malcolm A Chamberlain ('Mac'), Major D W Babbage, Mrs R H Parker, J D Evans, Reginald H Parker, Lieut W Bijur, John W Hamilton, Lucy Hermelin, Howard F T Smith

Sitting (left-right) Eileen M Hollington, Sgt H N Porter, Charles S Williams, Richard G Pendred, Sgt G Hurley, Miss S M Castor, Nigel S Forward, Mrs Howard F T Smith

Jean Davies		Joan Watkins		Joyce Robinson

The Three Js

C.S.M. Alfred Sugar (1906-2007) Age 100

COLOSSUS

At Bletchley Park, on 26 January 2008, Tony Sale (right), standing in front of the Colossus machine which he and his team of experts rebuilt, presented a trophy to Joachim Schueth, a German software engineer. Using a modern computer, Joachim had decrypted a message transmitted on a Lorenz SZ42 cipher machine. It took him 46 seconds to do it; the rebuilt Colossus took 3 hours and 45 minutes.

The Enigma machine

THE SPECIAL MODEL OF ENIGMA USED BY THE ABWEHR

STANDARD 3-ROTOR ENIGMA, WITH PLUGBOARD,
USED BY ALL GERMAN ARMED FORCES

she worked hard to increase the amount of money donated. Of the £9 million given for aid to Russia, £6,700,000 was collected by Mrs Churchill's fund.

In the last year of the war, Mrs Churchill, invited by the Russian Red Cross to visit the Soviet Union, travelled widely across that country from March to May 1945, accompanied by Churchill's old secretary Grace Hamblin. Stalin met Clementine and she was awarded the Red Banner of Labour. During this tour she saw much of the devastation of the country and spoke to many survivors. Back home after the end of the war in Europe, she was awarded a GBE, becoming a Dame of the Grand Cross of the Order of the British Empire. Mrs Churchill wrote an interesting account of her travels, which was published by Hutchinson in 1945 with the title: *My Visit to Russia*.

BP AND THE BARD

More than sixty years ago several of us log-readers arrived at the pink hut at 0001 hours on the first of January, 1943, ready for the night-shift. What a way to celebrate the new year! But Sergeant Newte, a lecturer in English literature at Lampeter College in civilian life, who always reminded me of the melancholy Jaques in *As You Like It,* was there, to cheer us up with a quotation from that play :

> Then, heigh-ho, the holly!
> This life is most jolly,

he chanted in lugubrious voice. Sometimes, having difficulty with his logs, he could be heard mouthing curses from the plays of Shakespeare. One such was part of King Lear's curse on his daughter Goneril if she should ever have a baby:

> Let it stamp wrinkles on her brow of youth.
> With cadent tears fret channels in her cheeks.

'Cadent, cadent,' he exclaimed, 'what a word!'

When Laurence Olivier's film *Henry the Fifth* was released in 1944, most of us saw it in London long before it came to our two local cinemas at Bletchley and Fenny Stratford. My friend Eric Plant, a Manchester university graduate, who worked in the Treasurer's department of Manchester City Council in his former life, was so deeply impressed by the film that for months he carried with him everywhere a tattered paperback copy of the play, quoting his favourite passages to anybody who would listen. As for me, during many hours spent in the bookshops of London, Oxford and Cambridge - all easily visited from BP - I had built up a complete set of the excellent Old Temple pocket-sized volumes of Shakespeare. One of these was always in my battledress pocket.

Many plays were produced at Bletchley by other sections, but I do not recall any of Shakespeare's. Nevertheless, we had our chance in London and in Oxford and Cambridge. Donald Wolfit and John Gielgud were the two stalwart producers of his plays during the war. I remember Gielgud's Macbeth in Oxford in the summer of 1942 and Donald Wolfit as King Lear in Cambridge later the same year.

Yes, there were many devotees of William Shakespeare in our section and no doubt his voice was heard all over BP. There was always an apt quotation for every occasion. It is fitting that this one from *King Henry V* is now inscribed on a plaque in the entrance hall of the mansion at BP:

> The King hath note of all that they intend
> By interception which they dream not of.

These words of the Duke of Bedford in Act II, Scene 2, neatly summarise our own 'strange, eventful histories'.

FIRE IN THE CAMP

If you were unlucky your name would appear on Part II orders, demanding your service the following day for 24 hours on Fire Picket. Colonel Fillingham himself, loving the daily ritual, would usually inspect the daily changing of the picket at 1700 hours in the square outside the guardroom. What happened if you were on duty in the Park during your 24 hour stint I do not remember. Presumably in emergency you would have been summoned to the camp to man the stirrup pumps.

The only fire we ever heard about took place one afternoon in 1944. My friend and fellow log-reader Alfred Sugar told me the story. That afternoon, off-duty and quietly reading in the camp library hut, he heard a cry of FIRE! Leaving his book, he left the library and found a young lance-corporal rushing around shouting FIRE. Alfred, a sergeant-major at that time, ran quickly towards one of the camp huts from which smoke was pouring. There was no evidence that Colonel Fillingham and his staff or even that day's picket were aware of the fire, so Alfred, gathering several other off-duty Intelligence Corps soldiers on the way, collected stirrup-pumps and buckets of water from other huts and before long had the fire doused. Alfred thought at first of telephoning the local fire brigade, but when he saw that the fire was put out, he decided not to. It was now late afternoon and while they were all congratulating themselves on a job well done, the young lance-corporal who had sounded the alarm approached Alfred and said: 'Excuse me, sergeant-major, but may I go now, I'm due on fire picket at 5 o'clock.'

HITCH-HIKING

Not many at BP wished to stay in Bletchley or in their billets on days off duty. Those of us in the army camp found it too depressing to stay there and although there was nothing to stop you leaving the camp and sitting by the lake at BP on a summer's day with a good book, the lure of London enticed many of us to spend our days off there. With its concerts, theatres, cinemas, restaurants, even in wartime its glamour remained. To those like me, who had lived only in country towns, London was the romantic 'Baghdad of the west' that Robert Louis Stevenson knew. If I had been at BP during the days of the London blitz in 1941-2, I would not have been so keen to go there. But, after 1942, the chances of meeting with a bomb with your name on it were remote, even in the days of the doodle-bugs and rockets later on in the war.

Always keen to save money on transport, most of us in uniform hitch-hiked when we could. On a day off duty it was so easy to walk a mile or so to the east of Bletchley town to the village of Fenny Stratford, through which passed the main road to London, via the ancient town of St Albans. It was more difficult for a civilian to hitch a ride, but there were many car drivers or truck drivers who would stop when they saw a soldier, an airman or a sailor, male or female, in uniform. Sometimes you were carried only a handful of miles, but often you had a free ride into London, or to the outskirts, from where you could travel by tube (underground railway) to your destination in the West End or wherever you wished to go.

One day I stopped an empty Royal Air Force aircraft recovery vehicle. There was no room in the cab with the driver but he said I was welcome to sit or stand on the 60-foot flat trailer behind. It was uncomfortable, but at least I had the opportunity of testing whether the carrier would move ahead of me if I jumped in the air or whether I should land in the same place. (I did). My friend Frank Higenbottam, the City Librarian of Canterbury before the war, but then an Intelligence Corps Sergeant at BP, hitched a lift to London and found that the driver who stopped was a Colonel in the redcaps (the military police). The friendly colonel asked no questions and even stopped at a cafe halfway to London and treated Frank to a coffee.

You were not always lucky when travelling long distances. On one extended sixty-hour break I hitch-hiked to Yorkshire to spend a couple of nights at my sister's farm. Short lifts only on the Great North Road delayed my progress. At last I arrived at Aberford at about 0100 hours, with a two mile walk on a minor road to bring me to the farm. Jean and her husband Arthur, the farmer, were not expecting me until the next day, and I had difficulty rousing them. The barking dog eventually woke them. To simplify matters Jean lifted her still-sleeping four-year old daughter Sheena into their bed, releasing hers for me. Great was her astonishment in the morning to see her uncle Jim in her bed. It was a good weekend and on the way back I had some good lifts. But in the evening, stranded on the outskirts of

Northampton, still quite a way from Bletchley, I had a stroke of luck. Seeing an army camp I asked the sentry if he knew where I could find a bed and breakfast place in Northampton. He called the sergeant of the guard. 'No', he said, 'but you can sleep in the guard-room cell if you like. We've no prisoners at present.' I spent a comfortable night and they woke me in the morning with a large mug of tea. I was soon on my way to Northampton station to catch an early train to Bletchley. I enjoyed a leisurely breakfast at the YMCA on the station there, and by 0900 hours I was at my desk ready for work.

THE JAPANESE NATIONAL ANTHEM

Most of the women log-readers were in the ATS, the women's army; several, however, had been recruited from the women who had joined the Royal Air Force. These were WAAFs. In their Air Force blue uniforms they stood out among the many more numerous ATS girls wearing khaki.

One of our WAAFs was Muriel Bell, a dark-haired beautiful girl, taller than most and slim. I never knew how she came to be in the WAAF or how she came to Bletchley as a log-reader. Like most of the girls she was young enough not to have had a job before joining the services. Many were straight from school; some came after a year at university and others having just graduated.

Muriel's parents had lived in Japan before the war and she was born there. With her good knowledge of the language she ought to have been working in the Japanese section rather than with us. My Japanese was limited to a few words from the national anthem, which we used to sing at the grammar school I attended at Beverley, Yorkshire, in the 1920s. Our music teacher, Mr Malkin, affectionately known to the boys as 'Bug-whiskers', had multiple copies of an ancient tattered nineteenth-century book with the title *National Anthems of the World.* Every week we would sing these anthems, oblivious of the fact that some of the countries no longer existed. The one which appealed to me was the Japanese, with its haunting and melancholy melody. Underneath the music were printed phonetically the sounds of the Japanese words; these I remember we sang with great gusto although they had no meaning for us. At home I discovered that the melody could be picked out on the piano, using the black keys only.

One day at work Muriel Bell was talking about her childhood in Japan. 'Do you know the Japanese national anthem?' I asked. 'Of course', she replied. She began to sing the words softly. I joined in and together we sang the whole anthem, to the delight of our fellow log-readers.

Nearly sixty years after I had learned those words at school, I was staying in the guest-house at St Paul's University in Tokyo, where my wife was lecturing. Across the road from the guest-house we could see the playground of a large school. On the first morning I woke to hear the children singing their national anthem with great fervour. We could see hundreds of schoolchildren standing to attention in the playground. The ceremony was repeated every morning. These were the words they sang, familiar to me from my schooldays:

> Kimigayo wa
> Chiyo ni yachiyo ni
> Sazareishi no
> Iwao to narite
> Koke no musu made
>
> *May the reign of the Emperor*
> *Continue for a thousand, nay, eight thousand generations*
> *And for the eternity that it takes*
> *For small pebbles to grow into a great rock*
> *And become covered with moss.*

The words come from the 9th century, but the music, composed by Hiromori Hayashi, an Imperial court musician, was first performed in 1880 on the Emperor Meiji's birthday.

LES FLEURS

Morfudd Rhys remembers that she had been offered a job as a linguist in the Foreign Office and was posted to Bletchley Park, where she translated telegrams from Spanish and Portuguese sources. Morfudd recalled that 'there were only two of us in that section. Fortunately we got on very well. My superior, Marjorie Price-Hutchinson referred to me as the *incinerator*, as I managed to get through the translating pretty quickly.'

One warm sunny day in early June 1942, they were both sitting by the lake after lunch at the cafeteria. Being civilians, they both wore colourful summer dresses. As they sat, enjoying watching the swans on the lake, a group of elderly Frenchmen came by. They stopped. '*Ah*', said one, '*Les fleurs parmi les fleurs !* (The flowers among the flowers!) .

'A sweet nothing to remember all these years ' wrote Morfudd.

I met Morfudd many years after the war when I discovered that she was the aunt of Nansi, the wife of my second cousin, twice removed, Simon Thirsk. Later in the war, Morfudd had gone to live in La Paz, Bolivia with her father, who became British ambassador there.

Marjorie, her BP colleague, became a Baroness when she married Ulrich von Schippenbach, a farmer who owned an estate near Malaga in Spain.

LILI MARLEEN

Several of us on the day shift decided to go to the theatre at Northampton one evening to see the actor Donald Wolfit in *King Lear*. After the play ended we left the theatre, with old Wolfit still taking a bow, looking completely exhausted as he clutched the curtain. We had to run to the station to catch the train back to Bletchley. Like all trains from the north during the war it was crowded. But the journey was short and we stood in the corridor talking about the play. Three or four ATS girls, in high spirits, started singing some of the popular songs of the day. Suddenly, one of them silenced the others when she began to sing in German. We guessed that she was from BP. The song was *Lili Marleen* and the girl, with her lovely contralto voice, seemed to be word perfect.

This song, with its haunting melody and sentimental words, became popular with Rommel's soldiers in the Afrika Korps, when it was used as a theme song by a German radio station broadcasting from Belgrade. It has a curious history. The words, by Hans Leip, a poet-painter of Hamburg, were written in 1915, when he was in the army waiting to go to the western front. In his poem, his unmarried soldier is thinking of the girl he left behind outside the barrack gate.

> *Vor der Kaserne, vor dem grossen Tor*
> *Stand eine Laterne, und steht sie noch davor,*
> *So woll'n wir da uns wiedersehn,*
> *Bei der Laterne woll'n wir stehn.*
> *Wie einst, Lili Marleen.*

> In front of the barracks, in front of the big gate,
> There stood a lamp-post and it still stands there.
> Let's hope we see each other again there,
> And stand by the lamp-post,
> As we used to do, Lili Marleen.

Hans Leip himself composed a melody for his song, but it was shortly before World War II that a German, Norbert Schulze composed the well-known melody. The record, used as the theme song by the Belgrade radio station, was made just before the war, by the Swedish singer Lale Andersen. From Rommel's soldiers the song passed to the men of the British 8th Army; it soon became one of the best-known songs of the war, with an English version recorded by Bing Crosby, Vera Lynn, Marlene Dietrich and others. Like *Tipperary* in the Great War, which was also a pre-war song adopted by soldiers, and *We'll meet again*, Vera Lynn's plaintive song in World War II, *Lili Marleen* tells of lovers parted by the war; their appeal was universal because so many millions were separated from their loved ones.

As the train drew into Bletchley Station the girl ended her song, drawing a round of applause from those of us in the corridor. The song ends sadly, for it is clear that the young soldier has been killed. But he intends to return to the lamp-post by the barrack gate to see his Lili.

Aus dem stillen Raume, aus der Erde Grund,
Hebt mich wie im Traume dein verliebter Mund.
Wenn sich die späten Nebel drehn
Werd' ich bei der Laterne steh'n
Wie einst, Lili Marleen.

Out of the silent resting place, out of the earth's embrace
I'm lifted as in a dream by your loving lips.
When the night mists are drifting
I'll stand again by the lamp-post,
As we used to do, Lili Marleen.

GENERAL NYE'S VISIT

About six months after our section, the Central Party, moved entirely from Beaumanor to Bletchley Park in the spring of 1942, we heard that Lieutenant-General Archibald Edward Nye, Vice-Chief of the Imperial General Staff, would be visiting BP and that he would be including our section, the log-readers, in his tour. He was the first distinguished visitor we had seen, although we had heard stories of a visit earlier in the war by Winston Churchill, the Prime Minister.

Probably Churchill had suggested to General Nye that he should spend a few hours at BP to find out how the vital intelligence about the enemy was gathered. We had good warning of the visit and we were asked to tidy our desks to give some appearance of order to our untidy surrounding; in particular that we should hide our coffee and tea mugs. These, of all shapes, colours and sizes, normally stood close at hand on our bare trestle-table desks. It is said that Alan Turing, the Cambridge mathematician, chained his coffee mug to a radiator. We log-readers must have been more law-abiding than his colleagues, for I do not remember losing mine, which often roamed but never disappeared.

We awaited General Nye with interest, for we had heard that he was one of the few soldiers who had risen from the ranks to general. Born in 1895, he was a regular army man, who had served in the Great War, and was later commissioned in the Leinster Regiment. Twice wounded, he was awarded the Military Cross.

As the General walked through our hut, escorted by several men we did not know, who were probably heads of departments at BP, he paused at several desks to speak to log-readers. The party was soon on its way to other huts. In the brief minutes he was with us, my impression was of an alert, vigorous no nonsense-general. As soon as the door closed, out came the mugs and we returned to our log-reading. To celebrate the occasion and to amuse my friend Corporal Parlow, who at that time sat at a desk opposite me, I composed a Shakespearean account of the visit, written on a sheet of office paper, now creased and yellow after more than sixty years.

GENERAL NYE

Act I, scene 1

Enter General Nye with officers. A peal of ordnance. Alarums and several half-hearted excursions. Hautboys. Exit a bleeding sergeant. Cries of 'Second front now' and 'Hide the mugs' (a)

GENERAL NYE :

Let me have men about me that are fat,
Sleek-headed men and those that sleep o'nights.
Unlike yond Parlow, who, with furrowed brow
Pores o'er his books at dead of night and daily plots my downfall.
Lithgow (b), I tell thee I like not his looks.
Do thou set watch upon such fellows.
These upstart corporals,
Grown swelled in head and drunk with petty power
Have often grown to mighty puissance and have swayed the world with iron Sceptre.
These double-chevronned creatures of the marsh (c)
Do sometimes rise like Hitlers or Napoleons, and do seek
To overthrow King George and his most noble Generals
(Myself being one). Go smell them out
And send them o'er the main.

Exeunt omnes. Enter the bleeding Sergeant.

a) An old custom was to hide all domestic utensils whenever there was a visit by the King or his officers. Cf. Falstaff's 'Empty the jordan' (Henry iv,Part 1)
b) Major Lithgow, our Admin. Officer
c) Schlegel (and Dr Strabismus of Utrecht according to J.B.Morton), suggests that this is a phrase in a contemporary speech by Adolf Hitler, who, speaking of the English said: 'They are not men, they are marshy beings'.

Corporal Parlow was greatly amused and showed it to everyone in the section. Unfortunately, my satirical Shakespearean parody proved to be prophetic. Within a week of General Nye's visit, Parlow was posted to Cairo to another branch of intelligence; later he was sent to India. He survived the war but I never saw him again. Several years after the war I saw an article by him about India, which appeared in *The New Statesman.*

General Nye also served in India, but long after Parlow had been demobilised. He was appointed governor of Madras and later became the United Kingdom High Commissioner at Delhi.

THE NOSEY PARKER

The Nosey Parker was an annual publication which you will not find in the subterranean vaults of the British Library or in the National Archives at Kew. I may possibly be the only person who has a complete set It first appeared in September, 1946, when most of us in the Intelligence Corps at BP had been thankfully demobilised. This brilliant venture began after CSM Alfred Sugar, a log-reader in SIXTA, returned to his peacetime job as a journalist and publicity officer for the Co-operative Society, in Manchester. He wrote to a few of his old BP colleagues, offering to compile and issue annually a news circular composed of excerpts from their letters. This he proposed to duplicate on his Gestetner stencil machine and send to any old friends who wrote to him of their activities. A good response persuaded Sug (his familiar name at BP, pronounced as in the first syllable of sugar) to issue Volume 1, number 1, which contained many interesting stories of our various adventures on return to civilian life – some to pre-war jobs – others searching for new careers.

Volume 1, number 2, published a year later, in September, 1947, was entitled *The Nosey Parker, with which is incorporated Military Training Excuse Note, Chairborne Chronicle, Penpushers' Friend, Pram-pushers' Post, Four-fifty-eight Flyer, Guardroom Gazette and The Blancoist.*

Sug continued printing *The Nosey Parker,* each annual issue including generous extracts from our letters, many of which recorded the births of numerous babies in the post-war years. The arrival of so many babies tempted Sug to rename the annual *Baby Bulletin or Crèche Chronicle*. Issue number 4 bore the sub-title : *The Journal of Those who Stud at Ease*. By 1950, *issue number 5* had a new sub-title *: The Journal of Those with a Wonderful Future Behind Them*.

The letters had, of course, no mention of the work at BP, which was not revealed to the general public until the mid-1970s. But occasionally cryptic references to our work as log-readers found their way into our letters. Number 6 appeared as *The Nosey Parker, with which is incorporated Sans Culotte, the Journal of Those Without Breeches of Security*.

By 1953 Sug began to doubt whether enough letters would arrive to make possible another issue. His warning revived interest for a time, but in 1957 it was obvious that *The Nosey Parker* was reaching the end of its days. In the final issue of October, 1957, only five of us had written to Sug during the year. He ended the last issue with these words:

It's sad closing down.
I hope the twelve years of continued contact has given you as much joy as it has to Win (his wife) and myself and that the cessation of N.P. won't mean an end of the letters. It's rather like packing the kit-bag for the last time and saying goodbye at the hut door to staunch old friends whose company one has valued through the years. But the time has surely come, so good luck to you all, and

                          Cheerio,
                          Sug.

I and others continued writing to Sug occasionally, but gradually, towards the end of the twentieth century, we heard of the deaths of many of our old colleagues. During the last five years I wrote to him many times, enclosing drafts of the chapters of this book. He always replied promptly, with wit and humour, correcting my script with his journalist's expertise and recalling wartime stories.

Sug's first wife died and he had married Jean, with whom he lived happily in his retirement, travelling much in this country and abroad. After a short illness, his brain still as active and alert as in the Bletchley days, Sug died on 26 June, 2007, having reached the age of one hundred the previous year.

ROOFERS ON GUARD

More than sixty years later it is difficult to picture myself on the roof of the mansion at Bletchley Park. Yet the entry in an old diary I kept during the war records that on 26th April, 1944, a hot sunny afternoon, I was called away from my desk to take part in a military exercise. Corporal Codd, a fellow log-reader and I were told to station ourselves on the roof with a walkie-talkie set, from which vantage-point we would have a complete view of the park. Nothing much happened. The sun beat down and we both had a feeling that there was something unreal about our situation. The others taking part in the exercise had gone to other places in the park, or outside in the town for all we knew. I remember the crackling noises of the walkie-talkie set and faint incomprehensible voices in the earphones. I was a sergeant at that time, so technically I was in charge of my small detachment. We were obviously forgotten men, so after a while, although enjoying the sunshine, I suggested to Corporal Codd that we should go back to work.

The Home Guard at BP was a haphazard affair. In Bletchley town there was probably a highly efficient Home Guard company, like the one my father, a Great War veteran, was running in Beverley, Yorkshire. Ours at BP was composed partly of men like me who had been in the real army before coming to BP and partly of civilians who were expected to take part in the Park Home Guard. The women at Bletchley, who far outnumbered the men, were not involved in these activities. Meetings were irregular and we had the impression that whoever had been asked to organise the unit was not enthusiastic about his mission. I remember several lectures. One, about hand-grenades, was pointless without a practical demonstration. Another was a dreary talk about military law, delivered by another log-reader, Corporal Parker, a barrister in civilian life. After the war I heard that he had become a judge.

What we were supposed to do in the case of a German descent upon BP was never revealed. We had no weapons, ammunition or hand grenades and I doubt whether there was, anywhere in the park, a collection of arms and munitions. The park was surrounded by a high metal fence and I have read that a small contingent of the RAF Regiment guarded the place; but we never saw any such body of men.

Had the Germans dropped a party of parachutists on BP they would have had no difficulty taking the place over. The huts and later the more substantial blocks stood open twenty-four hours daily, with nobody checking you in or out. Alone on a night shift, as happened sometimes, or with several other log-readers present, we would have had to surrender immediately if the enemy had come.

THE SHIFT SYSTEM

When we, the log-readers of the Central Party, arrived at BP in May 1942, we soon learned that we had to work through the 24 hours of the day, in three shifts: midnight to 9 a.m., 9 a.m. to 4 p.m. and 4.p.m. to midnight. Some hated the night shift, but I found it interesting to be working quietly through the night with a much smaller number of colleagues than on the day shift. The one-hour break in the middle of the night, joining the crowds of civilians and service men and women of all ranks in the brightly-lit cafeteria for a hot dinner, provided a pleasant interlude, with time on the way back to enjoy the stars, the moon and a walk round the lake.

The drawback of the night shift was the difficulty of sleeping in the daytime; this was not usually difficult in a civilian billet, but when we moved into the army camp, sleep was interrupted by the tramp of hob-nailed boots of fellow hut-dwellers who had occasion to return to their hut during the day. CSM Alfred Sugar, a journalist before the war, a popular member of the log-reading team, known to us as Sug (pronounced Shug), remembered an incident in his hut in the camp:

During the worst of the winter we tried to keep the coke-fired stove alight all night. One night, the last man returning after midnight from the evening shift, came in quietly because most of us were asleep. Taking his boots off and tiptoeing silently to the stove, he lifted off the red-hot cover using the tongs, letting them both drop on the concrete floor. Then, shovelling up enough coke from the floor to fill the stove, he dropped the stove-lid into position with a clang. At last, having woken everybody up, he thoughtfully picked up his boots and tiptoed to his bed.

Sometimes in the dark it was difficult to find one's own bed in the crowded hut. One story on this topic was also told by Sug. His neighbour Frank Higenbottam had risen in the night to visit the latrine. Returning to the hut:

...he mistakenly got into the empty bed next to his, whose owner had a sleeping-out pass. 'I knew I was in the wrong bed', said Frank, 'when in the morning I put out my hand to get my teeth out of my boots and they weren't there'.

On one occasion during the first months at BP I found that I was the only person on the night shift. Mrs Judith Whitfield, a civilian in charge of the allocation of duties, suddenly became aware that I was alone. 'Corporal Thirsk', she said, one morning as I finished my shift at 9 a.m., 'You seem to be all on your own on the night shift. You must find it very lonely, would you like somebody to join you?' She transferred a young ATS girl from days to nights. But I do not now remember who it was or whether she was good company.

Best of all I preferred the evening shift. You avoided the hubbub and bustle of the day-shift which employed by far the most log-readers. On evenings, in a much more tranquil atmosphere, work did not seem so arduous. And when midnight came you looked forward to a good night's sleep and the prospect of a whole day before you, to be lazy or busy as you pleased until 4 p.m. came again.

In the huts and later in the blocks that we inhabited, mugs of coffee sustained us, especially on the night-shift. It was real coffee too, which you could purchase already ground in sealed tins. Those who added milk had to make do with powdered milk stirred in hot water. For, although liquid milk was delivered to houses throughout the war, it would have been difficult to obtain it inside the park.

THE SMOKERS

It was Alfred Sugar, a fellow log-reader at BP during World War II, who told me when I telephoned him recently that, in his mind's eye, he had a picture of a pipe rack on my desk at Bletchley, with five or six tobacco pipes of various shapes. I say desk, but we only had bare trestle tables, with no covers on them. That Alfred, born in 1906, should have had this vision of my pipe rack stored in his memory for the best part of a lifetime, seemed to me remarkable, especially because he had not thought about it during all those years since the war.

I gave up smoking many years ago and the pipe rack probably found its way to a charity shop. But in the Bletchley days most of us were smokers and there were no rules about not smoking. What clouds of cigarette and pipe-smoke filled the huts and later the much larger rooms in blocks D and G ! Yet nobody complained and nobody ever thought at that time that smoking could damage health. We had never heard of passive smokers. The women smoked also but not as much as the men. Cigarette smokers easily outnumbered the pipe smokers.

Tobacco was never rationed during the war and although sometimes one shop would run out of a particular brand of cigarette or tobacco, there would be another shop nearby which had stocks.

Although there was no ban on smoking at work, I remember one occasion when one of the ATS girls produced an elegant pipe with a metal stem, filled it and puffed away contentedly as she got on with her work. The news spread around quickly as others came to watch such an extraordinary event. Most of us had never seen a woman smoking a pipe. Somebody in authority, alarmed at the interruption to work, asked her to desist. She agreed to smoke only cigarettes but I am sure that she carried on pipe smoking during her free time.

Smokers are a dwindling tribe and nowadays you see them standing outside office buildings furtively puffing at their cigarettes. Do the smokers at GCHQ nowadays nip outside the front door to have a few puffs after their tea-break?

TORPEDOED

Sitting at my trestle-table desk all day or evening and on the night shift, trying to cope with the flood of paper 'logs' which never dried up, it was sometimes difficult to believe that out there in the real war, the dreadful slaughter of men, women and children continued.

My job as a traffic analyst did not include work on the German navy but in other departments at BP and at the Admiralty the cryptologists and the traffic analysts were striving to win the Battle of the Atlantic.

A first-hand account of the horrors of that battle came to me in January 1943, when a letter arrived from my old ship-mate Reg Palmer. Reg and I had been through infantry training together in 1940, later being transferred to *The Royal Artillery, Maritime Regiment,* at Liverpool, where, as port-gunners, we manned the guns on merchant ships. We slept on board while the ships discharged their cargoes and loaded up again, which often took two or three weeks.

After I transferred to the Intelligence Corps, Reg became a sea-going gunner on merchant ships, voyaging all over the world. Already he and Dawson Todd, another of my friends, had been on several voyages together in convoy across the Atlantic, without so far encountering German submarines. Reg's letter brought news of their escape from death after their ship had been torpedoed by a U-boat.

Picture, Jim, a ship laden to the hatch with cargo, making her way smoothly across the ocean. Everyone on board thinking about home … and then, if you can imagine, three terrific explosions. A mad scamper across a deck with a list of 40 degrees - the smell of cordite, heated arguments and flying debris. Imagine again the ship taking her final plunge with a few shipwrecked fellows like Toddy and me to hear her death-groan. And what a groan!

Reg and Dawson and the crew were lucky to be picked up by a British naval corvette after more than a week in open boats in the south Atlantic. Both of them survived the war after more voyages. Both of them lived to enjoy their grandchildren.

V 2

Towards the end of the war, in 1944, the V-2 rockets began to fall on London and the south-east. Hitler named his V-1 and V-2 weapons *Vergeltungswaffe* (Reprisal weapons). At that time a small group of us log-readers was analysing radio traffic between German units which were concerned with the launching of these V-2s. There was nothing we could do, for the logs indicated only the times of launching, giving no clue about their destination.

Unlike the V-1, popularly known as the doodle-bug, flying bomb or the buzz-bomb, which announced its approach with a buzzing sound easily distinguished from the sound of an aeroplane, the V-2 was silent. The passage of this long-range liquid-fuelled weapon, with its exploding warhead, was incredibly swift. No sound was heard until the rocket exploded on arrival from a great height, causing widespread destruction of people and buildings. At Bletchley, more than fifty miles from London, we were far beyond the reach of either of these weapons.

Usually, it was the mothers and fathers, wives and daughters who received the telegrams announcing the deaths of their sons and husbands, or that they were missing. Less often it was the men and women in the Forces who heard news of the deaths of their families in air-raids. One morning in 1945 I wearily finished a night-shift and returned to my hut in the army camp just outside Bletchley Park. Alone in the hut, a sergeant sat on his bed sorting out his kit. He worked in another section, but I knew him well as one of the sixteen in our hut. As I prepared to go to bed, he told me that he had just heard that his wife and two children had been killed in London when a V-2 rocket had completely destroyed their house and the houses of all their neighbours. He was about to go to London on compassionate leave to bury any remains of his family he could find.

BIOGRAPHIES

How fascinating it would be to read the biographies or autobiographies of the ten thousand and more men and women who worked during World War II at Bletchley Park or its outstations. For each one of them had a tale to tell and each played a part, however small, in the defeat of Nazi Germany, Japan and their allies. Alas, during the sixty years and more since the war ended most of the ten thousand have died, many of them without ever telling their spouses or relations what they had been doing. But in the archives of the Bletchley Park Trust are some biographical and autobiographical details. Perhaps one day somebody may publish these as a *Who Was Who at Bletchley Park*.

My aim here is to record briefly the lives of those whose names come to mind, either because they headed sections at BP, or made important contributions to the decryption of enemy ciphers, or analysed and dealt with the intelligence derived from the messages.

I have not included those who dealt with intelligence derived from decrypted Enigma messages, or other sources, who were not at Bletchley. There were many such people, working in London and elsewhere, whose work was of tremendous importance, particularly those at the Admiralty. Their contribution has been recorded in other books and, in any case, my book is about Bletchley Park and its inhabitants. I have not written of the talented Polish cryptologists who first broke into the Enigma machine before the war. They did not work at BP and their story has been told in other books.

Nor have I written of the many talented Americans who came to BP later in the war, whose valuable contributions to the work of Huts 6 and 3 and other departments, have been told well and thoroughly by Thomas Parrish, in his book *The Ultra Americans,* first issued by the New York publisher, Stein and Day, in 1986. Although at first some of the British resented the arrival of the Americans at BP, they were soon accepted and we enjoyed their company.

I would like to have written about the heroic deeds of men of the Royal Navy and allied navies in rescuing code books, intelligence material and even Enigma machines from U-Boats and other vessels. The story of the deaths of Lieutenant Anthony Fasson and Able Seaman Colin Grazier, who, while serving on the British destroyer HMS *Petard*, boarded the captured German submarine U-559 to retrieve intelligence material, has moved many. To the horror of their shipmates they were drowned as the submarine suddenly sank to the bottom of the Mediterranian, after they had gone inside again to seek more material. Tommy Brown, a sixteen year old seaman who had helped them, escaped. The first two were awarded the George Cross, posthumously. Tommy was given the George Medal. This event and other successful captures have been told by David Kahn in his book *Seizing the Enigma* (Souvenir Press, 1992), and in other books.

Few, I hope, will disagree with my choice of those about whom I have written. They do not include some outstanding men and women still living, for, although urged to do so, I feel that those who are still with us have a right to their privacy. Long may they survive!

Some may complain that nearly all the biographies are of men. The truth was, however, that during the war there were very few women in charge of sections or in senior positions. The pattern of management in war and in peacetime at that period almost precluded women from occupying senior positions. My wife Joan Watkins, whom I first met at Bletchley in 1944, although agreeing with this truth, has reminded me that there were many hundreds of women, like herself, who were called to BP because of their specialist knowledge – in her case German language. She added that:

...as the men had been subject to conscription since the beginning of the war and most of them were already serving in different theatres of war, there were few men left when more hands were required after 1942 at BP. So fresh searches began in the universities and schools for young women in their teens and early twenties and many women with German and other qualifications arrived at this stage of the war. All around me in the Fusion Room there were many women of my age, between twenty and twenty-three years old, who had either just completed modern languages degrees or had interrupted their courses because of the requirement to do war work. With us worked civilians and soldiers slightly older, doing the same work. The only difference was that they were paid more. Let it be said, however, that although these personnel have not qualified for inclusion in this biographical section, all of them worked valiantly and many of them, men and women, went on to have distinguished careers after the war.

Of those I have written about, I met only four. I am aware of the difficulties and dangers of summing up a person's life in a couple of pages. What does one really know about other people, even if one has lived and worked with them? In each of us that 'hidden self' Matthew Arnold spoke of in his poem *The Buried Life,* eludes the biographer, let alone the individual himself.

I hope that my short biographies offend none of the children and grandchildren of my subjects, for I have tried to paint true portraits of a remarkable group of people whose work helped to shorten the war. We must always remember that they were mainly young men and women, who had a zest for living and who had the stamina to use their brains for long hours, often through the night.

Many of them far outlived the three score years and ten the Psalmist spoke of, surviving until their eighties and even nineties. Which proves perhaps that overworking the brain in youth does not wear it out. If any of their descendants have corrections or wish to comment on my short biographies of their forbears, I shall be pleased to hear from them.

ALEXANDER CRAIG AITKEN (1895-1967)

Had a Turkish sniper's bullet found twenty year old Alexander Aitken, the British academic community would never have known one of the most remarkable mathematicians of the 20th century. For Alexander Aitken, a New Zealander, took part in and survived Churchill's disastrous Gallipoli campaign. Born at Dunedin, New Zealand, on 1st April 1895, he was the eldest of the seven children of William Aitken and his wife Elizabeth. His grandfather, also Alexander, who became a farmer near Dunedin, had emigrated from Lanarkshire in Scotland.

Aitken had won a place at Otago University, New Zealand, but his studies in mathematics and languages were interrupted by the beginning of the Great War in 1914. Volunteering for the army, he soon arrived at Gallipoli, fortunately for him, a few weeks before the withdrawal of all troops. Moving then to the western front in France, he was commissioned in the field. It was then that his luck ran out, for, severely wounded in the battle of the Somme, he was invalided home in March 1917. Alexander wrote a book about his days in the army, but this was not published until 1963, with the title *Gallipoli to the Somme: Recollections of a New Zealand Infantry Man.* It won the Hawthornden prize.

Alexander was married in 1920 to Mary Betts, a lecturer in botany at Otago University, where he had now returned. Graduating in mathematics, French and Latin, he spent the next three years teaching at his old school. In 1923, awarded a postgraduate scholarship, he and his wife sailed for Scotland, the home of his paternal grandfather. There he became a lecturer in mathematics at Edinburgh University, achieving a DSc. in 1926.

During the inter-war years Aitken wrote many mathematical books and papers and became a popular lecturer, who would sometimes entertain his students by demonstrating his astonishing mental calculations. In a paper about Dr Aitken's mathematical abilities, which appeared in *The British Journal of Psychology* in 1962, the psychologist I.M.I.Hunter gave his opinion that Aitken's skill

....possibly exceeds that of any other person for whom precise authenticated records exist. Professor A.R. Collar believed that Aitken had also in large measure the kind of mystical insight into problems which characterised, for example, Isaac Newton.

When World War II came, Alexander was recruited to Bletchley Park as a Foreign Office civilian, joining Turing, Welchman and the other brilliant mathematicians in Hut 6. Being of an older generation than most, he was always known as 'Dr Aitken', rather than by his first name; most of us were known by our first names. An exception was Alan Turing, who was affectionately called 'Prof.' It was not until after the war in 1946 that he became Professor Aitken, having succeeded to the Edinburgh chair of Mathematics. I remember being called to his small room in Block G when I was reading logs containing traffic about the launching of V2 rockets. Dr Aitken wished to know about the times of rocket launches. I found him a pleasant and courteous man who examined my notes with care, bringing them close to his eyes, although he was not wearing spectacles. In his room was an Enigma machine.

Alexander's experiences in the Great War haunted him until the end of his life for, like many mathematicians, he had a phenomenal memory. He was a lifelong lover of music and the playing of his violin, which he had carried everywhere, even in the army, must have helped to soften the bitter memories of soldiering in France. He is remembered by his students as a warm and gentle man and a brilliant lecturer. Dr Aitken became a Fellow of the Royal Society in 1936.

HUGH O'DONEL ALEXANDER (1909-1974)

Hugh Alexander was born in Ireland, the son of William Alexander, a professor of engineering at University College, Cork, and his wife Hilda Bennett, who came from Birmingham. When her husband died, Hilda went back to England with Hugh and his three younger siblings. There he attended King Edward's School, Birmingham, where he excelled in chess; when still at school he won the British Boys' Chess Championship at Hastings, in 1926.

Obtaining a mathematics scholarship, he went to King's College, Cambridge, obtaining a first in that subject in 1931. His brilliance at chess occupied much of his time during the 1930s and in 1939 he was in Buenos Aires, playing for the English team. In 1934 he married an Australian woman, Enid Crichton, nine years older than him, the daughter of a sea captain. They had two sons, the older one, later Sir Michael Alexander, became a notable diplomat.

Having taught at Winchester School during the 1930s, Hugh left to become head of research at the John Lewis Partnership in London. The war put an end to his brief service there and in February 1940 he came to Bletchley Park, joining Hut 6, where the German air force and army Enigma ciphers were broken. Soon however he moved into Hut 8, which dealt with German naval Enigma, as deputy to Alan Turing.

In October 1941 he, with Turing and two colleagues, wrote a letter to Churchill appealing for more staff. Their wish was granted. When Turing went to the USA in 1942, Hugh became head of Hut 8; he had been acting head for some time, for Turing hated administration. Alexander, described later by a colleague as 'a model manager who treated his cryptographers as colleagues and was remarkably tolerant of our foibles', turned Hut 8 into a highly efficient section, passing decrypted messages to the naval section in Hut 4.

It was thanks to Turing and Alexander's efforts and those of many other cryptographers that the Battle of the Atlantic was finally won, albeit after many periods when the German naval Enigma cipher proved impregnable.

At the end of the war Alexander returned briefly to the John Lewis Partnership. Soon however he was tempted back to Government Communications Headquarters, which had now moved to Cheltenham. There, as head of a section, he remained until his retirement at the age of sixty-two. Alexander had only a brief retirement, for he died in 1974 at the age of sixty-four. Enid, his wife, died in 1982, at the age of 82.

In his retirement Alexander continued his lifelong interest in chess, becoming chess correspondent of a number of newspapers and periodicals. It has been said that but for the war he might have competed for the World Championship title.

His greatest achievement, however, was his work at Bletchley Park, where he presided over the activities of Hut 8, 'delighting his friends and colleagues with his gaiety, humour and warmth.'

DENNIS BABBAGE (1909-1991)

It would be interesting to know whether Dennis Babbage was a descendant of the famous nineteenth-century Englishman, Charles Babbage, a Cambridge professor of mathematics whose pioneer work on calculating machines sowed the seeds which produced the twentieth-century computer; for Dennis was also a brilliant mathematician, one of that glorious band, many of them from Cambridge, who, with others at Bletchley Park, decrypted German ciphers during World War II.

Born in London in 1909, Dennis attended St Paul's School, where his mathematical bent was revealed early. His scholarship to Magdalene College, Cambridge, followed; there he passed the examinations with ease, achieving his PhD by 1933. A research fellowship was followed by his appointment to a university lectureship at Magdalene. It has been said that he was truly the golden boy of the college establishment in those pre-war years, when brilliant mathematical papers flowed from his pen.

The war took him from Cambridge to Bletchley Park in 1939 along with Alan Turing, Gordon Welchman and other mathematicians. Unlike those two civilians Dennis was a major in the army. Soon he became head of a research unit in Hut 6 where he studied improvements the Germans were frequently making to their cipher machines. Every day brought a new challenge to Hut 6, but somehow the Enigma ciphers continued to be decrypted.

In a passage from a memoir Dennis wrote many years later he remembered that exhilarating chapter in his life:

I shall never forget the spring and early summer of 1940. Wonderful weather, France collapsing , yet a liberating feeling that now at last we were on our own; and then the first real breakthrough, which ultimately became a flood, into the decoding of Enigma. In this I had some modest part and for all those extraordinary years there was the feeling of being close to the centre.

However, he also confessed that his six years at Bletchley covered a period of bereavement and personal unhappiness.

Returning to civilian life after the war, he remained at Cambridge for the rest of his days, director of studies in mathematics and, as tutor and senior tutor; later he became a senior fellow (1982-1991). His association with Magdalene College had lasted sixty-four years and as a Fellow for sixty years.

Several generations of Cambridge mathematical students must have been sad when they heard of his death in 1991.

CHARLES BECKINGHAM (1914-1998)

Born in February 1914, at Houghton, Huntingdonshire, less than six months before the beginning of the Great War, Charles Fraser Beckingham was the only child of Arthur Beckingham and his wife Alice Shingles, a nurse. Arthur was a painter, an Associate of the Royal Society of British Artists, who was nearly sixty when Charles was born. Charles was nick-named 'the professor' at the age of eight because of his precocious mind. When, in old age, Charles met by chance a childhood neighbour whom he had not seen for seventy years, he recalled the details of their boyhood friendship, even remembering the names of his friend's teddy bears. His father died when he was only six, leaving his mother short of money.

At that time it was almost impossible to go to university without financial help from parents or by the aid of grants. However, Charles did well at Huntingdon Grammar School, winning not only a county scholarship but also the much-prized state scholarship. At Queens' College, Cambridge, he read English. In addition to his studies he continued his boyhood interest in oriental subjects, reading widely on the subject both in history and geography.

Charles's first job after graduation was as a temporary assistant cataloguer in the Department of Printed Books at the British Museum. There, in a boring job re-cataloguing books for a new edition of the catalogue, he continued his oriental studies and began to learn Arabic.

When the war came, Charles was not called up immediately. But, by 1942, he was in uniform and was transferred to the Intelligence Corps after basic training. There followed a period at the Naval Intelligence Division of the Admiralty, preparing, with others, the Admiralty's *Handbook to Western Arabia and the Red Sea coast*. Finally, released from this job in January 1943, he spent the rest of the war at Bletchley Park, engaged on cryptographic work. At the end of the war, Charles married Margery, the only daughter of John Ansell, a conductor and composer. They had one daughter, Carolyn, but Margery died in 1966, leaving Charles a widower for thirty-two years.

Rather than returning to the British Museum at the end of the war or choosing an academic career for which he was well equipped, Charles stayed on with the Bletchley organisation, moving with them under its new name, GCHQ, to Cheltenham.

In 1951 he retired from that post, moving to Manchester University as a lecturer in Islamic studies, a late comer to the university world. Before the end of the decade he succeeded to the professorship. Travels in Cyprus and Ethiopia followed and in 1965 he was invited by the School of Oriental and African Studies, University of London, to become Professor of Islamic Studies, an offer which he accepted. Later he became head of the Near East and Middle East department of the School.

Charles had a flair for classical and modern languages. Both the Royal Asiatic and the Hakluyt societies elected him as their president. By then he had edited in the 1960s an *Atlas of the Arab World* and for many years had been engaged in translating and editing the final volume of the Hakluyt Society's annotated translation of the fourteenth-century Arabic narrative *The Travels of Ibn Battuta* (volume 4,1994). Charles was amused to tell people that the translation, begun by Sir Hamilton Gibb twenty-eight years earlier, had taken longer than Ibn Battuta's journeys. His last work, with Bernard Hamilton was *Prester John, the Mongols and the Ten Lost Tribes (1996)*, a subject which had interested him for many years, and on which he had already written two books with G.W.B. Huntingford .

On his death a fine tribute appeared in the Hakluyt Society's annual report (1998) :

As a university lecturer for thirty years, he was remembered by his students as much for his approachability and the personal encouragement he gave them, as for the lucidity of his presentations. But no tribute is complete that fails to acknowledge those subtle qualities of personality – integrity of mind, breadth of interest, sense of humour, gentleness – that made this most likeable of men such agreeable and rewarding company.

John Shipman of the British Yemeni Society, paid tribute to Charles in these words:

...an eminent scholar who will be warmly remembered for his wit and humanity and for the generosity with which he shared his immense learning with others.

Charles died on 30 September, 1998, in his eighty-fifth year. He had been living for some time with his daughter Carolyn, in Sussex.

RALPH BENNETT (1911-2002)

Not many academic historians have the opportunity of making history and of subsequently writing about it. But Major Ralph Bennett, of the Intelligence Corps, worked in Hut 3 at Bletchley Park, writing intelligence reports based on decrypts of the German Enigma messages provided by Hut 6. These reports, compiled by Ralph and his colleagues, influenced the actions taken by allied military generals throughout the war. Long after the war ended and after the secret of Bletchley Park became generally known, Ralph who had returned to his job as a historian at Cambridge, wrote four books about the work at Bletchley Park, which relied heavily on the vast collections of Ultra material in the Public Record Office. In his study of this material, he applied the rigorous analysis of an academic historian, aided by his own memories of handling the intelligence more than thirty years earlier.

Ralph Bennett was born in October, 1911, the son of a veterinary surgeon in Romford, Essex, England. Educated at a new state grammar school, the Royal Liberty School, in that town, he proceeded to Magdalene College, Cambridge, with which he was to be associated for sixty-four years. An athletic young man, he became interested in rowing, an activity he pursued for most of his life. Choosing to be a medievalist, he was advised by Geoffrey Barraclough, a fellow Cambridge historian who later also served at BP. In 1935 Ralph spent a year in Munich working on his thesis on the early Dominicans and on learning German.

Returning to Cambridge after the war as a university lecturer, Ralph took a big part in the administration of Magdalene College, first as Director of Studies in history for twenty-seven years. He also served as steward and lastly as President of the college from 1979 to 1982. He had many interests and although he did not write much on his subject, he introduced generations of students to the medieval world. His book: *First Class Answers in History (*1974*)* was a popular guide for students. The author of the obituary notice in *The Times* summed up his devotion to his students:

Many generations of Magdalene men appreciated his concern for them: trenchant yet warm-hearted, conscientious and cheerful, he was the kindliest of men.

In 1977 when the first Ultra material was declassified and made available at the Public Record Office, Ralph, now retired, decided to write a book, based on the records and his own memories, which would confute some of the inaccurate accounts of the work at BP which had appeared. In this enterprise he was encouraged by his publisher son. The first book, published two years later, was *Ultra in the West: the Normandy Campaign of 1944-45*. (1979) This was followed ten years later by *Ultra and Mediterranean Strategy* (1989) and in 1994 by *Behind the Battle:Iintelligence in the War with Germany,1939-1945*. Finally, in 1996, he published a collection of his articles and lectures on intelligence, with the title *Intelligence Investigation: how Ultra changed History*. These four publications are essential reading for anybody who wishes to study the history of intelligence during World War II. Ralph also wrote a more personal essay about his work in Hut 3, which appears as Chapter 2: *The Duty Officer, Hut 3* in *Code-breakers: the inside Story of Bletchley Park*, edited by F.H. Hinsley and Alan Stripp. (OUP, 1993).

In 1939 Ralph married Daphne Meyler. They had two sons both of whom graduated at Magdalene College. Daphne was a royal biographer and author of many books. She died in 1996. In 1985, they had left Cambridge to live near the Public Record Office at Kew, where he spent so many hours of research on the Ultra material. Ralph died in August, 2002, in his 91st year.

FRANCIS BIRCH (1889-1956)

When the Great War began in 1914, Francis Lyall Birch, usually known as Frank, was a young man of 24 who had already gained a double first in the history tripos at King's College, Cambridge, after school at Eton College. The third son of John Birch, a banker and his wife Charlotte Stopford, Frank volunteered to join the Navy; as an able seaman he served on ships in the Atlantic and the Dardanelles.

In 1916, recruited to Room 40, the Royal Navy's cryptographic section, he joined his friend from Cambridge days, Alfred Dillwyn Knox (Dilly). There he worked as an analyst of decrypted German messages. After the war Frank returned to Cambridge, where, as a Fellow of King's, and a lecturer in history, he remained until 1928. It was then that he left the academic world to become an actor and producer of plays.

Mrs Penelope Fitzgerald, the novelist, a niece of Dilly Knox, remembers Frank Birch several times in her entertaining book *The Knox Brothers* (1977):

Birch was a many-sided human being - a rather dull historian, an acceptable drinking companion, a mysterious private personality, a brilliant talker and a born actor.

When World War II was looming, Frank was called in with others by Alastair Denniston, the chief of GC&CS, the successor to Room 40, to advise him how to recruit men suitable for the department. On the outbreak of war in September 1939,

Frank joined the naval department of GC&CS at Bletchley Park.. In June 1941 he succeeded Clarke as head of the naval section (Hut 4), responsible for all naval cryptanalysis, except Enigma ciphers. Hut 4 was also responsible for translating and analysing decrypted messages from the Japanese, Italian, German, French and Spanish navies.

In 1942 Frank went to Washington DC with Edward Travis, who had replaced Denniston as head of GCCS, to negotiate an Anglo-American agreement to collaborate on naval cryptographic work.

In his biography of Frank Birch in the *ODNB*, Ralph Erskine writes that, although Frank

... was not a born leader and at times had a heavy-handed managerial style, which was an unwise approach to GC&CS's free spirits, he cared deeply about his staff and was highly popular with the junior members of his section in consequence.

After World War II Frank was appointed chief of the historical section at GCHQ, as GC&CS was now called. One of his tasks was the compilation of an internal *History of British Sigint*, which has not been published, but can be seen in the National Archives.

Frank died much younger than many of his contemporaries, at the age of 67. His wife Vera Benedicta, daughter of Henry Charles, fifth Viscount Gage, survived him. They had no children.

WILLIAM FRANCIS CLARKE (1883-1961)

William F. Clarke, affectionately known as 'Nobby', the nickname given to many of that surname, was the son of an eminent Conservative member of Parliament, Sir Edward George Clarke (1841-1931), who became Solicitor-General. His mother, Kathleen Bryan, Sir Edward's second wife, had only one child.

After education at Harrow School and Magdalen College, Oxford, Nobby became a barrister in 1906. The next year he married Dorothy Mainland; they had one son and two daughters. With every prospect of a future similar to his father's, he settled down to a legal career. Revelations in an unpublished memoir, *My way to Room 40*, in the National Archives at Kew, show that Nobby had a 'sneaking desire' before the Great War began to join the Royal Navy and go to sea.

When war came in 1914 he might have realised this dream had it not been for a failed eyesight test and the fact that he was over thirty years of age. Instead he was commissioned as an assistant paymaster. It was about a year later that fate intervened, in the shape of Admiral Reginald 'Blinker' Hall, director of the intelligence division of the Admiralty. With his good knowledge of German, and legal background, Nobby was a promising recruit for Room 40 OB (Old Building, Admiralty), joining Hall's group of young men devoted to cryptography. One of the lessons he learned there, wrote J. A. Maiolo in his biography of Nobby in the *Oxford Dictionary of National Biography (*ODNB) was the importance of 'information gleaned from wireless interception, rather than code-breaking'. In other words, the value of what we now call traffic analysis.

After the war he and a colleague, Frank Birch, compiled a history of Room 40 which was critical of the way intelligence was handled by the Navy.

When the Great War ended, the war cabinet decided to form a peacetime cryptographic organisation out of the remains of Room 40 and other units, to be known as the Government Code & Cipher School (GC&CS). There had been long arguments about the name, and it is said that Nobby Clark, hearing that his salary would be only £500 year, suggested the name 'Public Benefactor'. He joined the new organisation from the beginning in 1919 in their new home at Watergate House, Adelphi, London. The first director was Admiral Sir Hugh Sinclair, who remained in charge until his death in 1939.

At first Nobby was concerned mainly with diplomatic traffic, but in 1924 he was put in charge of a new naval section within GC&CS, a post he held until 1941.

Moving to Bletchley Park (BP) at the beginning of World War II, along with the whole staff of GC&CS, which included a number of the veterans of Room 40, Nobby dealt mainly with the decrypting of Italian naval ciphers.

Unlike some of his colleagues he decided to retire in October 1945 at the age of sixty-two. He died in 1961, having passed his seventy-seventh birthday. He is buried at Selworth church, near Minehead, in Somerset.

JOAN CLARKE (1917-1996)

Joan Elisabeth Lowther Clarke, a Londoner, was born near Dulwich Park, a district about four miles south of the River Thames. Her mother, Dorothy Elizabeth Fulford, had married William Kemp Lowther Clarke, an Anglican clergyman. Joan was the youngest child and had three older brothers and one sister. She was educated at the nearby Dulwich High School. From there she moved to Newnham, one of the women's colleges at Cambridge University, to read mathematics. With a double first in that subject Joan was looking for a job in 1940.

Gordon Welchman, the head of Hut 6 at Bletchley Park at that time, had known her when he tutored her in geometry for part two of the Cambridge mathematical Tripos. Looking for likely talent, he interviewed her early in 1940, telling her that the work 'did not really need mathematics but mathematicians tended to be good at it.' This, of course, was without telling her the nature of the job. Joan arrived at Bletchley Park on 17 June, 1940 and was given a chair and desk in a room in Hut 8 where Alan Turing and two others were working on German naval Enigma messages. Plunged straight into the work of decryption, Joan soon mastered the rudiments. Before long she found herself alone in a hut on a night shift, wondering, no doubt, what on earth she was doing there.

As a civilian employed by the Foreign Office, the problem of pay had to be tackled. Colleagues in the army and the men in the Foreign Office had salaries much greater than hers. Some increases followed her regrading as a linguist, which she was not. One of her first jobs was to use the very first British *bombe*, which had been designed by Alan Turing. It was a machine for recovering Enigma daily keys. For a brief period in 1940 Joan helped in another department to decrypt the German railways' cipher, named *Rocket*. She returned to naval Enigma in Hut 8 in March 1941, using, with considerable success, keys taken from the captured German armed trawler *Krebs*. Some material had also been recovered from the patrol boat *München*.

Joan Clarke had been working with Alan Turing for less than a year when he proposed marriage in the spring of 1941. A few days later he told her of his doubts about the success of a marriage, because he had 'homosexual tendencies'. They did not make public their engagement although some colleagues knew how close they were. Joan was happy to continue the relationship, but before the end of the year, Alan decided that the engagement should end. They remained friends.

After the war Joan continued working with GC&CS, now GCHQ, moving with them to Cheltenham. There she worked until her marriage in 1952 to Lieutenant-Colonel John Murray, a fellow-worker, a retired army officer who had served in India. They had no children. Ten years later, in 1962, Joan returned to GCHQ finally retiring fifteen years later, in 1977, at the age of sixty. When Sir Harry Hinsley worked on the five volume history, *British Intelligence in the Second World War*, Joan helped him with part of Volume 3, an account of Polish, French and British work on the decryption of Enigma.

In Joan's biography in the ODNB, Ralph Erskine pointed out that Joan 'was unique as the only female cryptanalyst to work in Hut 8.' He added:

Her acute intelligence enabled her fully to hold her own with her co-workers in Hut 8, and to make a significant contribution to its work in helping the allies to win the battle of the Atlantic, among other successes.

One of her closest colleagues at BP, Rolf Noskwith, described Joan as 'Kind and always good-tempered, but rather reserved.'

Joan died, a widow, in September 1996 in her eightieth year, at her home in Headington, Oxford.

JOSHUA COOPER (1901-1981)

Although geniuses were plentiful among the thousands who worked at Bletchley Park during World War II, there were only a few who combined their brilliance with eccentricity. Turing and Dilly Knox come to mind. Another was Joshua Edward Synge Cooper, known to all as 'Josh', who was a popular figure at Bletchley Park during the war and later at GCHQ, Cheltenham.

Josh was born at Fulham, London, in April, 1901, the eldest of the four sons and one daughter of Richard Edward Synge Cooper, chartered engineer, and his wife Mary Eleanor, the daughter of William Burke. His parents were both Irish. Josh's great-grandfather, Edward Joshua Cooper, a Fellow of the Royal Society, and a notable astronomer in Victorian years, wrote several books on the subject; he was also a member of Parliament for Sligo county from 1832-41.

From Shrewsbury School, where one of his teachers was Ronald Knox, a younger brother of Dilly Knox, the cryptographer, Josh proceeded to Brasenose College, Oxford. After classical studies there, Josh came to King's College, London, to read Russian and Serbian. With a first-class degree in those subjects in 1924, he had a brief period of teaching. But in 1925 A.G.Denniston, the director of GC&CS, was seeking recruits. One of these was Josh, who was introduced by a family friend, Charles Morgan, the novelist. He was to remain with the organisation until his retirement from GCHQ at Cheltenham in 1961.

In 1936, Josh, now an old hand at GC&CS, was seconded to the Air Ministry as head of the section which analysed intercepted radio traffic. He remained head of this air section until 1943, when he again became employed by the Foreign Office.

Aileen Clayton, the author of *The Enemy is Listening* (Hutchinson,1980), who joined the Women's Auxiliary Air Force (WAAF) in 1939, was asked in the spring of 1941 to go to BP to discuss a type of clear German traffic which her unit was intercepting, which appeared to be concerned with Luftwaffe night-fighters. At BP she was handed over to the air section to be interviewed by Josh Cooper. In her book she remembers him as one of the most unforgettable people I have ever met. A brilliant mathematician, and much younger than he appeared to be at first sight, he was the archetypal absent-minded academic - slightly deaf, incredibly unkempt in his dress, dark hair which he constantly brushed back with a vaguely irritated gesture, often thereby dislodging his thick spectacles. Yet one was aware of an inner brilliance, of an intelligence far beyond the realms of the normal human being.

Although, as D.R.Nicoll, the author of Josh's biography in the ODNB points out,

...his eccentricities were much embellished in the telling ... and arose from his concentration on the subject occupying his mind

there is one event, bordering on slapstick comedy, which has been written about several times, and was authenticated by Professor R.V. Jones, who was at BP at the time. A captured Luftwaffe pilot was to be interviewed by Josh and two others, hoping they would learn something about German Air Force communications. The young officer-pilot was paraded before them, clicked his heels, gave the Nazi salute and barked *Heil, Hitler!* Taken by surprise, Josh scrambled to his feet, returning the salute and greeting. Then, realising what he had done, he sat down quickly, missing his chair and landing on his back under the table.

After the war Josh moved to Cheltenham with GCHQ, becoming an assistant director in control of research work. The ODNB records that:

Cooper demonstrated the great range of his mind and his ability to comprehend in fields such as mathematics and physics which were outside those in which he had been educated. He realised very early the potential significance of the post-war development of computers and ensured that his colleagues understood it too.

Before the war, in 1934, Josh married Winifred Blanche de Vere, the daughter of Thomas Frederick Parkinson, a civil engineer in India. They had two sons, the elder of whom died in 1956. Josh Cooper died at the age of eighty at Amersham in Buckinghamshire. His wife and younger son survived him. He had enjoyed twenty years of retirement, during which he returned to Russian studies, producing a *Russian Companion* for Pergamon Press in 1967. He also translated *Four Russian Plays,* which was published by Penguin Books in 1972.

EDWARD CRANKSHAW (1909-1984)

Edward Crankshaw was in Moscow during the war from 1941 to 1943, a member of the British Military Mission to the Soviet Union. Before that he had worked in London with the Central Party, a department of MI8, dealing mainly with traffic analysis. After his Moscow days he came to Bletchley Park with the rank of major, where for a short period he was in charge of SIXTA, the department of Hut 6 concerned with traffic analysis. I remember that, soon after his coming to BP, he visited each of us log-readers separately, sitting in turn at our desks, questioning us about our work.

Major Crankshaw was a small man of slender frame, whose unusual background had brought him to BP. Born in London in 1909, the elder son of Arthur Crankshaw and his wife Amy Bishop, Edward, unlike many of his contemporaries at BP, had decided not to go to university. Instead, 'in a first display of his romantic and headstrong side' (ODNB), he went alone to Vienna at the age of eighteen, supporting himself by teaching English at a language school. Edward not only became fluent in German, he also studied German and Austrian history. On his return to England, he lived in Hampstead, London, with his wife Clare Carr. There, in the early 1930s, they entertained many Austrian, German Jewish and other refugees, including the German dramatist Ernst Toller, some of whose plays Edward translated.

Edward had no regular job and his only income came from earnings from journalism, book reviewing and as a dramatic critic. His first book on *Joseph Conrad*, was published in 1936. It was about this time that he and Clare abandoned London, to live in the small village of Sandhurst, near Hawkhurst in Kent. There they lived frugally until war came. To the surprise of his left-wing friends, he had joined the Territorial Army in 1936. When war came in 1939 Edward was quickly recruited to intelligence work, partly because of his fluent German.

At first he worked in London, in MI8, where he endeavoured to work out the general pattern of Luftwaffe communications by means of traffic analysis and the study of call-signs. In 1941 he was seconded for duties with the British Military Mission in Moscow. There he had some success in swapping intelligence with his Russian colleagues, becoming fluent in the language.

During his stay in Moscow he developed an enormous admiration for the endurance of the Russian people and the Soviet army battling against hardship and death. After the war he wrote frequently in the *Observer* about the state of the Soviet Union. But in spite of his hatred of the Soviet system, he never lost his faith in the people.

In the 1960s Crankshaw began to write a number of books based on diligent research. In 1963 appeared *The Fall of the House of Habsburg*; in 1969 appeared his biography of *Maria Theresa* and in 1976 *The Shadow of the Winter Palace*, a study of nineteenth century Russia. Reviews of books and articles on the Soviet Union continued and Crankshaw became known as one of the leading kremlinologists.

Edward Crankshaw died at the age of seventy-five at his home in Kent after a long illness. He continued writing to the end of his days, even when unable to leave his bed. He and his wife had no children.

ALEXANDER DENNISTON (1881-1961)

The Scotsman who was to become head of the GC&CS from its foundation in 1919 until 1941 was Alexander Guthrie Denniston, who preferred to be known as Alastair. The eldest child of Dr James Denniston, a medical practitioner and his wife Agnes Guthrie, he was born in December, 1881, near Greenock on the Clyde. His father died at sea, leaving Agnes to bring up her family on very little money. Alastair was a bright scholar, good at classics, mathematics and languages. An excellent athlete, although a small man, he was chosen later to play hockey for Scotland in the Olympic Games of 1908. From Bowden College in Cheshire he progressed to the universities of Bonn in Germany and the Sorbonne in Paris. Having completed his studies, Alastair at first taught German at Merchiston Castle, a notable public school in Edinburgh. From there he moved to a post teaching German at the pre-Dartmouth naval preparatory school at Osborne in the Isle of Wight.

When war came in 1914, Alastair was recruited to the establishment known as 40 OB, a branch of naval intelligence which had been set up in Room 40 in the old building of the Admiralty. Under Admiral 'Blinker' Hall, a small staff at the beginning of the war dealt with the interception, decryption and interpretation of German and other messages in cipher, sent by wireless or cable.

After the war, the government decided to keep on a cryptographic department which was established in 1919 and was named the Government Code and Cypher School (GC&CS). Alastair Denniston was appointed head. In 1917 he married Dorothy Mary Gilliat, who was working in Room 40 at that time. She was the daughter of Arthur Gilliat, a business man. They had one son and one daughter.

GC&CS had a lean time during the inter-war years in the 1920s and 1930s. The government was unwilling to provide funds for much increase in staff, from the original twenty-five employed in 1919. However, Alastair managed to cope with the increasing complexity of ciphers employed by foreign governments. It is said that we were able to decrypt most of the ciphers used throughout the world except those employed by Germany and Russia.

With World War II looming, Alastair began looking for new recruits. Realising that the services of more and more mathematicians would be required, he made contact with the universities, thereby insuring that on the outbreak of war these mathematicians would immediately join them.

Shortly before the war, in July 1939, Denniston, with Dilly Knox and a third person who may have been Stewart Menzies, then deputy head of the intelligence services, visited Poland at the invitation of the Polish cryptographers. Alastair appreciated the technical help the Poles provided and their subsequent gift of a reconstructed German Enigma machine.

The move to Bletchley Park on the outbreak of war was successfully accomplished, although, understandably, it took some time to become established there. Alastair was not a great administrator, and the rapid increase of staff as the new recruits flooded into Bletchley Park made his life difficult.

In 1941 he became ill and was operated on for a stone in the bladder. Orchitis followed and he was off work for many weeks. After a long convalescence he returned to BP in June 1941 where Commander Travis, his deputy, had been holding the fort. In July, apparently at his own initiative, he undertook two journeys, to Canada and the United States of America, flying via Newfoundland. Although America was not yet in the war, he met William Friedman, the leading American cryptologist, thereby laying the foundations for subsequent Anglo-American co-operation in the handling of Ultra material. The second visit, to Canada, followed a week after his return. Alastair's health had returned but inside BP there were calls for change. Ultimately the decision to remove him from office must have been that of Menzies, who by now had succeeded Admiral Sinclair as head of the secret service. Alastair remained in command until the end of January 1942, when he moved to London as deputy director in charge of commercial and diplomatic traffic. There in Berkeley Street, although a disappointed man, he headed a successful department until the end of the war.

Alastair was described by one as 'a very self-contained Scot, perhaps a little dour', and by another as 'a small, bird-like man with bright blue eyes.' But another description of him is given by Aileen Clayton, in her book *The Enemy is Listening* (Hutchinson, 1980*)*. Aileen, a young WAAF officer, had been sent to BP by the Air Ministry in 1941 to discuss interception problems and learn how the cryptographic centre worked. She wrote:

Bletchley Park was under the control of Commander Alastair Denniston, a quiet, middle-aged man, who seemed more like a professor than a naval officer. It was to him I had to report and I was immediately impressed by his kindness and by the courtesy with which he greeted me. I was a very junior officer and abysmally ignorant of things cryptographic.

In his biography of Commander Denniston in the ODNB, Professor Hinsley wrote that:

By his willingness to delegate, his trust in subordinates, his informality, and his charm he set his stamp on the character of the place, particularly in the early war years in Bletchley Park. More than any other man, he helped to maintain both the creative atmosphere which underlay its great contribution to British intelligence during the Second World War and the complete security which was no less an important precondition of its achievement.

After his retirement in 1945 he taught French and Latin at a Leatherhead preparatory school. Alastair died at the Memorial Hospital, at Milford-on-Sea, Hampshire on New Year's day, 1961.

WILFRED DUNDERDALE (1899-1990)

Wilfred Albert Dunderdale, or 'Biffy' as he was known to many of his friends, was born in Russia in December 1899, the son of a British shipowner. Educated in Russia, he was studying naval engineering at the University of Petrograd when the Russian Revolution came in 1917. The Royal Navy, which was involved with other countries in the attempt to crush the Bolsheviks after the Great War, enlisted his help because of his knowledge of the Russian language. Dunderdale was recruited by MI6, at a time when guns of the Royal Navy were trained on Constantinople, fearing a Turkish plot to seize the city. Dunderdale's assistance in this action was important. The Sultan Muhammed VI, deposed in 1922 by Kemal Aturturk, was carried into exile in the British battleship *Malaya*. Dunderdale, provided with a large amount of English sovereigns, was sent ashore to pay-off and repatriate those members of the Sultan's harem who were foreigners.

In the 1920s he was posted to Paris, where he remained until France fell in 1940, still working for MI6. His job was to liaise with French intelligence (le deuxième bureau). A writer in the *ODNB* wrote that Dunderdale:

...spoke several languages well, and was debonair and a wonderful host. There was about him an element of the pirate; he was a romantic with enormous vitality and a gift for friendship.

Over the years he became a close personal friend of the Frenchman, Colonel Gustave Bertrand, who was the bureau's chief signals officer. Shortly before the outbreak of war in 1939 the Polish cryptographers gave Bertrand two Enigma cipher machines which they had constructed, one for France and one for Great Britain.

These were brought from Poland to Paris in a diplomatic bag. On the 16th of August, Colonel Bertrand, assisted by Dunderdale, came over by ship and boat train to Victoria Station, London, handing the Enigma machine to Colonel Menzies, then the deputy head of British intelligence, who was waiting at the station to receive it. It was a historic moment. And I missed it by two days! I had spent a couple of weeks in France on holiday that August. Had I returned to England two days earlier I could have said in later years that I had been on that station, even on the same boat-train, on that memorable day. This gift from the Poles, who had better success in the decryption of pre-war Enigma messages than the French or the British, was of enormous value. Britain declared war little more than a fortnight later, on the third of September,1939.

After the fall of France in 1940, Dunderdale came to London where he was allowed to set up a small office near MI6 headquarters, because he could not stand the routine of a large organisation.

Married three times but with no children, Commander Dunderdale died in New York, at the age of ninety.

THOMAS HAROLD FLOWERS (1905-1998)

Thomas Flowers, known as Tommy by all his friends, born in Poplar , in London's East End, the son of Thomas Flowers, a bricklayer, and his wife Mabel Emily Richardson. He had one sister, born when Tommy was five years old. Having seen her, he said that he would have preferred a Meccano set. Tommy proved to be a boy of remarkable determination. He won a scholarship that gave him entry to a technical college until the age of sixteen. There followed a four-year apprenticeship at the Royal Arsenal, Woolwich, during which time, by studying at evening classes as an external student, he achieved a degree in engineering at the University of London.

His first job was as an electrical engineer at the Post Office, at the age of twenty-one. But by 1930 he had moved to the famous Dollis Hill Post Office laboratory in north-west London. There he concentrated on the application of electronic technology to telephony; he also became an expert on the uses of thermionic valves. It was in the mid-1930s that Tommy married Eileen Margaret Green, the daughter of a conveyancing clerk. They had two sons.

The *bombe*, the device which proved essential for the decrypting of German Enigma messages, was of no use for cracking non-morse messages enciphered on the Lorenz machine, a type of teleprinter which used the Baudot code rather than the Morse. Max Newman, the Cambridge mathematician, was head of a section at BP which became known as the 'Newmanry'. His team of mathematicians devised an electro-mechanical device known as Robinson, named after Heath Robinson, the cartoon artist who devised elaborate machinery for executing simple tasks. Robinson was not as successful as they hoped and it was at this stage that Tommy Flowers was brought to Bletchley, possibly at the suggestion of Alan Turing, who knew his work.

Tommy, with his knowledge of electronic valves, proposed that an enormous machine, later christened *Colossus*, should be built, containing no fewer than 1,500 valves. Work began at Dollis Hill in February 1943 and Flowers and his co-workers built the first *Colossus* in less than a year. Improved versions came later, which achieved tremendous success in decrypting the messages sent on the Lorenz machine. About ten *Colossi* were working by the end of the war. The Germans only used Lorenz for messages passing between the highest levels of the German command, for example between Hitler and his commanders. Unlike the Enigma machine it was not used in the field. Although the *Colossus* was a team effort, it was thanks to Tommy Flowers, with his vast practical experience gained at Dollis Hill, that the enterprise was successful and helped to shorten the war. When it ended, Tommy went to Germany with an intelligence-gathering unit.

Tommy Flowers returned to Dollis Hill after the war, in charge of electronic switching, which led to subscriber trunk dialling throughout the telephone system. He also worked on the electronic random number generator ERNIE which produces the numbers of winning premium bonds.

Tommy died at the age of ninety-two at his home in Mill Hill, London, in October 1998, survived by his wife Eileen after a marriage which had lasted sixty-five years, and by their two sons and three grandchildren.

HUGH FOSS (1902-1971)

With his tall lanky figure - he was well over six feet - red hair and beard, Hugh Rose Foss was one of the more colourful inhabitants of Bletchley Park.

Born in 1902 in Kobe, Japan, he was one of the five children of Hugh James Foss (1848-1932), Anglican Bishop of Osaka, and his wife Janet Ovans, twenty-two years younger than her husband. Hugh came to England and was a pupil at Marlborough College. After graduating from Christ's College, Cambridge, he joined the Government Code and Cipher School (GC&CS) in 1924, which had only been established by the government in 1921.

In the 1920s and 1930s GC&CS was busy advising the government on the use of codes and ciphers and in decrypting the secret messages of many foreign nations. During this period the development of cipher machines was rapid. The German

Enigma machine, designed originally for commercial use, was being adapted by the Germans for military use. Copies of these earlier simpler machines were purchased by GC&CS and by the Americans and others. Foss and his colleagues had some success in decrypting messages which had been intercepted.

From Queen's Gate in Knightsbridge, GC&CS moved to new quarters in Broadway, Victoria, London. In 1932 Hugh married Alison Graham. They had a daughter and a son. It was at this time that Hugh, although not a Scotsman, became interested in Scottish dancing and joined the Chelsea Reel society. He composed Scottish jigs and, according to Anselm:

…probably did more to extend the Scottish dance tradition into novel areas than anybody before him or after him.

Since his childhood in Japan, Hugh had been fluent in Japanese. Before the war he had investigated the possibility of decrypting Japanese machine ciphers and in 1934 he broke the cipher in use by naval attachés at Japanese embassies abroad.

As war loomed the department became more and more interested in the German Enigma machine. Hugh, with Dilly Knox and Alastair Denniston, the head of GC&CS, took part in meetings with the Polish cryptographers, who had made far more progress in decrypting pre-war German Enigma than the British. But Enigma was being improved and made more difficult as the war approached.

When GC&CS moved to Bletchley Park in September1939, Hugh at first worked in Hut 8, dealing with the German naval Enigma ciphers. But with the coming of the war with Japan, he became head of the Japanese naval section, in Hut 7. In the spring of 1942 Hugh travelled to Washington DC with a small delegation, to brief the Americans on progress with Enigma and to persuade them to concentrate on the Japanese ciphers.

After the war Hugh decided to stay with GC&CS, which subsequently was renamed GCHQ. He retired at the age of fifty-one in 1953, moving to Kirkudbrightshire, in Scotland. His interest in Scottish dancing continued. Hugh died at his home in Scotland at the early age of sixty-nine, two days before Christmas 1971, having enjoyed 18 years of retirement.

HARRY GOLOMBEK (1911-1995)

It would be interesting to know what Harry Golombek replied to the standard question: 'Do you play chess?' at his interview for recruitment to Bletchley Park. For Harry had been a chess expert since boyhood, taught originally by his older brother, and he had already won the London Boys' Championship before he left school.

Born in south-east London in 1911, Harry was the younger son of Barnet Golombek, a London grocer and his wife Emma Sendak. He had three sisters. His grandparents had migrated to England in about 1903, coming from a Jewish community in Poland. At Wilson's Grammar School, Camberwell, to which he had gained a scholarship, Harry shone in modern languages and mathematics. From school he went on to King's College, London, but left in 1932 without completing his degree.

Already before the war Harry was well-known in British and international chess circles, having played in three Olympiads, at Warsaw, Stockholm and Buenos Aires between 1935 and 1939. He was in fact in Argentina when the war began, in the British Chess team, with Milner-Barry and C.H.O'D.Alexander, with both of whom he later worked at BP. Harry was a soldier in the Royal Artillery from 1940 to 1942, before he was selected for transfer to BP, largely because of his chess and language skills. There he worked in Hut 8 from 1942, tackling the German naval enigma ciphers, under the leadership at first of Alan Turing. Although undoubtedly the most brilliant mathematician of his time, Alan was not a brilliant chess-player. It is said that when Harry played a game of chess with Turing, and defeated him, Harry would then turn the board around and show Alan how he might have won.

After the war a great part of his life was dedicated to chess. As a player, an editor of chess magazines, a regular contributor to the BBC's radio chess magazine and chess correspondent of *The Times,* he was never idle. According to the *Oxford Dictionary of National Biography,* Harry:

...also enjoyed a distinguished career as a chess official and administrator. From 1952 until 1985 he served on the rules commission of FIDE, the international chess federation, which is responsible for the rules of chess, and was the British delegate to FIDE's annual conferences for most of the period.

Harry was captain of the British team in five of the nine chess Olympiads which he attended.

At the age of seventy-four he was awarded the title of international grandmaster emeritus. He also produced more than thirty books on chess, either as editor, author or translator. One of his best known books was about José Capablanca, the famous Cuban chess champion *Capablanca's hundred best games* (1947). Another which he edited was *The Encyclopedia of Chess* (1977), later published as a Penguin handbook in 1981.

It should not be thought that chess was Harry's only interest. He was a great reader, a collector of books, with a keen interest in the arts, especially in opera and the ballet. In *Who's Who* he listed his recreations as *Music, the stock exchange and the theatre*.

Almost a lifelong bachelor, Harry married in the late 1980s, but separated from his wife soon after.

NIGEL DE GREY (1886-1951)

Nigel Arthur de Grey was one of the talented young men who served in the Great War in the famous Room 40 OB (Old Building), the Department of the Admiralty concerned with intelligence and particularly with the interception and decryption of messages in code or cipher. Under the direction of Admiral 'Blinker'* Reginald Hall (1870–1943), whose staff occupied a number of rooms in the old Admiralty building, but retained the designation Room 40, Nigel de Grey and his colleagues had great success in reading enemy messages. It was Nigel and his colleague the Reverend W. Montgomery, of the Westminster Presbyterian College, Cambridge, who together decrypted a message from the German foreign minister Zimmerman to the German legation in Mexico. The revelation of that news was one of the factors that persuaded President Wilson and the United States government to declare war on Germany in 1917. Zimmerman had requested the German legation to tell the Mexicans that if war started between Germany and the United States, Mexico would be offered the restoration of three American states if they would come in the war on Germany's side.

Nigel was born in 1886, the son of Arnold de Grey, Rector of Copdeck in Suffolk, and his wife Margaret Fane. Having completed his schooldays at Eton College he tried to join the diplomatic service instead of going to a university. Unfortunately, he failed part of the examination but found a job with William Heinemann, the publisher, in 1907. At the end of 1910 he married his second cousin, Florence Gore. They had two sons and a daughter.

When the Great War began in 1914, Nigel, joining the Royal Naval Volunteer Reserve (RNVR), was posted to Belgium as an observer in the balloon section. His posting did not last long for he was transferred to naval intelligence in Room 40 in the old building at the Admiralty. His career in intelligence ended during the Great War with a posting to Italy, our ally, with the rank of Lieutenant-Commander; there he liaised with the Italian director of naval intelligence.

In the inter-war period Nigel became head of the Medici Society, which published old prints. His many varied activities included shooting, gardening, amateur acting and cricket.

At the beginning of World War II he was invited, with several of Admiral Hall's 'old boys', to join GC&CS, which was the name given to the cryptographic organisation that had carried on, with a skeleton staff, through the twenties and thirties. With Dilly Knox and others who had worked with him in the Great War, Nigel de Grey contributed greatly to the successes of BP during World War II. Michael Loewe recalls that Nigel assembled a large group of people in the open air at BP to announce that the German war had ended.

When the war was over, Nigel decided to stay with the organisation which, under its new name GCHQ, moved firstly to Eastcote, near Harrow, Middlesex, and subsequently to Cheltenham, Gloucestershire, about a hundred and twenty miles west of London. He became deputy director of GCHQ, retiring in 1951 at the age of sixty-five, and looking forward to a long rest from mental labours working in a pottery he had recently bought. But his retirement was short, for he died in May 1951, after a heart attack in Oxford Street, London.

*Admiral Sir William James, in his biography of Hall: *Eyes of the Navy* (1955), wrote that thousands of naval officers remembered Hall's 'dynamic figure, with piercing eyes and that facial twitch' which accounted for his nickname 'Blinker'.

PHILIP HALL (1904-1982)

Philip Hall, the son of George Hall and Mary Laura Sayers of Hampstead, London, lived through his childhood without a father. George Hall had left the family without providing maintenance for the boy or his mother, who earned her living as a dressmaker. Philip's grandfather Joseph Sayers at first came to their aid. But in 1910, Laura, with her twin sister Lois, and her two other twin sisters, bought a house in Well Walk, Hampstead, which they ran as a boarding house. Having won a scholarship to Christ's Hospital School at the age of eleven, Philip remained at this school as a boarder during the years of the Great War. He joined the school's officer training corps as a young cadet.

Philip excelled in mathematics at school and came to love the subject, winning medals in his final year in both mathematics and English. Fellow pupils remembered him at school as 'likeable and cheerful, with a sense of humour, gentle and reserved.' Philip proceeded to King's College, Cambridge in 1922, having won an open scholarship in his final school year.

With the encouragement of Arthur Berry, the assistant tutor in mathematics at King's, Philip developed an interest in group theory, influenced by the magnificent work of William Burnside on *The Theory of Groups*. Graduating in 1925, Philip won a scholarship enabling him to spend another a year at King's College. It was at this time that he spent a summer in Italy learning the language, later studying German in London. Philip, then having decided to embark on an academic career, submitted a mathematical dissertation to that end. His efforts were rewarded by his election to a fellowship at King's College, Cambridge, in 1927. Years of important mathematical studies followed, including his most famous essay: *A Contribution to the theory of groups of prime power order*. Later it was said of Philip that the fact that 'the growth group theory was one of the major mathematical topics of the twentieth century was largely due to him.'

When World War II came, Philip went to GC&CS at Bletchley Park, probably recommended by one of his Cambridge colleagues. There he worked at first on Italian ciphers, but later on Japanese diplomatic ciphers; at this time he learned some Japanese. During the years at BP Philip lived in Little Gaddesden with his mother and aunt who had moved there to get away from the bombing in London. His journey to Bletchley each day was partly by motorbike and partly by train.

After the war Philip returned to Cambridge where he was promoted Reader in 1949. In 1953 he succeeded Professor Mordell to the Sadleirian Chair. Influential mathematical papers proceeded from his pen throughout the following years and when his collected work was published in 1988, six years after his death, one reviewer wrote that

... this book consists of almost fifty years of publishing by one of the greatest mathematicians of this century.

The reviewer also referred to

... his universal kindness and his invigorating enthusiasm for mathematics and the world in general.

Apart from his mathematical studies, Philip loved English, Japanese and Italian poetry. His other loves included music, flowers, and walking in the country. He was, however, almost a recluse, for he avoided large gatherings of people, but was happy in the company of one or two close friends. J.E. Roseblade, one of his students, who wrote the life of Philip in the *Oxford Dictionary of National Biography*, spoke of his

...wide interests in both the sciences and the humanities, with an encyclopaedic knowledge and prodigious memory.

Philip never married and lived alone most of his life. He died on 30th December 1982, in Cambridge. His ashes were interred in his mother's grave in Impingham churchyard, near Cambridge.

FRANCIS HARRY HINSLEY (1918-1998)

Professor Sir Harry Hinsley, who long after World War II was commissioned to edit and write the main part of the official history of British intelligence in World War II, came from a humble background in Walsall, near Birmingham, England, where he was born in 1918, about a fortnight after the end of the Great War.

The son of Thomas Henry Hinsley, an iron works waggoner and his wife Emma Adey, Harry progressed from the local elementary school to Queen Mary's Grammar School, Walsall, winning a scholarship in 1937 which took him to St John's College, Cambridge, to read history. By 1939 he had gained a first in part one of the historical Tripos; but he never finished his degree or obtained any other degree. World War II had intervened. Harry, an impecunious student, had been hitch-hiking through Germany on his own that summer and only just got back to England in time.

Interviewed at St John's by Commander A.G. Denniston and Colonel John Tiltman, who were looking in the universities for possible recruits to intelligence, Harry found himself, 'pitchforked into Bletchley Park at the age of twenty.' Working at first on the organisation of the German navy, based on traffic analysis, he was in regular liaison by telephone with the Admiralty Operational Intelligence Centre, (OIC). He had the impression that the Admiralty at first had little interest in any information he gave them. But gradually, with the supply of intelligence obtained from traffic analysis and decrypted German naval Enigma messages, the Admiralty began to value his work. So much so, that he had more than one invitation to visit Admiral Tovey's flagship at Scapa Flow. The work was 'onerous and exciting', wrote Harry. Later he recalled that:

Bletchley was like a university. We lived the anarchic lives of students. There was a tremendous social life, parties, amateur dramatics, lots of young ladies and lots of young men.

His liaison work continued until the summer of 1944, interrupted by visits to Washington DC 'to discuss collaboration with the United States in the production and distribution of Ultra intelligence.' He described his work:

...as on the one hand debating with the Admiralty about the significance of the contents of the decrypts and, on the other, attempting to apply traffic analysis and operational information from the Admiralty for the benefit of the cryptanalysts in their daily struggle to solve the Enigma settings.

There is no doubt that the work of Harry and his colleagues helped to win the battle of the Atlantic. After D-Day, Harry became more and more involved in negotiations with Washington.

Harry's future wife Hilary, the daughter of Herbert Francis Brett-Smith and his wife Helena, also worked at BP. They were married soon after the war in April 1946. Returning to St John's College, Cambridge, where he was to spend most of the rest of his life, Harry was promoted steadily. Appointed a research fellow while still at BP, he became a lecturer in history in 1949, a Reader in the history of international relations in 1965 and Professor in 1969. He also served as President, 1975-79, then Master of his college from 1979 to 1989. Finally he was appointed Vice-Chancellor of the University of Cambridge, serving from 1981 to 1983. Harry was knighted in 1985.

The monumental five volume *British Intelligence in the Second World War,* (HMSO, 1979-1990), occupied him for several years. Most of the early volumes were written by Harry himself after much research in unpublished archives. Sir Maurice Oldfield, former director of MI6 remarked that: 'there are hardly any names in it. You get the impression that the intelligence war was won by committees in Whitehall.' Harry, however had been told not to include names of people. Later he co-edited a smaller work: *Code-breakers: the Inside Story of Bletchley Park* (OUP, 1993), in which he wrote an entertaining chapter about his own experiences.

Before the secrets of BP were generally known, and before his history of British intelligence appeared, Harry had produced in the post-war years many historical works on the subject of British naval history, Hitler's strategy, sovereignty, and nationalism. Of these books his study of *Power and the Pursuit of Peace (*Cambridge University Press, 1963), is said to be his most important book. Harry was a popular lecturer. A lively picture of his seminars appears in the introduction to his *Festschrift*.

Gently and often amusingly directed from behind clouds of pipe smoke, current research students could try out their latest interpretations of their material, describe what archives they had found ... The sessions could often be exhilarating and provided at once a sense of companionship and a sense of the broad scope which international relations offers ...

Harry died of lung cancer in hospital at Cambridge in February 1998 in his eightieth year, survived by his wife Hilary, who died soon afterwards, and their three children.

LEONARD JAMES HOOPER (1914-1994)

Known to everybody who worked with him as 'Joe', Sir Leonard James Hooper, born in 1914 in East Dulwich Road, Camberwell, London, less than a fortnight before the Great War, was the son of James Edmund Hooper, a copywriter for a pharmaceutical firm and his wife Grace Lena Pitts, a head mistress. Proceeding from Alleyn's school at Dulwich to Worcester College, Oxford, Joe achieved a first class honours degree in modern history. He also excelled in cross-country running.

With the war looming, Joe abandoned a D.Phil thesis on the English Jesuits of the seventeenth and eighteenth centuries and joined GC&CS in August 1938, moving to Bletchley Park on the outbreak of war. Working on cryptanalysis in the Italian air section, he progressed to take charge of the Japanese Air Force section.

After the war, Joe, like a number of his colleagues, decided to continue working in intelligence at GCHQ, the successor to GC&CS, at Cheltenham. Working his way upwards, he became assistant director at a time when the supposed threat of an attack on the west by the Soviet Union occupied the minds of politicians and the armed forces.

The writer of *The Times* obituary of Joe wrote that:

…the one item always missing from Joe Hooper's desk was a pending tray: He never left for home until everything had been cleared.

Whether this is a wise procedure is to be doubted; for some matters arising must be mulled over and slept on. However, his brisk methods of work led him to the post of deputy director in 1960 and finally to the directorship of GCHQ in 1965. After eight years in the chief position, during which he established a close relationship with the American National Security Agency (NSA), he became the Government's intelligence co-ordinator, and deputy secretary in the Cabinet Office. From this important post he retired in 1978, spending his time at his home in Cheltenham. Michel Herman wrote of Joe in the ODNB:

British intelligence since 1945 has not produced towering figures, but for twenty-five years Hooper was held in unusually high regard nationally and internationally. He was a major figure in the peacetime development of signals intelligence as a well-managed, large-scale, high-technology enterprise with an intimate transatlantic relationship.

Joe was married three times, firstly to Hilda Sefton Jones, an officer in the women's air force (WAAF) in 1942. They had one son. After that marriage ended in 1949, Joe married Ena Mary Osborn, a Foreign Office worker, in 1951. This marriage also ended in divorce in 1978. Later that year he married Mrs Mary Kathleen Horwood, a retired civil servant who had also served at Bletchley and GCHQ.

Joe died in his eightieth year in Cheltenham, survived by his third wife, Kate.

ERIC MALCOLM JONES (1907-1986)

To have left school at fifteen years old, to have been placed in charge of Hut 3 at Bletchley Park in 1942, when thirty-five, and to have succeeded to the directorship of GCHQ at Cheltenham at forty-five, was the astonishing record of Sir Eric Malcolm Jones.

Eric Jones was born in April, 1907, in Buxton, Derbyshire, England, the third in a family of four sons and one daughter. Their father and mother were Samuel Jones and Minnie Florence Grove. Samuel was head of the textile manufacturing firm, Samuel Jones and Son of Macclesfield, Cheshire. Leaving King's School, Macclesfield, at fifteen, Eric joined the Manchester branch of the family firm. But by the time he was eighteen he had set up a textile agency on his own. Four years later he married Edith Mary ('Meg') Taylor, the daughter of Sir Thomas Taylor, a silk merchant of Macclesfield. They had one son and one daughter.

When the war came, Eric, rather than waiting to be called up with his age-group, enlisted in the Royal Air Force Volunteer Reserve in 1940. Posted to air ministry intelligence, he rose to the rank of squadron-leader and in 1942 was sent to Bletchley Park to stand in temporarily as senior officer in Hut 3. By that time the task of supplying round-the-clock intelligence to the various commands made necessary a stricter routine in the department. Ralph Bennett, one of the air advisers in Hut 3, wrote in his book: *Ultra in the West*, that:

...changes of such magnitude posed problems of administration, organisation and authority on a scale not previously encountered ... The steadying temperament and business experience of Squadron-Leader Jones, who became head of Hut 3 at this juncture, ensured that the process of adaptation was smooth, and guided Hut 3 calmly until the end of the war.

Stuart Milner-Barry, later head of Hut 6, wrote of Eric Jones in an essay: *Hut 6: Early days*, in *Codebreakers*, edited by F.H. Hinsley and Alan Stripp, (OUP,1993):

Jones was not a scholar or an academic ... he was a genuinely modest man who regarded himself as having little to contribute compared with the boffins with whom he was surrounded; in fact he was a first-rate administrator who was liked and trusted by everyone.

By April 1943, Commander Travis, director of GC&CS, confirmed Eric's appointment as head of Hut 3, and he was promoted to the rank of group-captain.

From 1945 to 1946, Eric was in Washington DC representing the British in discussions with the Americans which formed the basis for post-war Anglo-

American co-operation in the field of signals intelligence. Returning to England, Eric decided to stay on with GCHQ, moving with them to Cheltenham. With his wife, he bought Bredons Hardwick manor, a house near Tewkesbury, where he and his wife and family cultivated a fine garden.

Eric became deputy director of GCHQ in 1950 and succeeded Sir Edward Travis as director, in April 1952. But after eight years in charge, he decided to take early retirement.

D.R. Nicoll in the ODNB, wrote of Eric Jones:

A man of the highest integrity, it was said of him that corruption was unthinkable in his presence.

Eric's wife Meg died in 1984 after fifty-five years of marriage. Eric died at a nursing home in Gloucester on Christmas Eve, 1986, in his eightieth year, survived by his son and daughter.

DILLWYN KNOX (1884-1942)

Known to colleagues at Bletchley Park as Dilly, Alfred Dillwyn Knox was the second son of the Reverend Edmund Knox, who became Bishop of Manchester, and his first wife Ellen Penelope, the daughter of Thomas French, Bishop of Lahore. Dilly had an older brother, 'Evoe', one-time editor of *Punch* magazine and two younger brothers; he also had two sisters. Their mother Ellen died when Dilly was only eight years old.

From Eton College Dilly arrived at King's College, Cambridge, in 1903. Studying for the classical tripos, which he passed in 1907, he was much influenced by the scholar and poet, Walter Headlam, Fellow of King's, who inspired Dilly's lifelong love of Greek literature. As a Fellow of King's himself, in 1909, he inherited Headlam's unfinished work on Herodas, publishing a book on the subject in 1922.

When the Great War came in 1914, Dilly who had acquired a motorbike, saw himself as a dispatch-rider. But he was short sighted and although he maintained that this would not affect night riding, he was quickly turned down. More suitable for a man of his unusual intellect and his love of puzzles and paradoxes, he was invited to join ID25, the Department of naval intelligence better known as Room 40 OB. There he took part in the solution of many cryptographic problems. Along with other colleagues, he decided at the end of the war to continue working in intelligence, although he had firmly intended to return to Cambridge as a Fellow. So, through the 1920s and 1930s, he worked for the Government Code and Cipher School (GC&CS), the successor to 40 OB. He had married Olive Rickman in 1920.

They had two sons. In 1921 Dilly bought Courn's Wood, a woodland house in the Chiltern hills, near High Wycombe, in Buckinghamshire. From there he commuted to London to his job at Room 40. A couple of years later he was offered the chair in Greek at Leeds University, which he refused.

Dilly moved to BP at the beginning of World War II and was installed in The Cottage at the rear of the mansion. He had some success before the war in cracking Italian messages enciphered on a primitive type of Enigma machine which the Italians had adopted. During the war a more complicated machine was used, but Dilly, with the aid of his girls - a team of gifted young women – decrypted Italian naval messages. Their greatest success was when they enabled Admiral Cunningham to win the naval battle of Matapan by revealing Italian plans and locations in the Mediterranean, destroying or crippling much of the enemy fleet.

The German Abwehr (Secret Service) also used a modified Enigma machine, less complicated than that used by the Luftwaffe or the German army. Dilly, although mortally ill with cancer, had broken the Abwehr cipher, largely working at his home at Courn's Wood, assisted by one of his girls, Margaret Rock. Mavis Lever was another of his girls, and Dilly claimed that with their help everything was possible. 'Give me a Lever and a Rock and I will move the Universe', he said. After his death in 1943, the department, known as ISK (Intelligence Services Knox) increased in size, employing more than a hundred staff in one of the new blocks.

One of the least physically robust of the four talented Knox brothers, whose history was told eloquently by his niece, Penelope Fitzgerald, in her book *The Knox Brothers (*1977), he had already had one operation for cancer. In 1942 he underwent a second operation. In *The Times* obituary notice, Maynard Keynes, an old friend since Eton College days, described him as: 'Sceptical of most things except those that chiefly matter, that is, affection and reason'. Dilly, in spite of his descent from devout Christians was hostile to Christianity and did not believe in a life after death. His son Oliver Knox, in an article in *The Oldie (*March 2000) wrote of:

...the greatest passion of my father's life - Greek scholarship, to which all other activities, including his eminent career as senior cryptologist at the Foreign Office, came as an unfortunate if necessary distraction, a passion that was closer to his heart than his family, or his friendships made as a Fellow of King's College, Cambridge.

LESLIE LAMBERT (1883-1941)

The son of Thomas Lambert, a hosiery manufacturer and his wife Kate Everington, Leslie Harrison Lambert was born in 1883 at Basford, near Nottingham. After school at Rugby, one of England's ancient public schools, he was articled to a surveyor for seven years. He became interested in magic, at first as an amateur, but later as a professional magician and a member of the Magic Circle.

During the Great War, his early dabbling in wireless telegraphy proved of great value. Interception of foreign radio signals was in its infancy, largely depending on the work of radio hams. With two other hams, one a barrister and the other a retired colonel landowner, Leslie manned an old coast-guard station at Hunstanton on the Norfolk coast. These 'voluntary interceptors' were later augmented by many specially trained operators. After the war Leslie became a full-time member of GC&CS, engaged partly on administrative duties.

In 1933, Leslie and others in the department, using direction-finding equipment, tracked down a Soviet spy station operating from a London suburban house. Commander Denniston, in charge of GC&CS, later described this episode as 'perhaps the earliest example of D/F success.' Leslie continued to work in the department, moving to Bletchley with his colleagues at the beginning of World War II.

To his friends and neighbours he was no doubt known just as one who worked at the Foreign Office. But Leslie was a man who loved mysteries, from the time when he first practised magic. It was in 1924, after a conversation with Rex Palmer of the BBC, that he was engaged to broadcast a story on the wireless, as it was called in those days. He chose to use the pseudonym A.J. Alan for this and subsequent broadcasts. This led to much speculation about the author of such fascinating stories. The first one he read, in 1924, *My adventure in Jermyn Street*, was a tremendous success and listeners clamoured for more. He read the stories in a conversational, urbane style, and his plots were akin to those of O.Henry (William Sydney Porter, 1862-1910), the American short story writer, whose speciality was the surprise ending.

His broadcasts became more and more popular with the listening public, who looked forward to his friendly opening: *Good evening, everyone!* which became the title of his first book of stories, published in 1928, by Hutchinson. Leslie preserved his anonymity, although according to the *Oxford Dictionary of National Biography* (ODNB):

…only once, in 1933, did anyone successfully guess his true identity. This was a listener in Jamaica who remembered Alan's voice from his schooldays in Rugby.

Leslie was a tall slim man who wore a monocle. He was married but had no children. Living in London at Holland Park for most of his life, he and his wife also had a bungalow at Potter Heigham, on the Norfolk coast, where he kept his boat *Muggins*.

He had a serious operation in 1937 and, although continuing to work at BP in spite of poor health, he died in a nursing home in Norwich in December 1941, at the early age of fifty-eight.

CLIVE LOEHNIS (1902-1992)

Sir Clive Loehnis, known from his childhood and by his colleagues as Joe, did not work at Bletchley Park during the war. I am including him here because of his close collaboration with Harry Hinsley and others in the naval section at BP when he was working at the Operational Intelligence Centre (OIC) of the Admiralty in London; also because, after the war, he became the head of GCHQ at Cheltenham.

Joe's father, Herman William Loehnis, a barrister of the Inner Temple in London, died when he was about to take silk, when Joe was only two years old. He was an only child, although an older brother had died as a baby. Joe's mother was Vera Geraldine Wood, and his paternal grandfather was a business man in Tsarist Russia. The family appears to have emigrated from Austria during the Napoleonic wars.

After turning down a scholarship to Winchester School when he was at Lockers Park prep school, Joe proceeded to the naval colleges at Osborne, Dartmouth and Greenwich. The Great War ended before Joe was ready for action, but shortly afterwards he served as a midshipman in the battle cruiser HMS *Renown*, on a grand tour of the Far East, with Edward the young Prince of Wales.

It was at this time that Joe qualified as a signals officer. He achieved rapid advancement, and was soon serving on the battleship *Nelson* as flag lieutenant to the commander in chief, Atlantic. Joe married Rosemary Beryl Ryder in 1929 and they had two children, Serena Jane and Anthony David.

In 1935 Joe retired early from the Navy, tired of life at sea and preferring to live at home with his family. With another naval friend he became a film producer. But after three years making minor films, he was suddenly called to the Admiralty at the time of the Munich crisis in 1938. When the war started the following year, Joe was transferred to OIC at the Admiralty. Then in 1942 he became liaison officer between the centre and GC&CS at Bletchley, where he had close contact with Edward Travis, then the director of BP and Harry Hinsley, in the naval section. It was this co-operation together with the work of the cryptanalysts that was largely responsible for the success of the anti-U-boat campaign after the dire sinkings of merchant shipping earlier in the war.

Towards the end of the war, Joe, now a commander, with Sir Edward Travis, Rear-Admiral Rushbrooke, director of naval intelligence (DNI), and Harry Hinsley, embarked on a world tour which took them to the Middle East, India, Ceylon,

Australia, New Zealand and the USA. Their aim was to make sure that the resources of British signals intelligence were smoothly transferred to the Japanese theatre of war as soon as the German war was finished. A second reason for the trip was that the British wished to foster post-war collaboration on intelligence between Britain and the Commonwealth and the USA. The new American President Truman agreed, and issued a secret order authorising collaboration on signal matters, including cryptanalysis between Britain and America. An Anglo–US conference took place in the spring of 1946, under the chairmanship of Sir Stewart Menzies, chief of the British secret service.

Joe was demobilised in 1945, but began work as a civilian at GCHQ, Cheltenham. He made rapid progress, from membership of the directorate in 1951, to deputy director in 1954, and from 1960 to 1964 he was director of the whole establishment.

Joe was an efficient administrator, presiding over GCHQ during the difficult period of the Cold War. Although some of the staff were not pleased with his naval officer manner, he did attempt to get to know them all personally. In 1959, skidding on ice in his Jaguar car, he had serious injuries which took him off work for six months; he had been driving daily from London to Cheltenham. Joe died in London, at his home in Eaton Place, Belgravia, in May 1992, of pneumonia followed by a stroke, in his 90th year.

GEORGE CUNLIFFE McVITTIE (1904-1988)

George McVittie was born in the ancient port of Smyrna in Turkey, in June, 1904. His father, a business man in that city and his mother Emily Caroline, the daughter of George Weber, an Alsatian, had two more children after George, another son and a daughter. In August 1922 Smyrna and its hinterland, which had been awarded to Greece, was attacked by Turkish forces, led by Mustapha Kemal. The city was sacked, but fortunately the McVittie family was on holiday in England at the time. They lost everything and never returned.

George, who had been privately educated by tutors in Turkey, began to work in London with his father. Later he proceeded to Edinburgh University to read mathematics and scientific philosophy. His early interests had included archaeology and star-gazing. With a first-class master of arts degree under his belt, George moved to Cambridge University, where he studied under the supervision of Sir Arthur Eddington, the professor of astronomy. In an autobiographical sketch in 1975 he listed a formidable number of subjects in his postgraduate research: they included unified field theories, spherically symmetric solutions of Einstein's equations, cosmological investigations, classical hydrodynamics and orbits of particles in general relativity. After gaining a Ph.D, he lectured at Leeds and Liverpool universities. In 1934 he married Mildred Bond, daughter of John Bond, professor of education at Leeds University. In 1936 George was appointed Reader in mathematics at King's College, London and published his first book, *Cosmological Theory,* in 1937.

Soon after the beginning of World War II George was invited to join GC&CS at Bletchley Park. After a brief training under Colonel Tiltman and Josh Cooper, George was placed in charge of a meteorological section attached to the air section in Hut 10; its object was to crack the weather codes used by Germany and its allies. From small beginnings the section grew rapidly until, by the end of 1943, sixty people were employed. George was a good administrator and organiser, but also excellent at breaking ciphers. An enormous number of weather reports was decrypted daily, providing allied commanders with valuable data which influenced their plans of action.

One particular decryption of a weather message led to the breaking of the German U-boat's Enigma cipher which had for nearly a year defied all the efforts of Hut 8. The decryption of this German weather cipher, coupled with information from a captured Code Book, enabled Hut 8, in December,1942, to break the Enigma Shark cipher, by providing a 'crib', or likely plain German text. As a result, allied shipping losses in the Atlantic were considerably reduced. Our convoys could now be directed to follow courses across the Atlantic which avoided waiting U-Boats.

George returned to King's College in 1945 at the end of the war, staying there until 1948, when he was appointed Professor of mathematics at Queen Mary College, London. After only four years, George was offered the chair of astronomy at the University of Illinois, USA, in 1952. There, during the next twenty years he built up an astronomical centre of world class. The department, using a radio telescope, mapped part of our own galaxy, making many discoveries.

When Arthur C Clarke, the science fiction writer and author of *2001: a Space Odyssey* was asked why he said that *Hal*, the talking computer in the novel and the film, was 'born' in Urbana, Illinois, he explained that:

My mathematics tutor at King's College, Cambridge, when I took my first degree in 1947-48, was the distinguished cosmologist George McVittie ....During the 1950s, George moved to the US, where he took up a post at the University of Illinois, Urbana. I was happy to pay this fitting tribute to him, for I am now sure he must have been involved in establishing the Supercomputer Center in Urbana.

Retiring from the University of Illinois in 1972, George returned to England, to Canterbury, where he was appointed honorary professor of theoretical astronomy at the University of Kent. He continued lecturing in astronomy and mathematics until he was eighty-three. Although his numerous books and papers are dependent on mathematics and hence difficult or impossible for many to read, George did attempt in his book, *Fact and Theory in Cosmology* (Eyre & Spottiswoode, 1961), to make cosmology understandable to the general reading public.

George was elected a Fellow of the Royal Astronomical Society in 1931 and of the Royal Society of Edinburgh in 1943. In 1934 the International Astronomical Union honoured him by naming a newly-discovered asteroid after him (No.2417).

George died in Chaucer Hospital, Canterbury, in 1988, in his 84th year. He had no children.

STEWART GRAHAM MENZIES (1890-1968)

The designation 'C' has long been used by the heads of British intelligence ever since the first holder of the office, the eccentric naval Captain Mansfield Smith, changed his name to Cumming. The initial letter of his adopted surname has been used by all his successors. When Stewart Menzies was appointed 'C' in 1939, after the death of his predecessor Admiral Sinclair, his duties included overall supervision of the Government Code and Cipher School (GC&CS). 'C' did not often visit Bletchley Park during the war, and most of us working there had no knowledge even of his existence. But because of his constant involvement throughout the war in the intelligence derived from decrypted Enigma and other cipher messages, his everyday contacts with Winston Churchill and the Joint Intelligence Committee (JIC), his biography is included here.

Sir Stewart Graham Menzies was born in 1890 in Westminster, London, at 46 Upper Grosvenor Street, the second son of John ('Jack') Graham Menzies, who inherited a fortune from his father Graham Menzies, the founder of an empire of whisky distillers. Stewart's beautiful mother was Susannah West Wilson, one of the daughters of Arthur Wilson, who with his older brother (the first Baron Nunburnholme), inherited from their father Thomas Wilson, a ship owning firm at Hull which became one of the largest and wealthiest in the country.

Somebody once said that Stewart's father, nicknamed 'Hellfire' Jack, never ceased sowing his wild oats. The result was that, occupied with horse racing, gambling, unstable commercial investments and alcohol, rather than applying himself to the prosperity of the distillery, Jack soon spent his fortune. What was worse, he contracted tuberculosis, and, isolating himself from the family, died at the early age of 50 in 1911. Stewart's mother Susannah married the following year Lieutenant Colonel Sir George Holford of the Life Guards, who was an equerry in waiting to Queen Alexandra and extra equerry to King George V.

Stewart was twenty-one at the time of his mother's second marriage. He had gone to Eton College at the age of 13. There he was a popular boy who loved sport and was a good athlete. A fellow pupil once spoke of his 'quality of indomitability'; another praised his physical stamina. Scholastically he excelled, winning prizes in French and German, both of which languages would prove useful in later life. Electing to be a soldier rather than proceed to university, Stewart joined the Grenadier Guards. But he soon tired of soldiering on foot and transferred himself to the Household Cavalry. With his love of hunting and horses from an early age - about the only common interest he had with his father - the cavalry suited him better.

Then came the Great War. Transferred to the front almost immediately, Stewart spent the next thirteen months fighting during the fearful battles of 1914 and 1915 when Britain's 'contemptible little army' (the Kaiser's words) strove to hold back the German onslaught. The casualty lists grew and many of Stewart's old Etonian friends were killed along with thousands of other ranks, mostly of the regular army. As a young subaltern, he was awarded the Distinguished Service Order (DSO). Later, in 1915, he was awarded the Military Cross (MC). It was at this time, recovering from a gas attack, although not wounded, that he transferred to an intelligence section at the General staff headquarters, then at St Omer. Later in the war he was appointed chief of counter-espionage and security to the British army in France. He ended the war with the rank of Brevet Major. Several fitness reports written by his seniors, have survived. General J. Charteris reported that Menzies 'had great tact, energy and is a good linguist.' Major W. Kirke wrote that 'the counter-espionage branch of Ib owed its success mainly to Menzies and the happy relations which existed between the British, French and Belgian services were largely due to the same cause.'

After the Great War he was appointed to an intelligence unit known as MI 1(c) which later became the Secret Intelligence Service (SIS), also known as MI 6. Although acting as deputy to the then 'C', he was not officially designated deputy until 1932. At this time SIS occupied rooms in Whitehall Court, above those where Bernard Shaw and other writers lived.

As Sinclair's right-hand man the twenty odd years between the two world wars, were a tranquil time for Stewart, compared with the busy years in France. He remained in the army and had time to follow the hounds and visit his favourite clubs. He was a great club man, spending many hours at Boodle's or White's. His interests in the activities of GC&CS continued during these years and, as an ardent anti-Bolshevik, he kept one eye on the extra-mural activities of Stalin and his associates. The department was short of money during the inter-war years and was not well prepared for action when World War II came.

Admiral Hugh Sinclair, who had been 'C' since the original 'C' died in 1923, had apparently bought Bletchley Park with his own money in 1938. He had moved down there with the staff of GC&CS at the outbreak of war, but died in November, 1939. The cabinet and Neville Chamberlain, the Prime Minister, were in favour of appointing Stewart Menzies to succeed Sinclair, but Churchill, then at the Admiralty, opposed the appointment. Later his objection was overruled, and Stewart now began his long reign as 'C'.

The anonymous writer of his biography in the first edition of the Dictionary of National Biography wrote that:

...the stamina and toughness Menzies displayed during the war years, 1939-45, came as something of a surprise to those acquainted with his easy and affluent way of life between the wars. Running his service and supervising GC&CS meant exceptionally long hours of office work, besides which he became in time a member of Churchill's intimate circle of war advisers.

Stewart continued to support the work of GC&CS throughout the war. He also promoted and supported Anglo-American co-operation in the field of intelligence. When he decided to retire in 1951, it was not because of ill health. He was still an ardent huntsman, believing, he once told a friend, that the exercise improved the state of the arteries; presumably those of the horse too. The cold war had changed the nature of intelligence-gathering which was now mainly in the hands of the technologists. He was also obviously upset by the defection of Kim Philby, a man he had trusted.

Whoever was appointed to be 'C' was destined to be enigmatic and a man or woman of mystery. But to those who worked with Stewart Menzies there was no enigma. Kim Philby, who, had he not been exposed as a spy, might have eventually succeeded Stewart as 'C', had definite views about his old chief. In his book *My Silent War,* published in 1968, the year of 'C's death, he wrote:

I look back on the Chief with enduring affection. He was not, in any sense of the words, a great intelligence officer. His intellectual equipment was unimpressive, and his knowledge of the world, and views about it, were just what one would expect from a fairly cloistered son of the upper levels of the British Establishment. In my own field, counter-espionage, his attitudes were schoolboyish – bars, beards and blondes. But it was this persistent boyish streak shining through the horrible responsibilities that world war placed on his shoulders, and through the ever-present threat of a summons from Churchill in one of his whimsical midnight moods, that was his charm. His real strength lay in a sensitive perception of the currents of Whitehall politics, in an ability to feel his way through the mazy corridors of power.

Also published in 1968, a book by Professor Hugh Trevor-Roper (later Lord Dacre) : *The Philby Affair: Espionage, Treason and Secret Services* included another view about 'C' by a member of his staff:

> I would like to take this opportunity to pay a brief tribute to him. No one would claim that he was a brilliant chief of the Secret Service. He was a bad judge of men and drew his personal advisers from a painfully limited social circle, which was quite incapable of giving him the support that he needed ... But all who knew him, however critical of the organisation, regarded him with respect. He was personally considerate, patently just, patently honest. These virtues were rare enough, in that world, to excuse any purely intellectual failing, and I remember him with affection.

Stewart Menzies was married three times. In November, 1918, a few weeks after the Armistice, he married Lady Avice Ela Muriel Sackville, daughter of the eighth Earl of Warr. After this marriage ended in divorce in 1931, he married Mrs Pamela Garton, the daughter of Rupert Evelyn Beckett (nephew of the first Baron Grimthorpe)and divorced wife of James Garton. Pamela died in 1951 after a long illness. The following year Stewart married Audrey Clara Lilian Chaplin, daughter of Sir Thomas Paul Latham, first Baronet. He was Audrey's fourth husband. Stewart had only one child, a daughter Fiona, born in 1934, by his second wife Pamela.

It was in 1967, when seventy-seven, that Stewart had a bad fall when hunting. Although not seriously injured, his health declined. He had a heart condition and died the following year on 28 May, 1968 at the King Edward VII hospital in London.

STUART MILNER-BARRY (1906-1995)

Sir Philip Stuart Milner-Barry was one of the brilliant British amateur chess players of the pre-war generation, and was winner of the first British Boys' Championship in 1923 at the age of seventeen. When the war came in September, 1939, he was in Buenos Aires playing in the Chess Olympics with two friends, Harry Golombek and Hugh Alexander. All three abandoned the tournament and returned to England by ship. They all served at Bletchley Park later.

Stuart was born in Hendon, north London, in September 1906, the second youngest of six children. He had one sister and four brothers. Their parents were Edward Leopold Milner-Barry, a school-teacher who later became a professor of modern languages at Bangor University and his wife Edith Mary, the daughter of Dr William Besant, a mathematician of St John's College, Cambridge. Educated at Cheltenham College and Trinity College, Cambridge, Stuart obtained firsts in the Classical Tripos (part I) and the Moral sciences Tripos (part I). Leaving Cambridge during the Great Depression, he became a stockbroker, an occupation which he did not enjoy. Chess was his all-absorbing interest. He played for England and was chess correspondent of *The Times* from 1938 to 1945.

Although not a mathematician, Stuart had known Gordon Welchman, the head of Hut 6, since pre-war Cambridge days. Welchman recruited Stuart along with his chess-player friends Alexander and Golombek. However, he had a knowledge of German and was able to help in their daily struggle to decrypt Enigma messages. By guessing a German phrase of several words and placing them under the text of an enciphered message, it was often possible to prepare a programme for the *bombes*, which would lead to the decrypting of the complete message. Such cases were known as cribs. Close relations were maintained between Huts 3 and 6 and 8, with frequent consultations about priorities and the use of the *bombes*, which were also used by Hut 8 to decrypt naval Enigma.

Long after the war in his chapter *Hut 6: early days (*in *Codebreakers*, edited by Hinsley and Stripp O.U.P., 1984) Stuart wrote that:

...there was a spirit of camaraderie which I think never failed us, even when the war generally seemed to be going badly, or when we found ourselves temporarily delayed in delivering the goods. There was a perpetual excitement about each day's break, at whatever time of the day or night it might come.

The story of the famous letter written to the Prime Minster by four of the code-breakers at BP has been told many times. Churchill had visited BP early in the war and was enormously impressed with the work of the code-breakers. However, in October 1940, Gordon Welchman, Alan Turing, Hugh Alexander and Milner-Barry, having tried without success to persuade Commander Denniston that more hands were urgently required, decided on the unusual step of appealing directly to the Prime Minister. It was not that they required more code-breakers and highly qualified personnel at that time; they required twenty more women clerks to operate the Hollerith machines and about twenty trained typists for Hut 6. They also asked for more Wrens to operate the *bombes*. The four signed the letter and Stuart Milner-Barry was chosen to deliver it in person to the Prime Minister. Later Stuart claimed that he was chosen because he was 'the most expendable member of the quartet', in case a head should roll. It was one of Stuart's favourite stories in later years when these matters could be spoken of.

When I attended the eightieth birthday of John Kirby, a fellow librarian who had worked in Hut 6, I met several old BP veterans, including Stuart whose wife Thelma was with him. He told me the story of the letter. He took the train to London and went to Downing Street, which in those days had no barriers at the Whitehall end. Knocking at number 10 and invited inside, he told a clerk that he had an important secret and confidential letter which he had to deliver to Mr Churchill in person.

Higher authorities were called. Unfortunately Stuart had no means of identification, although as a civilian he should have been carrying his identity card. After much argument, and having been assured by a high-ranking army officer that he would personally deliver the letter direct to Mr Churchill's hands, Stuart left the building, hoping for the best. The result could not have been better. Mr Churchill, with typical brevity wrote a note to Major-General Hastings Lionel 'Pug' Ismay, his essential link with the chiefs of staff, attaching it to the letter: 'Make sure they have all they want on extreme priority and report to me that this has been done.' For added emphasis, he attached one of his familiar labels: ACTION THIS DAY.

By September 1943, when Gordon Welchman had moved on, Stuart was promoted head of Hut 6 in charge of about 450 staff. He was in favour of complete collaboration with the Americans, urging them to produce more *bombes* to cope with increasing traffic.

After the war, Stuart, now forty-one, married Thelma Tennant Wells. They had one son and two daughters. He worked for many years after the war in the Treasury, becoming an under secretary in 1954. At the age of 60, the normal retiring age he became the ceremonial officer in the Civil Service Department, responsible for administering the honours system. Stuart died in Lewisham Hospital London on the 25th of March 1995, in his 89th year.

MAXWELL NEWMAN (1897-1984)

Max Newman was another Bletchley man among the few who were born in the nineteenth century. Maxwell Herman Alexander was the son of Hermann Alexander Neumann, a German secretary working in England, and his wife Sarah Pike, an elementary school teacher. After school in London Max won a scholarship to St John's College Cambridge. There he passed one part of the Mathematical Tripos before serving for three years in the British army during the Great War, when he changed his surname to Newman. Returning to Cambridge in 1919, he completed his degree and was elected to a fellowship of the college in 1923. From then until the outbreak of World War II in 1939, apart from his teaching at Cambridge, he studied in Vienna and spent a year at Princeton University. Newman's *forte* was the branch of mathematics known as topology, a subject on which he wrote many papers and a book, *Elements of the Topology of Pane Sets of Points (*1939).

Recruited to BP in 1942, he at first joined the section known as the Testery, under the leadership of Major Tester. This section was trying to decrypt German messages enciphered on the Lorenz machine. Unlike Enigma, the Lorenz cipher used teleprinter equipment; it was a non-Morse cipher. Max became dissatisfied with the methods used and put forward the idea of decrypting by using electronic machinery with tape and photo-electric cells. Turing, his younger Cambridge colleague, who had come to BP long before Max, helped with the design of a machine, together with Tommy Flowers, an engineer of the Post Office research station, and others. The machine was named Colossus and the section which used it, headed by Max, was known as the Newmanry. Soon Colossus was busy decrypting important German army messages. The Lorenz cipher was used by Hitler and the German High Command (OKW) for messages of strategic importance sent to army groups, which were usually of great value to us. Max's staff grew, until the Newmanry employed twenty cryptanalysts, six engineers and two hundred and seventy-three WRENs.

Max's biographer in the ODNB records that :

Newman ran his large section with the natural authority of a father figure, but in a democratic spirit. He took pleasure in the achievements of his staff, and originality flourished.

After the war Max was Fielden Professor of mathematics at Manchester University until 1964, where he persuaded the university authority to build a large computer. There followed three years abroad, at the Australian National University and at Rice University, Texas. He was elected a Fellow of the Royal Society in 1939.

Max Newman was a fine pianist and an excellent player of chess. He married Lyn Irvine. They had two sons. After her death in 1973 he married Dr Margaret Penrose, the widow of Professor Lionel Penrose. Max died in 1984 in Cambridge, survived by his wife, who died five years later.

DENYS LIONEL PAGE (1908-1978)

Of all the academics who found their way to Bletchley Park and who, after the war, achieved distinction in their pursuits, perhaps Sir Denys Lionel Page was the brightest luminary. To be recognised as one of the greatest classical scholars of the twentieth century and to have served as President of the British Academy for three years were no mean achievements.

His life, except for the years at Bletchley Park, was spent entirely in the academic world, very unlike the career of his father Frederick Harold Dunn Page, who was a chartered civil engineer with the Great Western Railway. Frederick married Elsie Daniels and Denys, born in Reading in May, 1908, had two brothers and two sisters. He won a scholarship in 1926 which took him from Newbury Grammar School to Christ Church College, Oxford. There he was greatly influenced by Gilbert Murray, the classical scholar famous for his translations of Greek tragedies. Denys won several prizes for Latin and Greek verse. In the examinations he obtained first-classes in Classical Moderations and Literae Humaniores. Sport was not neglected and Denys had a place in the college cricket team, gaining the reputation of being a demon bowler.

As a Derby scholar Denys spent a year in Austria at the University of Vienna, returning to Christ Church in 1931 to become a lecturer. In 1930 he married Katharine Elizabeth, the daughter of Joseph Michael Dohan of Philadelphia, USA. They had four daughters. During these pre-war years Denys already had several publications to his name. His special study of the early Greek lyric poets led to the publication, in 1942, of a volume of *Greek Literary Papyri*.

There seems to be a mystery about Denys's recruitment to Bletchley Park; perhaps Tiltman or some other head-hunter found him when visiting Oxford. At BP Denys worked under Oliver Strachey, an older brother of the writer Lytton Strachey. Oliver, who had been with GC&CS for many years in peacetime, with Dilly Knox, was in charge of a department which dealt with hand ciphers. Oliver was, in the main, concentrating on ciphers used by the German secret service (the Abwehr). The Abwehr also transmitted messages using a special version of the Enigma machine, but the non-machine ciphers were more easily decrypted. Denys Page, with his excellent German which he had learned in Vienna, proved to be so efficient in the job that, when Oliver Strachey went to Canada at the end of 1941 to help their cryptographers, he was appointed head of the section.

When the war in Europe ended, Denys headed a mission to the headquarters of Viscount Mountbatten, at Kandy and Singapore. Returning to Christ Church in Oxford he resumed research and teaching, serving also as senior proctor in 1948-9. In 1950 the chair of Greek at Cambridge became vacant. Page did not apply, but was offered the post and accepted it. With his family he moved to Cambridge. As a Professor at Cambridge he was a great success. Professor Hugh Lloyd-Jones, the author of his biography in the *Proceedings of the British Academy* (LXV, 1979) wrote that:

Page's arrival changed the atmosphere completely. Undergraduates were as fascinated as those of Oxford by his brilliant lectures, in which the necessary facts were set out with consummate learning and with crystal clarity, inferences from them deduced by cogent reasoning, and the whole performance, like that of a great advocate, rendered irresistible by the charm, liveliness, and intelligence of the performer.

Many publications came from his hand during the Cambridge years, including two which were based on lectures he gave in America at Bryn Mawr in 1954 and at Berkeley in 1958, *The Homeric Odyssey* (1955) and *History and the Homeric Iliad* (1959).

In the late 1950s Denys's wife's illness brought difficulties for him, which were somewhat alleviated when he was elected Master of Jesus College, Cambridge. His wife's renewed illness in 1973 caused him to retire from the chair two years earlier than he would have done. They moved to the peace of Northumberland, where Denys continued his research, making use of the library of the University of Newcastle. But in 1978 he was found to have lung cancer. He died in July of that year, working until the end. His wife died a few weeks later.

Page was elected a Fellow of the British Academy in 1952 and served as President of that institution from 1971 to 1974. At the end of his biography in the *Proceedings,* Professor Hugh Lloyd-Jones gave his opinion that in the 'work of editing and explaining the remains of Greek poetry Page's achievement is very great', but that 'he had little interest in philosophy, religion, or the history of ideas.' However, he continued :

Page's charm and gaiety delighted most of those who met him, often surprising those who had known only the somewhat formidable personality revealed in what he wrote.

ELIOT J.B. ROSE (1909-1999)

Wing-Commander Eliot Joseph Benn Rose, popularly known as Jim, was born into a wealthy Anglo-Jewish family in June 1909, at Palace Gardens Terrace, Kensington, London, the son of Ernest Albert Rosenheim, who later changed his surname to Rose. Jim had a brother and two sisters. His mother was Julia Eda Dula, the daughter of Eliot Levy (later Lewis), of Liverpool. His father, a mechanical engineer and early motoring enthusiast, served in the British army in the Great War, rising to the rank of lieutenant-colonel. Jim attended Rugby School, proceeding then to New College, Oxford, where he read Greats. For several years before World War II he helped to resettle refugees arriving in England from Nazi Germany; at that time he was a founder-member of the 33 Club for German Jewish refugees and secretary of Lord Baldwin's Fund for German refugees.

Jim volunteered to join the Royal Air Force at the beginning of World War II. After service as an intelligence officer with 609 squadron, he was transferred to Bletchley Park in 1941. There he worked in Hut 3 as one of the air advisers; their job was to evaluate decrypted messages coming from Hut 6, writing comments on the contents and drafting intelligence reports ready for transmission to commanders in the field, via the special liaison units. He became head of 3A, the air advisers' section but left BP later in the war. In 1943 he went to the USA to help to select suitable young American officers for work at BP, or as links with commanders in the field. While there he worked on British and American co-ordination of intelligence matters with Colonel Alfred McCormack of the Military Intelligence Special Branch.

In January 1945, now a wing-commander, he was appointed deputy director of Operational Intelligence at the Air Ministry in London. It was soon after this that he heard that Bomber Command was proposing to bomb the city of Dresden. Jim telephoned General Spaatz, head of the American air force in Europe, who confirmed that they and the British had decided on this plan because a German Panzer division was being moved through Dresden, to defend Hungarian oilfields. Jim knew through Ultra intelligence that the Panzer division was not going through Dresden. Spaatz replied that he would not bomb Dresden if the British agreed. Jim rang Wing-Commander Peter Calvocoressi at BP, the new head of 3A, who confirmed that the Panzer division's route was not through Dresden. He then tried to telephone 'Bomber' Harris, chief of Bomber Command, but found that he was away at the time. In the absence of Harris, Air Marshal Saundby, his deputy, refused to alter the plan, and so Dresden was almost obliterated.

After the war Jim married Pamela Gibson, the daughter of a London stockbroker, who had worked at BP in naval intelligence. They had two adopted children, a boy and a girl. His first marriage in 1940, to Molly Lipscombe, had ended in divorce. After demobilisation he became a journalist with Reuters in London. From 1948 he became literary editor of the Sunday newspaper *The Observer*, in the days when it employed some of the most influential literary critics of the day.

His next appointment, in 1951, took him with his family to Switzerland for a decade. At Zurich he was director of the International Press Institute, which, with financial support from the Ford Foundation, aimed to promote high standards in the newspapers of the world, and freedom of the press.

Returning to England, he directed the Nuffield survey of race relations until 1969, when the 'Rose' report, written in collaboration with Nicholas Deakin, was published with the title *Colour and Citizenship*.

Publishing was his next activity, first as an editorial director of the Westminster Press in the early 1970s, followed by the chairmanship of Penguin Books from 1974 to 1980. Among his many other interests he found time to be chairman and founder of the Runnymede Trust for fifteen years and of the Inter-action Trust for twenty years. At one time he was a special consultant to UNICEF.

In an account of his life in *The Independent*, Dipak Nandy wrote that:

…if there is one word which captures the essence of Jim Rose's personality, it is kindness. It was an unstinting, unsolicited generosity of spirit. With all his undertakings, he was a devoted family man and besotted with his grandchildren. He crammed three or four careers into one long life, and yet always found time to care for his innumerable friends.

Jim died on 21 May 1999, at Groombridge, near Tunbridge Wells, survived by his wife and two children. In another three weeks they would have been celebrating his ninetieth birthday.

EDWARD RUSHWORTH (1912-1975)

Major Edward Rushworth, known to all his colleagues at BP as 'Rush', was born in April, 1912, in the heart of the West Riding of Yorkshire, in the little township of Wyke, some four miles south of Bradford. His older sister and brother were both Victorians, being fifteen and twelve years older than him. The nickname Rush was affectionately given, but inappropriate. For Rush never appeared to be in a hurry, whatever the urgency of the moment; rather, he was a deliberate Yorkshireman, ever thoughtful before taking action.

The son of John Rushworth and Ada (née Johnson), both mill-workers, Rush came of a family that had been long committed to the temperance movement, his grandfather being one of the founders, in 1867, of the Wyke Gospel Temperance Mission. Rush attended the local elementary school before progressing to Bradford Grammar School. From there, a state scholarship took him to Queen's College, Cambridge, in 1931, to read Classics. In Part I of the Classical Tripos in 1933, he was placed in Class 1, with distinction in Latin verse composition and proficiency in Greek verse. The following year he was placed in Class 2 in part II of the same tripos. Having completed his degree he spent a further year there on the teacher training course. His first job was as Classics master at Hereford Cathedral School. But when the war came Rush forestalled call-up with his age-group by volunteering for service in the army. In the Royal Engineers, he was not the only sapper who proved to be a square peg in a round hole. Such skills as motor-bike riding and blowing up bridges he never mastered. His talents would clearly be of more use in another organisation where brains were of more importance than brawn, and so it was that Rush arrived at BP. Whether he had volunteered for intelligence work, or had been spotted, is not known.

At BP Rush was one of several other stalwarts in the Fusion Room (the subject of chapter 9 of this book) who reached the rank of Major. They spent much of their time liaising with Huts 3 and 6. Joan Watkins, who later became my wife, also worked in the Fusion Room. She clearly remembers:

...Rush's assiduity in performing his tasks. He was my boss and I have warm memories of working under him. He was a notably friendly, communicative colleague who obviously had considerable respect for the work of his women analysts. He plainly relished his job, which was crucial in helping to reveal the whole order of battle of the German armed forces. It was built up from close study of traffic analysis and of decrypted German messages from all sources. Rush was responsible for informing Hut 6 of any developments which might aid them in decryption; also in making connections concerning the movements of German units about which we message analysts wrote weekly reports.

Jean Davies, another young ATS student of German, who worked in the Fusion Room with Joyce Robinson and Joan Watkins, has memories of Rush:

I have a clear vision of Rush in the Fusion Room. He was a man with a strong Yorkshire accent (unfamiliar to me then), asking searching questions; then either he or Eric Morrison would go off to amend the huge wall map, covered in different coloured pins, which indicated German units and their dispositions. Rush obviously knew far more than we did about the material we were studying.

Part of the work was like trying to solve a gigantic jigsaw puzzle and at the same time juggling with a number of balls in the air; Rush, like many others, employed lateral thinking in solving problems, although this term did not come into use until long after the war.

Just before the end of the war, Rush was chosen to join TICOM (Target Identification Committee), a team of British and American experts sent to Germany to find out what their counterparts had achieved in their cryptographic departments. His wife Joyce would have known all about this expedition, but later, in the year before he died, he told Helen and Diana (good names for the daughters of a classical scholar) something of the expedition. Helen remembers:

The original plan was to parachute them into Berlin (not something he was keen on!). But because the Wehrmacht was crumbling and units were retreating south, they went to Bavaria instead. They visited Belsen, of course horrifying, and at Rosenberg were led to a buried Fish cipher machine that they dug up. Art Lewinson, one of the American cryptographers, who was not a German linguist, spoke to their prisoners in Yiddish, hoping that they would think that was how Americans spoke German. As well as bringing back the cipher machines, my father found Herman Göring's personal atlas when the group visited Berchtesgarten. This, along with other maps, is now in the Imperial War Museum. Also deposited there are the very illicit notebooks in which he recorded in his immaculate copperplate hand key things that he felt he needed to keep track of as he worked, often being in the Fusion Room for parts of each of the three shifts of each day.

Diana recalls that :

Rush was part of the debriefing team, somewhere in southern England, who interviewed the German personnel they had brought back to England along with their Fish and Enigma machines. Rush took photographs of the TICOM expedition and these were also deposited later in the Imperial War Museum in London.

In October 1945, soon after the end of the war, Rush married Joyce Robinson (one of my 'Three Js' in Chapter 11), who had been working in the Fusion Room for several years. While on their honeymoon, a message arrived at BP from the War Office, ordering him to go to Austria to join the army of occupation. Fortunately the W.O. had changed its plans by the time they returned to BP, enabling him to leave the army in January, 1946 and take up a post as Classics master at Manchester Grammar School. After three years there he moved in January, 1949, to University College, Leicester (later University of Leicester), as Lecturer and subsequently Senior Lecturer in Classics.

After leaving the army Rush became involved in work for the Liberal Party, and stood as a parliamentary candidate in Bradford South in the 1950 and 1951 elections and later in three more general elections in Harborough. Although unsuccessful in his attempts to become a member of parliament, he was elected to Leicestershire County Council where he became leader of the Liberal group. His activities in the Liberal Party consumed much of his time which might otherwise have been devoted to his special interest in Homeric poems. At that time it was not believed by classical scholars that historical facts could be discerned in the epic poems. Archaeology has since proved otherwise. Rush was a dedicated teacher who concentrated on the welfare of his students, to the detriment of his own research.

From childhood when he and his family all sang harmony parts in hymns at the local chapel, Rush was a lover of music. Before the war he enjoyed tramping in the Yorkshire Dales, no doubt with one eye on the landscape while the other was following his route on the old one-inch to the mile Ordnance Survey map. In those days I also tramped in the Dales, staying at Youth Hostels for one shilling a night; I do not remember meeting Rush.

In 1975 Rush had the opportunity of taking early retirement; but, when he was preparing for this he fell ill and died in his sixty-third year. His wife Joyce lived on until 2003; their two daughters and grandchildren flourish.

HUGH SINCLAIR (1873-1939)

Sir Hugh Francis Paget Sinclair deserves a place in the biographical section of my book because he was head of the Secret Intelligence Service (SIS) between the wars, from 1923-1939, having overall responsibility for GC&CS. Also it was he who bought Bletchley Park with his own money and brought the whole staff of GC&CS to BP, along with his own chef from the Savoy Grill, at the beginning of the war. He never saw the fruition of his labours, for he died in November 1939.

Hugh was born in Southampton, in 1873, the son of Frederick and Agnes May Sinclair. His father is described as 'gentleman' in the ODNB. Before the Great War, Hugh, who had joined the Royal Navy at the age of thirteen, specialised in work with torpedoes. His record of service was exemplary as he rose in the ranks. He married

Gertrude, the daughter of William Sydney Attenborough in 1907. They had two sons, Maurice Hugh and Derek Hugh. At the beginning of the Great War, Hugh, already nearly forty, was assistant director of the mobilisation division at the Admiralty. After a period at sea as captain of *HMS Renown*, he served as chief-of-staff of the battle-cruiser force for the last two years of the war.

Immediately after the war, on 3rd February 1919, when the director of naval intelligence, Admiral 'Blinker' Hall, retired, his deputy Captain Hugh Sinclair succeeded him. He was given the responsibility of forming the new government agency which was known as the Government Code and Cipher School (GC&CS). A tour of duty as head of the submarine service followed, which ended in 1923 when he was appointed chief of the Secret Intelligence Service (SIS), which included supervision of GC&CS.

His predecessor, Sir Mansfield Cumming, had always been known as 'C', the first letter of his adopted surname Cumming; Hugh, in his turn, was also known as 'C'. He was also known to his colleagues by the nickname *Quex*, after a leading character in a popular play by Sir Arthur Pinero in London in 1899, *The Gay Lord Quex*. The hero of the play was gay in the old meaning of the word, light-hearted and full of mirth; he was reputed to be the wickedest man in London. Hugh also had a reputation. He was a *bon viveur* who loved his cigars and wine and his lavish meals at the Savoy Hotel grill. His open Lancia car was well-known in London streets. He was divorced in 1920 and never married again. His unmarried sister Evelyn Beatrice Sinclair came to work at GC&CS and also looked after him.

Hugh was promoted to the rank of vice-admiral in 1926. In the inter-war period, the SIS was existing on a shoestring. The Soviet Union was seen as the chief danger to the country and Hugh was rivalled only by Winston Churchill in his hatred of Bolshevism. But by the mid-thirties the SIS began to take more interest in Italy, Germany and Japan. Likewise, GC&CS, headed by Alastair Denniston, was short of money during that period. By 1937, encouraged by Hugh Sinclair, Denniston visited many British universities looking for linguists and mathematicians who would be willing to join a GC&CS if war came.

Hugh's will makes no mention of Bletchley Park, which it is said he bought in 1938 with his own money, when various government departments refused to help. His two sons and Evelyn his sister were left £3,500 each, but Evelyn inherited the remainder of his unspecified estate. The subsequent history of the ownership of Bletchley Park remains a mystery.

Hugh died on 4th November 1939, at 8 Beaumont Street, Portland Place, London. His two sons, his sister and three step-grandchildren, survived him.

OLIVER STRACHEY (1874-1960)

Oliver Strachey, probably the oldest person to have worked at Bletchley Park during the war, was born in 1874 at Clapham Common, London. He was the third son of a large family of thirteen boys and girls born to Sir Richard Strachey, a former Lieutenant-General in the Royal Engineers and his wife Jane Maria Grant. Several of Oliver's brothers and sisters had notable careers, the most famous of them being Lytton Strachey, the author of the books *Eminent Victorians* and *Queen Victoria*, who created a new kind of biography in the early twentieth century.

Oliver's schooling was at Eton College. According to the ODNB, he was 'clever and good-looking, but also egotistic and somewhat feckless in his personal life.' Oliver did not go on to university. Instead, he studied music in Vienna for several years, later going to India as a traffic superintendent with the East India Railway Company, of which his father was chairman. India was not to his taste, so after a brief marriage to Ruby Mayer, which was soon dissolved, he returned to England. There was one child of this marriage, a daughter Julia. Back home he married Rachel (Ray) Costelloe, a feminist, the stepdaughter of Bernard Berenson, the American art critic. There were two children of this marriage, Barbara and Christopher. Oliver had no job, but he enjoyed the life and the parties in the Bloomsbury circle, where he played the piano. At this time he was living largely on his wife's income. Oliver was interested in his wife's concern about women's suffrage, and he served on the committee of the National Union of Women's Suffrage Societies.

The Great War came and Oliver was recruited to the War Office's code-breaking establishment MI1B, led by Major Malcolm Hay. He proved to be an excellent cryptanalyst. In 1916 he was sent to Egypt to set up a code-breaking unit there, surviving shipwreck when his ship was torpedoed.

After the war when the Government Code and Cipher School was founded in 1919, under the direction of Alastair Denniston, Oliver was one of the top three, appointed as a senior assistant. During the 1920s GC&CS had remarkable success in decrypting almost all the diplomatic messages of all nations. In 1934, Oliver, with Hugh Foss, decrypted messages produced by a Japanese naval cipher machine.

Gordon Welchman, in his book *The Hut 6 Story*, (new edition, 2000), remembers going to London from Cambridge before World War II, at the request of Denniston, the head of GC&CS.

I remember very little else about the preliminary indoctrination in London, except that I was very impressed by Oliver Strachey, a senior member of the staff, who during the coming war, would head an organisation known as Intelligence Services Oliver Strachey (ISOS). He seemed to be giving us an overview of the whole problem of deriving intelligence from enemy communications, and this may well have been a strong guiding influence on my wartime work.

Moving to Bletchley Park with GC&CS in 1939, Oliver was in a section concerned with decrypting German intelligence services (Abwehr) messages produced by non-cipher machine methods. The Abwehr also used the Enigma machine where possible, but hand ciphers when agents had no access to machines. The hand ciphers were of many different types and complexity, some of them proving impossible to solve.

Lord Dacre of Glanton, formerly Professor Hugh Trevor-Roper, Oxford historian, served in the British secret service, but was not at Bletchley Park. When working with MI6, he came to know Oliver Strachey, whom he described as:

…our regular contact at Bletchley. He was a long-serving epicurean professional cryptographer, not easily ruffled by such passing inconveniences as the outbreak of war.

Towards the end of 1941, Oliver was sent to Canada to be in charge of a code-breaking section known as the examination unit, in the Department of External Affairs. Oliver was sixty-seven and it is astonishing that a man of this age should have been sent on such a mission. But presumably he was a willing horse. While in Canada Oliver also decrypted Vichy French messages. He returned to BP in September, 1942.

Squadron-Leader F.W. Winterbotham, in his book *The Ultra Secret* (1974) remembered that:

Oliver Strachey was an individualist, tall, though a little stooped, with greying hair, broad forehead; his eyes, behind his glasses, always had a smile in them, as if he found life intensely amusing ... Oliver was also extremely musical. I believe he played several instruments, but he most enjoyed playing duets with Benjamin Britten on the grand piano in his rather untidy London flat.

Oliver's wife Ray died in 1940. In 1943 Oliver had a heart attack and, leaving BP, moved to a house in Gordon Square, Bloomsbury, London, living with two of his sisters. He died in 1960 in his eighty-sixth year.

DEREK TAUNT (1917-2004)

Derek Taunt, another young Cambridge mathematician, came to Bletchley Park in August 1941, shortly after the whole shape of the war had changed, when

Germany attacked the Soviet Union. Derek was born in November, 1917 and was educated first at Enfield Grammar School, followed by a course at the City of London School. From there he proceeded to Jesus College in the University of Cambridge, where, from 1936 to 1939, he was reading for the Mathematical Tripos, specialising in 'pure' mathematics. He had already approached Professor Hardy, a notable Cambridge mathematician, asking to be taken on as a research student, when the war started.

Registering with the joint recruiting board, Derek was quickly found work in the Ordnance Board at Chislehurst, 'analysing trial firings of new guns and ammunition and drawing up range-tables for them.' Derek was restive and wanted a more challenging job. His application for release passed through the usual channels. C. P. Snow, the novelist, was in charge of a body seeking to place square pegs in square holes. Derek soon found himself transferred to Hut 6 at Bletchley Park, the hut devoted largely to the decryption of the German Enigma ciphers. In charge was a fellow Cambridge mathematician, Gordon Welchman.

At first, billeted in a railway worker's home in Stony Stratford, Derek spent most of the first year at Bletchley working in Control. 'This section', Derek recalled in a chapter he wrote many years later in *Codebreakers*, edited by F.H.Hinsley and Alan Stripp (OUP,1993), 'maintained a constant contact between Hut 6 and the W/T (wireless telegraphy) stations intercepting the Enigma traffic.' Most of his colleagues, like himself, were in their early twenties, and, looking back he remembered that although Welchman and other seniors were more mature (they were in their thirties):

...the rest of us were like a bunch of enthusiastic undergraduates, our exuberance and in-jokes leavened by the civilising influence of the women members of the team. The universal feeling of comradeship in a demanding but exhilarating enterprise was palpable, contrasting vividly with my previous experience of civil service life, where formality and hierarchy were dominant characteristics.

After a year or so in Control, Derek was transferred to the Watch, where they had the use of a number of bombes, the devices which tested programmes and enabled them to decrypt German Enigma messages regularly, particularly the Red key used generally by the German Air Force.

'Life in the Watch was always demanding and never dull,' wrote Derek. He saw this section grow and grow until by 1943, it had to move to more spacious quarters in Block D, one of the new brick-built buildings which had been constructed.

During the last part of the war, Derek moved to a sub-section known as *Qwatch*. The name was a pun on the German word *Quatsch* (rubbish) and his task was to deal with less urgent but still important cryptographic problems. There were only three in

Qwatch: Derek, Bob Roseveare and Ione Jay. The last two married after the war, with Derek best man. One of their activities was the study of a key known as Brown, used by German scientists working at a station on the Baltic coast, who were experimenting with rockets.

The German war ended and the work of Hut 6 was finished. Some of the staff stayed behind to compile an official history of the department; others decided to stay with the organisation, moving eventually to Cheltenham. Army personnel had to wait for their discharge date and others returned to their civilian jobs. But Derek was posted to the Admiralty Research Laboratory at Teddington, where he worked for a brief period on aerodynamics. As soon as VJ-Day came, he returned to Cambridge to complete his Ph.D. Professor Hardy had retired, but Derek found that Professor Philip Hall, a specialist in Group theory, was willing to supervise him.

Derek spent the remainder of his career at his old college, Jesus, first as a Fellow, then as Cayley lecturer in mathematics. He also served as Bursar of the college and was President from 1979-1982. His interests included music, cricket, travel and walking. Derek had married the artist Angela Verren Chick in 1949. She and their two sons and a daughter, survived him when he died in July 2004, in his eighty-seventh year.

RALPH PATERSON TESTER (1901-1998)

Intelligence Corps Major Ralph Tester was one of only a handful of those at Bletchley Park who had a department bearing their own names. The *Testery* was a section in block B and later in block F, whose members, of both sexes and all ranks, worked on the decryption of the non-Morse traffic known as FISH.

Ralph was one of the eight children of a Kentish family. Born in June 1901, he was of that generation who were of the age to serve in both world wars. When the Great War ended in November, 1918, Ralph, a seventeen year-old soldier, was serving in France.

With the help of a godparent, Ralph was able to qualify in Edinburgh as a chartered accountant. In 1925 he moved to Berlin, working there as an auditor for the firm Price Waterhouse. In the course of his travels for the firm in Europe, he met and married Sigrid Laurell, a young woman who was working for the Swedish Shell Company. Leaving Price Waterhouse in 1930, Ralph began working for Unilever. His base was in Dresden, but he travelled extensively in Czechoslovakia, the Balkans and in Austria until the outbreak of war in 1939.

Back in England, where his wife and their son and daughter, who were born in Germany in the 1930s, had come several months earlier, Ralph joined the Home

Guard in London. With his fluent knowledge of German it was likely that Ralph would end up at Bletchley. Arriving there in 1942, he worked firstly on German police ciphers. It was later that Ralph was placed in charge of a new section which became known as the *Testery*. The Fish ciphers, transmitted by the Germans at high-speed on the Lorenz machine, proved more difficult to decrypt than Enigma. Nevertheless, William Tutte, with great perseverance, discovered the structure of the Lorenz machine, without having seen one. Work by Tester's team followed, but the final achievement leading to regular decrypting of the Fish ciphers, came only after the building of the giant Colossus machines.

Towards the end of the war, Major Tester was chosen to be a member of an Anglo-American team whose job was to search in Germany for information about German cryptographic methods, especially what progress they had made in decrypting allied traffic. The team, called TICOM, (Target Identification Committee), consisted of five British, including Major Rushworth of the Fusion Room, and four American officers, with radio operators and two drivers. Fortunately, they did not have to parachute into Germany (the original plan), for the war ended soon after they arrived in Heidelberg. After many adventures, they came back with several trucks laden with German cipher machines and other material; they also brought back a number of German prisoners of war, who had been working on the decryption of British, American and Soviet ciphers, and were willing to reveal their methods.

After demobilisation, Ralph returned to Unilever, working firstly in London and from 1949 to 1956 in Hamburg, where he still had pre-war friends who had survived. After his retirement Ralph returned to his native Kent, where his wife died in 1979. He then began to learn Swedish so that he could correspond with Sigrid's relatives in Sweden. In old age Ralph left Kent to live with his daughter near Oxford. He died in his ninety-seventh year, in 1998.

EDWARD THOMAS (1918-1996)

Born in May, 1918, at Walton-on-Thames, nearly six months before the end of the Great War, Edward Eastaway Thomas, a nephew of the poet of the same name, never saw his uncle, a soldier who was killed at Arras in 1917.

Edward went to two grammar schools, in Portsmouth and Guildford. At King's College, University of London, he studied languages under his professor, Sir Frederick Norman, who later also worked at Bletchley Park.

In 1940, having completed his degree, Edward joined the RNVR. After the usual seaman's training, he was posted to Iceland as a naval intelligence officer. There followed an unusual time of his life, during which he inspected a beached German U-boat, interviewed shipwrecked British seamen, and learned the Icelandic language. His main occupation, however, was as head of a direction-finding station, taking bearings on enemy submarines. Unfortunately, this station had been sited in the north of Iceland, designed to take bearings on Soviet submarines in the days before they became our ally. Orders to move the station to southern Iceland could not be carried out until May 1941 when the ice melted sufficiently to dig out the cables.

In February 1942, Edward was transferred to Bletchley Park to work in the naval section, Hut 4. Early in that year a twenty-four hour watch of naval officers became a part of Hut 3, which usually dealt with German army and air force messages. Named 3N, one of its tasks was to advise on naval problems arising from army and air force decrypts, particularly shipping intelligence relating to Italian and German convoys taking material to Rommel in North Africa across the Mediterranean Sea. Edward was part of this watch, busy translating and annotating German and Italian messages and passing his findings to the Admiralty. This team can be said to have played a major part in the defeat of Rommel and his army, by providing vital information which enabled the British Navy to sink many of the convoys, particularly those carrying the fuel he desperately needed for his tanks.

When the war in Africa ended in May 1943, Edward was posted away from BP to be an intelligence officer and adviser on signals intelligence to the Commander in Chief, Home Fleet, in his flagship, the battleship *Duke of York*, based at Scapa Flow. His knowledge of the German navy, gained at BP, was invaluable during operations off the Norwegian coast and on the Arctic convoys. One of his searing memories was the sight of the German battle cruiser *Scharnhorst*, destroyed by the Home Fleet in December,1943. He remembered the glowing red hot ship in the darkness of the Arctic, as she sank.

After the war, in 1946, Edward decided to stay on with the intelligence services. But instead of transferring to GCHQ at Cheltenham, he joined the Joint Intelligence Bureau, which had replaced the wartime Joint Intelligence Committee. He served on this body until 1970, when he retired at the early age of fifty-two. Edward was a man with many interests, a fine musician who played in local orchestras and was an expert gardener, who discovered a plant in Malaysia, which was named after him (*Fiffistigma Thomasii*). He also translated German books and was co-president of the Edward Thomas Society, devoted to the memory of his uncle, the poet.

However, these activities in retirement did not mean that he had left the world of intelligence completely. In 1971 he was persuaded to join the team, led by Professor Harry Hinsley, whom he had known at BP, which produced the official history: *British Intelligence in the Second World War*. He retired from this project in 1988, aged 70, on the publication of the fourth of five volumes.

Edward died on 22 January, 1996, at Dorking in Surrey, in his 78th year, survived by the twin children of his second wife Ruth, whom he had married in 1964.

JOHN HESSELL TILTMAN (1894-1982)

By the time John Tiltman retired from cryptographic work at the age of eighty-six he had become a legendary figure in Great Britain and the United States of America. For the last sixteen years of his career he was employed by the American National Security Agency (NSA) as a consultant and researcher. He had already reached normal retirement age in 1954 at GCHQ at Cheltenham, where he had worked since his World War II duties ended at Bletchley Park in 1946.

John was born in Bloomsbury, London, in May 1894, the youngest child of Alfred Hessell Tiltman, an architect, and his wife Sarah Ann Jane Kerr. Educated at Charterhouse School, he was unable to proceed to the University of Oxford, where he had been offered a place, because of changed family fortunes, following the death of his father. After teaching in several schools, John volunteered soon after the outbreak of the Great War in August 1914, joining the *King's Own Scottish Borderers*. Soon commissioned, he served with his regiment in France from October 1915 to May, 1917, when he was seriously wounded and awarded the Military Cross. Having recovered from his wounds, he served on the British Military Mission in Siberia in 1919. The next year he was attending a course in the Russian language when, on the point of returning to his regiment, he was asked to translate a backlog of decrypted Russian messages at GC&CS. John never returned to his regiment and was employed by GC&CS from then onwards.

For almost a decade after his arrival at Simla in India, where he had been posted as assistant to Colonel W. H. Jeffery, John was decrypting Russian diplomatic messages between Moscow, Kabul and Tashkent. During this time he also advised the Indian army on ciphers. In 1925 John retired from the army with the rank of captain, henceforth being employed as a War Office civil servant. Recalled to England in 1929, he was put in charge of a new military section of GC&CS. There he worked on Russian and Japanese ciphers and, with the help of Dillwyn Knox and others regularly decrypted messages sent from the Comintern (Communist International, the worldwide federation of Communist parties, run by Moscow), to the UK and other countries.

In the 1930s John began communicating with the French cryptographers after GC&CS had agreed to exchange information on Russian ciphers with the French. It was in 1933 that he went to Paris to meet Captain Gustave Bernard, head cryptographer of French military intelligence, with Colonel Stewart Menzies, who was at that time deputy head of the Secret Intelligence Service (SIS), now known as MI 6. At this time John had some success in decrypting Japanese ciphers, with the assistance of Lieutenant (later Colonel) Pat Marr-Johnson, a Japanese interpreter who worked at GC&CS.

On the outbreak of World War II in 1939, John was recalled to the army as a lieutenant-colonel, moving with GC&CS to Bletchley Park. Until the fall of France he was in close touch with Captain (later Brigadier-General) Bertrand and his fellow cryptographers. In the spring of 1940 John was in Finland, working with the Finnish code-breakers, who provided GC&CS with captured Soviet code books and other material. In view of later developments it was as well that Sweden refused to allow British forces to cross their land to come to the aid of Finland; it was also fortunate that Finland signed an armistice with the USSR soon afterwards.

Although John's expertise was in the decrypting of manual ciphers, he nevertheless made a number of contributions to the work on Enigma and other machine ciphers. One such success was his work on the Lorenz machine which led to the first decryption of this cipher. D.R.Nichol wrote in the ODNB that:

…as a solver of non-machine systems he was pre-eminent, through intuition, experience, and a dogged persistence, producing answers to problems of the most difficult and complex kind and constantly improving the speed and elegance of the methods used.

John had a finger in many pies. He set up crash courses in Japanese at Bedford, recruiting young undergraduates and graduates in classics, who were deemed to be capable of learning the language quickly. He visited the USA several times, taking a leading part in conferences there on Japanese ciphers. He was active also in recruiting young men and women from all over Great Britain.

In March 1944 John was promoted from the rank of colonel to that of brigadier, henceforth being known by fellow code-breakers in Britain and the USA as 'The Brig.'

From the beginning of the war John had advocated full co-operation with the United States of America on intelligence and cryptographic matters. Some British were reluctant to divulge our successes with Enigma, but John and others pressed for the sharing of intelligence with the Americans. This led, among other advantages, to a massive production in the USA of the bombes which were urgently required to facilitate the breaking of the Enigma ciphers.

After the war John continued to work at GCHQ, moving with them to Cheltenham. Although he retired at sixty, he continued to work there until he was seventy. It was then that he received an invitation from the National Security Agency (NSA), to work in Washington D C as a consultant and researcher. After ten years the director of NSA presented John with a scroll celebrating 'sixty years of distinguished cryptologic service.' One account of John describes him as 'a very smart military figure, a quiet man who did not laugh or smile much but with a dry sense of humour and great personal charm.'

John married Tempe Monica Robinson, the daughter of Major-General Oliver Robinson, of the army medical service, in 1926, in Simla, India. They had one daughter. After his final retirement from NSA in 1980, John moved to Hawaii, where his daughter Mrs Tempe Denzer, was now living. He died there in his 89th year, in August 1982.

EDWARD TRAVIS (1888-1956)

To have served in the Great War on the personal staff of Admiral Jellicoe, the Commander in Chief, Royal Navy, and in World War II to have been in command of operations at Bletchley Park, the headquarters of the Government Code and Cipher School, were two remarkable periods in the life of Sir Edward Wilfred Harry Travis.

Born in 1888 at Plumstead in Kent, not far from Woolwich, Edward was the son of Harry Travis, a civil engineer and his wife Emmeline Hamlyn. Known as Wilfred by his family and as Jumbo to his friends, Wilfred joined the Royal Navy in 1906, after school at Blackheath. By 1909 he was commissioned. On the outbreak of the Great War he was called to serve on the personal staff of Admiral Jellicoe. Subsequently he was transferred to cipher security.

After the war Edward decided to continue working at the Government Code and Cipher School, where he was appointed deputy to the head of the organisation, A.G. Denniston. Edward moved to Bletchley Park on the outbreak of World War II with all the others in the department. Gordon Welchman, one of the Cambridge mathematicians who later was the head of Hut 6 at BP, early in 1940 formulated a detailed organisational plan, involving much expansion of departments; it would also increase the cover of radio interception. Welchman, a civilian, must have felt some apprehension when he put his plan forward to Commander Travis. However, he found that this 'broad-shouldered man of heavy build', who stared at him over half-moon spectacles, approved his plan in full and, wasting no time:

...quickly obtained official agreement to the establishment of a new section in the BP complex, to handle the possibility of Enigma breaks on an interservice basis.

On another page of his book *The Hut 6 Story,* Welchman saw in Commander Travis some of Churchill's qualities.

He was definitely of the bulldog breed, and he liked to have things done his way, but he also had a great feeling for what it took to create happy working conditions. We in Hut 6 saw more of him while he was still deputy director than we did after he took on full responsibility for all the expanding activities of BP. He would get around to all our activities, making contact with staff at all levels, and he had the soft human touch.

In February 1942, Alastair Denniston, who had been head of BP, was removed, becoming Deputy Director (civil), in charge of diplomatic and commercial sections in London. Commander Travis replaced him as operational head of BP, with the title Deputy Director (services). He became in effect in control of the workforce of more than 9,000 men and women, for Menzies, the head of British intelligence, was nominally the chief, although not working at BP.

It is strange to realise now that Travis was completely unknown to the majority of the thousands who worked at BP and its out-stations. He was only known to the heads of sections or to those administrative staff who worked with him. The rest of us knew not who was in overall charge; nor were we interested in any part of BP other than the section in which we worked.

Far removed from his codebreaking days in the Great War and the 1920s, Travis built up and managed a colossal enterprise which became the greatest cryptographic establishment in the world. He remained Director of GCHQ until his retirement in April 1952.

Travis had married in 1913 Muriel Irene Fry, the daughter of William Henry Fry, an architect, and his wife Marion. They had two daughters, the elder of whom, Valerie, worked at BP during the war.

Sir Edward retired to his home at Pirbright, Surrey, dying there only four years after his retirement. He was cremated at Woking on St George's Day, 23 April, 1956.

ALAN TURING (1912-1954)

Alan, in whom the lamp of genius burned so bright ...he had real genius, it shone from him.

Professor Sir Geoffrey Jefferson (1886-1961)

Although most historians of intelligence matters would agree that the decryption of German Enigma and other ciphers at Bletchley Park during World War II was the result of team work, few would disagree that the outstanding member of the team was Alan Turing. From where does genius come? We can only speculate. One of the relatives of Alan's mother was the Irish mathematical physicist G.J. Stoney, a Fellow of the Royal Society, and professor of natural philosophy at Queen's College,

Galway, in the 1850s. Is it fanciful to imagine that Alan shared some of his genes with this notable physicist who had coined the word *electron* in 1891? Professor Stoney died in 1911, the year before Alan's birth. Alan's addiction to ingenious mechanical devices may have come from a gene provided by his grandfather Edward Waller Stoney, who, as well as spending most of his life as a railway engineer in India, invented *Stoney's Silent Punka Wheel,* which must have been a blessing to many who worked in India. However, John Robert Turing, Alan's other grandfather may also have contributed some genes to his grandson's stock, for he took a good mathematics degree in 1848 at Trinity College, Cambridge, but gave up the subject when he was ordained.

Alan Mathison Turing was born at Warrington Lodge, Maida Vale, London, on 23 June, 1912, the younger child of Julius Mathison Turing, of the Indian civil service, and his wife Ethel Sara Stoney, the daughter of Edward Stoney, chief engineer of Madras railways. Alan had an older brother, John, born in India in 1908. Their father returned to his job in India when Alan was about nine months old. Mrs Turing stayed a little longer, but joined her husband in September 1913, leaving fifteen month-old Alan and his brother to be fostered by a retired army couple at St Leonards-on-Sea near Hastings. Mrs Turing had intended to take Alan to India, but wrote later that 'owing to having slight rickets it was thought better to leave him in England.' Colonel and Mrs Ward had four small daughters; later three cousins of the Turings arrived. Alan's mother returned to England, spending the spring and summer of 1915 with her boys. But in the autumn, when Alan was little more than three, she sailed to India again, leaving the boys with Mrs Ward. Mr and Mrs Turing came back to England in the spring of 1916 and Mr Turing returned to India in the autumn, leaving his wife in England, not wishing her to face another voyage through waters patrolled by German U-boats. From 1916 to 1919, Mr Turing stayed alone in India. On his return he found it difficult to assert his authority over the young Alan, who was already showing signs that he was a maverick and one who seldom accepted the rules of the adult world. Both parents sailed again for India in the autumn of 1919 and when his mother returned in the summer of 1921 she found the vivacious boy she had left was now 'unsociable and dreamy'; his brother John was away at prep school.

At Hazelhurst, a small prep school near Tunbridge Wells, where Alan joined his brother in 1922, Alan became obsessed with chemical experiments. After 1924 the brothers spent holidays with their parents at Dinard in France, where Mr Turing had taken a house, thus becoming a tax exile who was allowed to live in the United Kingdom for six weeks only each year.

In the spring of 1926, Alan was accepted by Sherborne public school. His arrival there was unusual; arriving at Southampton from France, he found that because of the General Strike no trains or buses were running. Undeterred, he bought a map, left his luggage in Southampton and rode the sixty odd miles to Sherborne on his bicycle, which he had intended to take with him on the train. Breaking the journey he spent one night at a hotel in Blandford.

At Sherborne he had to become inured to cold showers and the usual public school fagging system. Alan shone only in the subjects that interested him, disappointing his teachers and his mother. Slovenly in appearance, untidy at all times, Alan was for a time a shy and solitary boy who exasperated some of the teachers. Mr Geoffrey O'Hanlon, Alan's housemaster at Westcott House, recalled in the Sherborne school magazine *The Shirburnian* (volume XLIV, summer, 1954), that Alan's contemporaries, boys and masters, 'knew him as clever, odd, unpredictable, and perhaps tiresome.' Others remembered him as 'an even-tempered, loveable character with an impish sense of humour and a modesty proof against all achievement'. But by the time he came to the school certificate examination, Alan's work had improved. He obtained a number of credits, including mathematics and additional maths. In the sixth form the young mathematics teacher, Mr Eperson, recognising Allen's excellence in the subject, let him go his own way.

...leaving him largely to his own devices and standing by to assist when necessary, allowing his natural mathematical genius to progress uninhibited...

At the age of fifteen Alan first became a friend of Christopher Morcom, a boy a year older than himself and from another house. Christopher, like Alan had a passion for science, mathematics and astronomy, subjects which they discussed endlessly. For Alan, who had been unable to find friends in his own house, his love for Chris was a revelation and they remained friends until the end of schooldays. Both boys were to go to King's College Cambridge, but Chris, taken suddenly ill, died of tuberculosis in February 1930. It was a parting which affected Alan deeply for the rest of his life.

At King's College Alan began studies for the mathematics degree (the tripos). He had some notable teachers and Alan devoted himself to the subject, soon gaining a reputation for brilliance. In 1934 he passed the examinations with distinction. Some of his rough edges were smoothed over during the Cambridge years. He enjoyed rowing and continued long-distance running, at which he had excelled at Sherborne.

A fellowship at King's College followed in 1935, a great honour for one so young. In 1937 he wrote a paper describing a universal computer which he called the Turing machine. From 1936 to 1938 he attended Princeton University in the United States, returning to his fellowship at King's with an American doctorate. Before the war began, he was approached by GC&CS. Denniston, the head of that government department, was looking for mathematicians and linguists who would be willing to join his service. And so it was that Alan turned up at Bletchley Park on September 4th, 1939, the day after Britain's declaration of war on Germany.

At BP Alan worked in Hut 8, which dealt with Enigma naval messages, including those from submarines (U-Boats). One of his first jobs was the design of a *bombe*, a much more sophisticated machine than the *bomba* which the Polish cryptographers had devised. Turing's machine, with the addition of a 'diagonal board' invented by Gordon Welchman, was vital in the decryption of Enigma enciphered messages. Alan's theories also contributed to the much larger machine known as *Colossus*, which led to decryption of the Lorenz ciphers. It was Professor Newman, however, who organised the production of *Colossus*, aided by Tommy Flowers, the engineer and others.

Alan, like most of the notable cryptologists, was unknown to most of the thousands who worked at BP. To those who did work with him he was always known as 'Prof' 'because he seemed to be omniscient in all matters scientific.' Andrew Hodges, whose book *Alan Turing: the Enigma of Intelligence* (1983), is the most substantial biography of anybody who worked at BP, saw Alan as the *genius loci* of Bletchley Park:

...shabby, nail-bitten, tieless, sometimes halting in speech and awkward of manner ... the foe of charlatans and status-seekers ...

Some have wondered whether Alan had what is now known as Asperger syndrome, a neurobiological disorder named after the Viennese physician Hans Asperger, which has been described as a type of autism. Lois Freisleben-Cook's description of Asperger syndrome almost sounds like an exact description of Alan:

... a few people with Asperger syndrome are very successful and until recently were not diagnosed with anything, but were seen as brilliant, eccentric, absent-minded, socially inept, or a little awkward physically.

She also mentions lack of eye contact and the habit of turning away at the moment of greeting a person. Lyn Irvine, in the foreword to Mrs Turing's biography of her son: *Alan Turing* (Heffer, 1959) remembered that Alan

...had a strange way of not meeting the eye, of sidling out of the door with a brusque and off-hand word of thanks.

In November 1942 Alan was sent to the United States for the purposes of liaison with American colleagues on the U-boat Enigma crisis and on the subject of scrambler telephones for use in top level communications. Soon, the decrypting of U-Boat signals was restored and the battle of the Atlantic had turned to the allies' advantage. C.H. O'D. Alexander had taken charge of Hut 8 in Alan's absence. On his return from America in March 1943, Alan, who was not a good organiser, became chief consultant on cryptanalysis.

As the war drew to a close Alan's pre-war idea that a universal machine could be constructed to replicate the processes of the human brain, which had been simmering on the back burner, became more and more his great passion. He was appointed to a post at the National Physical Laboratory on release from BP. There he began work on designing a computer. But in October, 1947, he decided to spend a year in Cambridge. But Newman, Alan's old BP colleague, had been appointed Professor of pure mathematics at Manchester University in 1945 and had obtained a very large Royal Society grant for the construction of a computer. In October 1948, Newman offered Alan the post of deputy director of the Manchester Computing Laboratory. Alan severed his long association with Cambridge and moved to the north, buying a house at Wilmslow, a small town south of Manchester. While at Manchester, Alan produced a number of important papers, including what his biographer Hodges described as 'the most lucid and far-reaching expression of his philosophy', which appeared in the periodical *Mind* (Volume 59, 1950). In 1951 he was elected a Fellow of the Royal Society.

Many who have written about Alan since his death have dwelled on his eccentricities – cycling to work at BP wearing his gas-mask to avoid hay fever, or burying ingots of silver in case of a German invasion, which he failed to find after the war. Others have spoken of his essential kindness, especially towards children. One wonders what Alan would have thought of all these attempts to 'pluck out the heart' of his mystery. Perhaps the most percipient views were those of Professor Sir Geoffrey Jefferson, the neuro-surgeon, an older man whom he first met in post-war Manchester. In a letter to Alan's mother, Sir Geoffrey wrote:

…Alan, as I saw him, made people want to help him, though he was rather insulated from human relations. Or perhaps because of that we wanted to break through. I personally did not find him easy to get close to …He was so unversed in worldly ways, so childlike it seems to me, so unconventional, so non-conformist to the general pattern …so very absent-minded. His genius flared because he had never quite grown up. He was, I suppose a sort of scientific Shelley.

Alan Turing was a homosexual. In the early 1950s anybody discovered engaging in homosexual activities was liable to be prosecuted. Alan's reporting of a theft at his house, led to police investigations about his relationship with the man accused of the theft. Alan was brought to trial in March 1952 and found guilty. He was given the choice of prison or oestrogen injections for a year. He chose the latter. A little over two years later he was found dead in bed of cyanide poisoning. At the inquest the verdict was suicide. He was forty-three years old. His father had died many years earlier, but he was survived by his brother and his mother. She wrote a biography of Alan and died still believing that his death was an accident.

WILLIAM TUTTE (1917-2002)

Professor Bill Tutte was another example of a student who changed horses in midstream. For, having gone to Trinity College, Cambridge to read chemistry, he returned at the end of World War II with different ideas: instead of completing his doctorate in chemistry he began studying for one in mathematics.

Born in Newmarket, Suffolk, England, in 1917, Bill was the son of an estate gardener, William John Tutte and his wife Annie Newell, a cook and housekeeper. The family moved frequently because of his father's job, but settled down in Newmarket when Mr Tutte obtained work at the Rutland Arms Hotel. Bill was just five years old when they moved to the village of Cheveley about three miles away. From the primary school in the village he moved to secondary school and on to Trinity College, Cambridge.

Although his main interest was chemistry, Bill was from schooldays fascinated by mathematical problems. He joined a mathematical society and then made friends with some of the Cambridge mathematicians. In 1941, Bill started work at Bletchley Park after a brief course on cryptography in London.

The Enigma machine cipher was being broken regularly, but another cipher produced by a machine known by the name of Lorenz, which enciphered teleprinter messages at high speed, proved a different kettle of FISH and was so named by the British code-breakers. The final cracking of Lorenz was the result of team-work. Colonel Tiltman achieved the first step, but it was Bill Tutte who, with dogged perseverance over several months, worked out the structure of the Lorenz machine without ever having seen it. At first, with the aid of a Heath-Robinson-like machine, some decrypting was achieved. But it was only when the first Colossus, an enormous computer-like apparatus, was built that success came on a regular basis. The importance of the decrypting of the Lorenz cipher was that, unlike Enigma, used extensively in the field, the Lorenz machine was only used for high-grade secret communications from Hitler to his generals or between Berlin and army groups. Some of the information gleaned from this source proved to be of enormous value. Professor Hinsley in the book *Codebreakers,* edited by F.H. Hinsley and Alan Stripp (OUP, 1994) wrote that, from the end of March, 1944 until D-Day the Lorenz link between Berlin and von Rundstedt, the Commander-in-Chief West, was broken.

All decrypts on this link ...supplied intelligence of crucial importance on Germany's appreciations of the Allied invasion intentions and on its own plans for countering them, together with much information about the state and disposition of its divisions.

After the secrets of BP were revealed, Bill Tutte wrote a paper: *Fish and I,* explaining the methods he used in working out the secrets of the Lorenz machine.

This, to my knowledge, has not been printed, but is available on the internet. In it, Bill explained why the authorities decided to concentrate on Tunny, the German army Lorenz cipher, used also by the Abwehr and the navy, instead of Sturgeon, used by the Luftwaffe.

One reason: resources were limited and it seemed better to make a full-scale attack on one cipher system than to make half-hearted attacks on both. Another reason: Enigma was supplying much information about the German navy and air force but little about the army

Bill, returning to Cambridge after the war, achieved his doctorate in mathematics in 1948. After graduation he was invited to a teaching post in Canada at the University of Toronto. It was at this time, in 1949, that he married Dorothea Geraldine Mitchell. They had no children. Bill stayed at Toronto until 1962, when he moved to Waterloo University, in Ontario, only five years after its inception. Bill and his wife made their home in West Montrose, a hamlet outside the city of Waterloo. They were both great walkers. There he spent the rest of his teaching days, retiring in 1984 after a long and successful career during which he published many books and more that than one hundred and sixty-eight mathematical papers. In retirement he was elected honorary director of the *Centre for Cryptography Research*, which had been established at Waterloo University. His wife Dorothea died in 1994 and Bill went back to England. But life in Canada appealed to him more so he returned to Waterloo in 2000, dying there in 2002 in his eighty-fifth year.

PETER TWINN (1916-2004)

Peter Frank George Twinn was probably the earliest mathematician to arrive at Bletchley Park, for he had been appointed before the war started to a post at GC&CS.

Peter was born at Streatham in south London, the son of a Post Office official, but went to school in the north and the south, first at Manchester Grammar School and later at Dulwich College. At the University of Oxford, at Brasenose College, he read mathematics, graduating in 1938. Having then won a scholarship for postgraduate studies in physics, he started this course at the beginning of 1939, but was still not sure what career he wished to follow. The uncertainties of life at that time between the Munich agreement in 1938 and the summer of 1939, were especially difficult for young people, and when he spotted a government advertisement announcing that mathematicians were required he decided to apply. No details of the post were offered in the advertisement or at the interview.

The job turned out to be with GC&CS, still in London at that time, in a building at Broadway, near St James's Park. Peter began work in February 1939 as an assistant to Dyllwyn Knox (Dilly), an eccentric classical scholar who also had a passionate interest in mathematics. After five minutes training, Dilly threw Peter in at the deep end to learn to swim in his own way. Before the war started in September 1939 the whole unit had transferred to Bletchley Park. In August, a replica Enigma machine, manufactured by the Polish cryptographers, arrived at BP; the Poles had given one copy to the French and one to the British cryptographers. This was of great help to the British team including Twinn, Turing, Knox and Welchman, who early in 1940 had made a breakthrough in decrypting Enigma messages. In a chapter on *The Abwehr Enigma* in the book *Codebreakers*, edited by F. H. Hinsley and Alan Stripp (OUP, 1993), Peter Twinn recalls a visit from Josh Cooper:

...at that time a senior officer in Bletchley, who reminded me of what I knew only too well, that I was the first British cryptographer to have read a German services Enigma message. I hasten to add that this did me little if any credit, since with the information Dilly had brought back from Poland, the job was little more than a routine operation.

Twinn later worked with Turing on breaking the German naval Enigma in Hut 4. When Knox became ill, Peter took on the decryption of the German secret service (the Abwehr) messages in 1942, pleased that he had three stalwart assistants, 'the gifted trio', Keith Batey, Mavis Lever and Margaret Rock. 'With this Lever and this Rock, I can move the world', Dilly had said.

After the war Peter took a job with the British Ministry of Technology and was in charge of hovercraft. He was later appointed secretary of the Royal Aircraft Establishment at Farnborough. His hobby was entomology and Peter, content with nothing but the best, studied the subject part-time at London University, achieving a doctorate. The subject of his thesis was the jumping mechanism of the click beetle.

Peter was a music lover who played the clarinet and the viola. At Bletchley he took part in musical concerts. At one of these he met Rosamund Case, a cello player who worked in the registry. They married in 1944 and had a son and three daughters. Peter died in 2004.

ALEXIS VLASTO (1915-2000)

Not all of the recruits to Bletchley Park who came from the University of Cambridge were mathematicians. One notable exception was Alexis Vlasto. Of a wealthy Greek family which had emigrated to England in the nineteenth century, Alexis was born in Liverpool in November, 1915. Educated at Eton College, he emerged into the real world in 1937 when he arrived at King's College, in the University of Cambridge, to read modern and medieval languages. With his fine intellect and thirst for languages, this quiet, reserved student - some called him laconic - mastered French and German and was turning to medieval languages and to Russian when the war began.

Recruits for the Japanese section at Bletchley Park were urgently required. Colonel Tiltman, the veteran cryptologist of Great War days, had, with the help of others, set up a six-month Japanese course at Bedford. Most of his colleagues at Bletchley had endured this difficult course, which was largely composed of young undergraduates or graduates in classical studies. But Alexis seems to have missed Bedford and arrived separately at BP. He had somehow acquired a knowledge of the language and by 1943 he was in charge of a team which was trying to decrypt the Japanese Air Force general cipher known as 3366. *The Times* obituarist described Alexis as 'a very quiet man with a nice ironic sense of humour.' Maurice Wiles, one of his colleagues, remembers that Alexis presided over the team 'with unfailing grace and wisdom.'

At Bletchley Park Alexis met again Jill Medway, a girl whom he had known before through membership of the Cambridge University Music Society. They were married in 1945, both returning to Cambridge, Jill to be head of music at two women's colleges, Girton and Newnham, and Alexis to work on his Ph.D. Having obtained a first in part II of the modern and medieval languages tripos, Alexis had, before war, been inspired to turn his attention to the Russian language, after hearing lectures by Elizabeth Hill, who later became the first professor of Russian in the University and a Dame.

After the war, he was elected to a research fellowship at King's College, which he held until 1950; at the same time he taught Russian under Elizabeth Hill's supervision. He proved to be an excellent scholar in the fields of Slavonic philology and Slav medieval history, At the end of his studies in 1953, he gained his doctorate with a thesis on intellectual life in the age of Catherine the Great.

After ten years as a university lecturer, he was elected to a fellowship at Selwyn College, serving there not only as director of studies in modern languages, but also as librarian and garden steward. His first major publication came in 1968: *The Entry of the Slavs into Christendom*. He remained a Fellow of Selwyn until his death. A second major work followed in 1986 with the publication of *The Linguistic History of Russia to the End of the Eighteenth Century*. Apart from his great interest in languages, Alexis had two other main pursuits, music and botany. An oboe player when an undergraduate, he was in after years a supporter of the College Music Society and the chapel choir. Later in life he was a great collector of plants and bulbs. Having enjoyed them in his garden in his lifetime he gave an extensive collection of bulbs to the University Botanic Garden, when nearing the end of his life.

Alexis died in July 2000 in his eighty-fifth year. His wife Jill had died thirty-two years earlier. He did not marry again and was survived by a son and daughter, Dominic and Alexandrina.

GORDON WELCHMAN (1906-1985)

'Welchman was a visionary, and a very practical visionary at that'. These are the words of Stuart Milner-Barry in his chapter, *Hut 6: the Early Days*, in the book by F.H. Hinsley and A.Stripp: *The Codebreakers* (OUP,1993). Paying tribute to the early work of the Polish crypt-analysts, Milner-Barry added that the main credit for the breaking of the German Enigma cipher should go to Alan Turing, Gordon Welchman and C.H.O'D. Alexander. But it was Welchman, he wrote, who

> foresaw much of what would be involved in the way of expansion of staff, machinery (the *bombes*) and all the other necessary substructure. And he had the fire in his belly that enabled him to cajole higher authority into supplying our needs. If Gordon Welchman had not been there, I doubt if Ultra would have played the part that it undoubtedly did in shortening the war.

William Gordon Welchman was born at Fishponds, in the parish of Stapleton, a village about three miles from Bristol. He was the youngest of the three children of William Welchman, a country parson and Archdeacon of Bristol and his wife Elizabeth Marshall, the daughter of the Reverend Edward Moule Griffith. Gordon had an older brother who was killed in 1914, and a sister. Their father had earlier been a missionary.

Gordon's schooldays at Marlborough College ended when he won a scholarship to Trinity College, Cambridge, in 1925. He sailed through the mathematical tripos during the years 1926-28, and, after teaching at a school in Cheltenham, returned to Cambridge to a fellowship at Sidney Sussex College in 1929.

In the late 1930s, Commander Alastair Denniston, the head of the GC&CS, realising that if war came they would have to move out of London and find more staff, began to visit the major universities, looking for possible recruits. Gordon Welchman agreed to attend a short preliminary indoctrination programme in London, where he was impressed with Oliver Strachey's views about deriving intelligence from enemy communications. He returned to Cambridge, having promised that he would report to the newly-acquired Bletchley Park if war came. Gordon continued lecturing in mathematics at Cambridge during 1939 and also working on a book about algebraic geometry, which he later put aside and published after the war.

On 4th September 1939, the day after Britain declared war on Germany, Gordon drove from Cambridge to Bletchley. Denniston greeted him and immediately sent him to see Dilly Knox, who was in charge of a group of people working on Enigma in a small building known as the cottage, which had probably been the coach house. Gordon formed the impression that Dilly did not like him. There must have been some jealousy on the part of the old timers who had worked through the inter-war years at GC&CS, seeing all the new recruits as Johnnys-come-lately. Whatever the reason, Gordon was turned out of the Cottage and sent to Elmers school, outside the park, to study call-signs and the preambles to Enigma messages. His banishment from the cottage, wrote Gordon in his book *The Hut 6 Story: Breaking the Enigma Codes (1982; revised ed. 1997)*, 'proved to be the real start of the Hut 6 organisation that was to develop.' Soon he returned to the Park and set up his stall in Hut 6, one of the hastily erected buildings near the Bletchley mansion. At first Gordon did a lot of recruiting new staff himself by approaching graduates and undergraduates from Cambridge and elsewhere. By 1941, however, it was decided to channel all recruitment through Dr C.P. Snow of Christchurch Cambridge, who later became known as a prolific novelist.

From his earliest days at BP Gordon saw the possibility of improving the primitive Polish *bomba*, until finally, renamed *bombe*, it proved to be the most important device in the armoury of the cryptanalysts working on Enigma. Designed largely by Alan Turing, the *bombes* were produced in large numbers by British and later American engineers. But it was Gordon's modification to the circuitry of the *bombe*, by the addition of a simple electrical circuit, known as the diagonal board, which increased its efficiency enormously. Turing agreed that it was a spectacular discovery.

Gordon was in close touch with a group known as the Central Party, which was concerned with call-signs and traffic analysis. Originally a branch of MI8, it had moved from London to Beaumanor, near Quorn in Leicestershire. I had joined this group a month before we moved to Bletchley in 1942. There we became part of Hut 6, and it was Gordon who urged the authorities to allow the traffic analysts to know that Enigma was being decrypted. From then on log reading became much more interesting and useful.

In 1943 Commander Travis, now the head of BP, having replaced Denniston, moved Gordon away from Hut 6 to be his assistant director for mechanisation. In this new capacity, one of his jobs was to carry on the Anglo-American technological liaison on Enigma and other problems which had been initiated by Alan Turing and Commander Denniston. This involved a visit to America in February 1944 on the *Queen Mary*. Gordon met many of the technical staff of the United States army and navy departments.

After the war, instead of returning to the academic world at Cambridge, Gordon was persuaded to become director of research at the John Lewis Partnership. But in

1948 he moved to the United States of America, to a post in the Mitre Corporation, where his work involved the development of secure communication systems for the United States forces. He became an American citizen in 1962 and remained there until his death in his eightieth year in 1985, at Newburyport, Massachusetts.

Gordon married Katharine Hodgson, a professional musician, the daughter of a captain in the Indian army, in 1937. They had one son and two daughters. After their divorce in 1959, he married Fannie Hillsmith, an artist. This marriage also ended in divorce. In 1972 he married his third wife, Elisabeth, a physiotherapist, the daughter of Wilhelm Huber, a Bavarian saw-mill owner and his wife, Myrtle Hussey, who was Gordon's second cousin.

FREDERICK W. WINTERBOTHAM (1897-1990)

Frederick Winterbotham published his book, *The Ultra Secret* in 1974; it was the first book which broadcast the secrets of Bletchley Park to the world, although, as I have told in another chapter, some of the secrets had already been revealed in the post-war years.

Frederick William Winterbotham was born in 1897 at Stroud in Gloucestershire, the only son and younger child of a wealthy solicitor, Frederic Winterbotham and his wife Florence Vernon Graham. His education began at a prep school in Eastbourne, after which he transferred to Charterhouse, one of the public schools of England.

At fourteen years old Fred was over six feet tall and still growing. At sixteen, in 1913, he contracted measles, followed by German measles. The doctor advised a long sea voyage to recover his strength. Fred set off on his own, no doubt fortified by funds from his father, on an adventure which carried him round the world, via Canada, Japan, Australia and New Zealand.

Back at Charterhouse he was already thinking about a degree course at Cambridge when the Great War began. Fred, who had already served in the school's Officer Training Corps (OTC), volunteered immediately, joining the Royal Gloucestershire Hussars. Training in England followed for more than a year, but in 1916, Fred, who had met an officer in the Royal Flying Corps, was persuaded to transfer to that unit. He enjoyed flying and was soon qualified and in France, engaging the enemy. But the following year he was shot down during an aerial dogfight over Passchendaele, and reported killed in action. Fred survived the crash with a broken nose and spent the rest of the war in a German prison camp. After the war he read his own obituary in a local newspaper. 'I never realised what a fine fellow I was', he wrote.

Finally released into civilian life, Fred studied law at Christchurch, Oxford, reading for the short degree course for ex-service men. It was in 1921, during his student days at Oxford that he met and married Erica Horniman, the daughter of F. J. Horniman, the tea merchant and member of Parliament who founded the Horniman Museum. Erica's father had left her a lot of money, so after a short period in his father's practice, which he did not enjoy, they decided to try their hand at farming in the Cotswolds.

During this period they had a son and two daughters. But Fred was restless and, leaving his wife and small children, went to Africa, hoping to find that farming in Rhodesia would be more profitable than in the Cotswolds. He returned disillusioned. Fred was now looking for a different way of earning a living.

Hearing of his plight, an old girlfriend talked about him to another friend in the Air Ministry, mentioning that Fred was seeking employment. An interview with Archie Boyle, head of the air intelligence section of the Air staff, followed. After more searching interrogations, Fred was asked, in his own words, ' to start up and operate an organisation in the Secret Intelligence Service (SIS) for the Royal Air Force, alongside those already in existence for the Navy and Army'. Ten crowded years followed, ending with the outbreak of World War II. Fred's particular job was to discover everything he could about the German Air Force, which had been increasing in size, in spite of the restrictions imposed after the Great War. To this end he travelled often to Germany 'on holiday', posing as an enthusiast for the Nazi regime, and, as an old flying officer from the Great War, became friendly with senior officials of the Luftwaffe. Although he knew some German, picked up during his time as a prisoner of war, Fred pretended not to know the language, so that his Nazi friends either had to speak English or rely on an interpreter. He soon found that Hitler had no wish to fight England, and that his main objective was to invade and defeat the Soviet Union. A meeting with Hitler himself convinced him of the Führer's hatred of Communism and of his determination to destroy it. Fred's reports were at first disbelieved by his superiors, but gradually some of them began to take notice.

From the beginning of World War II Fred became involved with Bletchley Park and the breaking of the German Enigma machine ciphers. To quote his own words in a letter to The Times Literary Supplement on 25 June, 1976 :

Although I was, for the purposes of 'cover', entered as a liaison officer in the Air Ministry list, I was, in fact, head of the Royal Air Force section of MI6 from 1935-1945; and when Ultra was first broken, I was given the job, by the Chief of MI6, of recruiting and training the personnel and setting up an inter-service unit at Bletchley for the translation, selection and distribution of Ultra signals to the Joint Intelligence Committee (JIC), chiefs of staff and to the commanders in the field. I was also made personally responsible for the selection and supply of important signals to the Prime Minister...

His Special Liaison Units (SLU) were attached to all commanders in the field, including the Americans. One of his tasks was the indoctrination of the British and American commanders before they were allowed to receive Ultra messages.

After the war Fred worked for the British Overseas Aircraft Corporation (BOAC) for several years until he finally retired to a farm he had bought in Devon. There he began writing his book *The Ultra Secret* , which was published in 1974. Although he was criticised for revealing wartime secrets, Fred had in fact been in touch with Admiral Denny, the head of the D-notice committee at the Ministry of Defence, who had approved publication.. The book was published in America in 1974 and in England later the same year. It was a bestseller and the royalties enabled him to give up the Devon farm and move to Kelloways Mill, an idyllic home in Dorset, with his third wife Petrea, whom he had married in 1947, after a second wartime marriage which ended in 1946. His first marriage, to Erica Horniman, had ended in divorce in 1939. Petrea died in 1986 and the following year Fred married Kathleen Price, an old friend who was now a widow.

Fred died in his ninety-third year on the 28th January 1990 at his cottage in Dorset, near Blandford. His last book, *The Ultra Spy,* an engaging autobiography, was published by Macmillan in 1989, the year before his death.

CHARLES WYNN-WILLIAMS (1903-1979)

Charles Eryl Wynn-Williams was one of that talented group of scientists who brought Colossus into this world, enabling the cryptographers to decrypt the Lorenz cipher used by Hitler and his generals for transmitting high-grade secret messages.

Charles was born in Wales in 1903, the son of a physics teacher and school inspector, and his wife Nell Wynn, the daughter of a shopkeeper of Llanrwst. Educated at Wrexham during the Great War and at the University College of North Wales at Bangor, Charles graduated in 1923. It was during his university days that he adopted the surname Wynn-Williams. The award of an open fellowship took him to Trinity College, Cambridge, where he was supervised by Sir Ernest Rutherford. His interest in wireless technology led him to research in electronic instrumentation for use in nuclear and radioactive physics. During the 1930s, the devices he constructed, according to the ODNB:

...opened up new avenues of research in nuclear physics and were widely copied (often with readily given advice from Wynn-Williams himself) in laboratories in Europe and the United States.

From his post as assistant lecturer in physics at Imperial College, London, where he had gone in 1935, Charles was seconded to Bletchley Park. There he joined the team of post office engineers who were developing the bombes used for decrypting the Enigma cipher messages; they were also working on the forerunner of Colossus, known as 'Heath Robinson', after the humorous drawings of the artist of that name. Later he worked on Colossus, which had been designed by Turing and colleagues.

Charles returned to Imperial College after the war, where he was appointed Reader in physics. He had married a school-teacher Annie Eiluned James in 1943. They had two sons. After his retirement in 1970, Charles returned to Wales, dying there nine years later at his home at Borth, Cardiganshire.

BLETCHLEY PARK
Traffic flow from interception to action

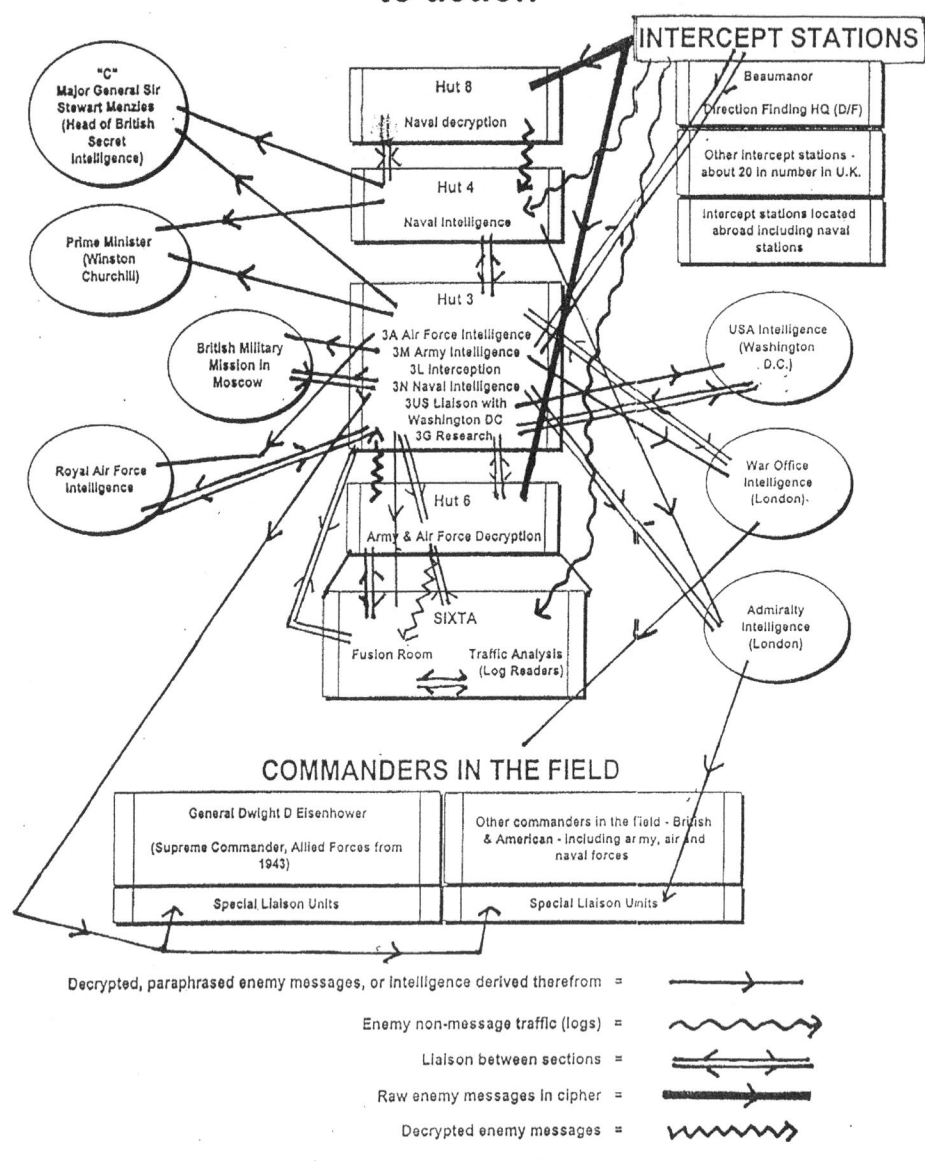

ENIGMA AND FISH CIPHERS

188

INDEX

Abbreviations 11-12
Ablutions 94
Abwehr 157 180
  records 64
  use of Enigma 64 165
Accoce, P. & Quet, P.
  The Lucy Ring (1962) 62
  description of book 83
Aid to Russia Fund 96
Aitken, Dr A.C. 117
  Gallipoli to the Somme (1963) 117
  professor at Edinburgh 118
Alan, A.J. *pseud.*
  Great War interception 146
  Good Evening, Everyone! (1928) 146
Alexander, Hugh
  head of Hut 8 118-119
  letter to Churchill 118
Americans
  at BP 94-95
Atlantic ocean
  torpedoed in 110

Babbage, Charles 119
Babbage, Dennis 119-120
  at Cambridge 119
'Baron'
  supposed agent at BP 68
Bax, Lt Rodney 20
Beaumanor 20
Beckingham, Charles 120-122
Bell, Muriel 100
Bennett, Ralph 122-123
Bertrand, Gustave
  delivers Polish Enigma replica 66
  Enigma (1973) 66
Bickerstaffe, Lt 79-81
Billets, civilian 39-40
Biographies 113-115
  difficulty of writing 114
Birch, Frank 123-124
Bird book 48
Blackout 96
Bletchley Park
  achievements 90
  bombs 55
  compared with beehive 9
  biographies 113
  cafeteria 21-22
  description of community 25
  flow chart 188
  Home Guard on roof 107
  libraries at 25
  poem about 69
  poets at 69-76
  secrets revealed 61
  transport 24
Blunt, Anthony 56
  passed intelligence to USSR 68
  stripped of knighthood 68
Bolitho, Squadron-Leader Hector 29
Bombes 133-134
  Welchman's contribution 183
Bono, Dr Edward de
  Lateral thinking 52
British Military Mission (Moscow) 67
Bureau Ha 86
Burgess, Guy 68

"C", see Menzies, Sir Stewart
Cafeteria 22-23
Cairncross, John 56
  passed intelligence to USSR 67
  worked at BP 68
Callsigns 48
Calvocoressi, Peter 95, 159
Central Party 20 49 52
  move to BP 21
  Welchman on 90
Churchill, Clementine
  Aid to Russia Fund 96-97
Churchill, Winston 13 61
  receives letter from BP 154
Clarke, Joan 125-127
  and Turing 126
Clarke, William F. 124-125
Clayton, Aileen
  visits BP 127
  The Enemy is Listening (1988) 41

Coffee
  on night shift 109
Colossus 134
Convoys 110
Co-op shop
  at Bletchley 96
Cooper, Joshua 127-128
  eccentricities 128
  Four Russian Plays (1972) 128
Corrin, Captain 15-17
Crankshaw, Edward 129-130
  views on Lucy Ring 85
  in Moscow 129

D/F see Direction Finding
Dacre, Lord
  The Philby Affair (1968) 63
Dansey, Claude 86

Davies, Jean F. 57
  marries Gordon Wallwork 59
Deacon, Richard *pseud* 64
Denniston, Alexander 130-132
  head of GC&CS 130
  service at 40 OB 130
  leaves BP 131
Direction Finding 41 43 44
Dresden 159
Dunderdale, Wilfred 132-133
  brings Polish Enigma replica 133

Edwards, Freddie
  friendship with Websters 31
  lateral thinking 52
  recruited 30-31
Enigma machine 64 135

Farago, Ladislas
  The Game of the Foxes (1971) 64
  on Abwehr records 64
FSP see Field Security Personnel
Field Security Personnel 17
  training at Winchester 33
  rejected soldiers 34
Fillingham, Colonel 79
  his gimlet eye 79
  retinue 79
  stickler for saluting 80
Fire picket 98
Firnberg, Major 44
Fish traffic 168

Flowers, Thomas H. ('Tommy') 133-134
  contribution to Colossus 134
  experience at Dollis Hill 133
Foote, Alexander
  and Muggeridge 84
  Handbook for Spies (1949) 85
  radio transmitter to Moscow 84
Fortitude South 43
Foss, Hugh 134-135
  early days at GC&CS 134
  employed by GCHQ 135
  fluent in Japanese 135
Friedman, Colonel William F. and wife
  construction of Purple replica 62
  greatest feat of cryptanalysis 66
Fusion Room 51-53

GC&CS, see Government Code and Cipher School
Geheimschreiber 44-45
Golombek, Harry 135-137
  work in Hut 8 136
  Encyclopedia of Chess (1971) 136
Government Code and Cipher School
  formation 127
  move to BP 26
Grey, Nigel de 137-138
  deputy director GCHQ 138

  service in 40 OB 137

Hall, Bunty 23
Hall, Philip 138-139
  Cambridge mathematician 139
  Italian and Japanese ciphers 139
Hasek, Jaroslav 95
  Schweik in the camp 77
  The Good Soldier Schweik (1929) 77
Hewett, Joyce, see Peasegood, Joyce
Hinsley, Francis H. 140-141
  liaison with Admiralty 140
  on the Lucy Ring 85
  pitchforked into BP 140
  British Intelligence in the Second World War (1975-1990) 141
Hitchhiking 99
Home Guard
  BP's own Home Guard 107
Hooper, Leonard J. 141-142
  director of GCHQ 142
  Italian and Japanese ciphers 142
Huts, The 23
Hyrons, Mrs Jean see Seabury, Jean
Hyrons, James
  RN bunting tosser 37

Intelligence Corps 14
Intercept operators 41
Intercept stations 41 188
Interception 41-45
  French and Russian logs 89

Japanese ciphers
  Decryption at BP 32
  Japanese language 100
  Course at Bedford 32
Japanese National Anthem 100
Jones, Mr & Mrs and family 39-40
Jones, Eric M. 143-144
  Director of GCHQ 144
  head of Hut 3 143
Jones, R.V. 128

Kahn, David
  revealed location of BP 65
  The Codebreakers (1968) 65
  Seizing the Enigma (1992) 114
Knowles, Sgt M.C.
  poem about the camp 78
Knox, Dillwyn ('Dilly') 144-145
  interwar at GC&CS 144
  joined 40 OB 144
  Italian naval cipher 145
  work on Abwehr cipher 145
Kursk, Battle of 56

Lake, the 101
Lambert, Leslie see Alan, A. J. *pseud.*
Lateral thinking 52 161

190

Libraries
  at BP 25
  at the camp 80
Lili Marleen
  sung in German 102
Liverpool
  blitz, May 1941 14
Loehnis, Clive 147-148
  at Admiralty 147
  at sea in RN 147
  Director, GCHQ 148
  liaison with BP 147
Log reading
  introduction to 20
  refusal to read allied logs 89
  the job 47
Lorenz machine, see Fish traffic
Lucas, F.L.
  career at Cambridge 75
  experience in Great War 75
  visit by American 95
  work at BP 75
Lucy, see Roessler, Rudolf
Lucy Ring 83-88
  activities 83
  Muggeridge on 84

McCormick, Donald, see Deacon, Richard *pseud*.
Maclean, Donald
  passed intelligence to USSR 68
McVittie, George C. 148-150
  astronomy at Illinois 149
  Meteorological section at BP 149
  U-boat Enigma 149
Mansion, The
  coffee in 23
  Home Guard on roof 107
  shower in 94
Menzies, Sir Stewart G. 63 150-153
  appointed 'C' in 1939 152
  overall supervision 150
  congratulates BP staff 91
  served in Great War 151
MI8 20
Milner-Barry, Stuart 153-155
  head of Hut 6 155
  visit to 10 Downing Street 154
Moore, Len
  Z17 (1996) 42
Muggeridge, Malcolm
  revealed BP secrets 62-63

Newman, Maxwell 155-156
  served in Great War 155
  work on Lorenz cipher 155
Newte, Corporal 20 97
Nosey Parker
  history of publication 105
Nye, Lt-General A.E.
  visit to BP 103

OKW
  at Bendlerstrasse, Berlin 87
  Ruland works at 87
Olla podrida 93
  meal in Madrid 93
Osborn, 'Bobbie'
  poem about BP 69-70
Owen, Iris M
  So many Lives (2000) 42

Page, Denys L. 156-158
  work on Abwehr ciphers 157
Parlow, Corporal
  in Shakespearean parody 103
Parrish, T.
  The Ultra Americans (1986) 95
Peasegood, Joyce
  recruited 34
  Foreign office pay 35
Peters, George
  recruited 32
Philby, Harold ('Kim')
  passed intelligence to USSR 68
  revealed secrets 65
  My Silent War (1968) 65
Plant, Eric
  arrives at BP 20
  returns to depot 90
Poets at BP 69-76
Polish cryptologists
  contribution to breaking of Enigma 64 133
Prince, F.T. 73-75
  Italian ciphers 73
  pre-war poetry 73
  marries Elizabeth Bush 73
  Poems (1938) 73
Purple cipher machine 62 64

Q-code 47

Radio Security Service 45
Recruitment to BP 27-37
Red Army 49
Reed, A. and Fisher, D.
  Operation Lucy (1981) 85
Reed, Henry
  Japanese section 72
  poem: *Naming of Parts* 72-73
  service before BP 73
  A Map of Verona (1946) 73
Rhys, Morfudd
  translates Spanish 101
Rigold, Stuart E. 81
Robinson, Joyce 58
Roessler, Rudolf ('Lucy')
  activities in Lucerne 83
  anti-Nazi 83
Rose, Eliot J.B. ('Jim') 158-160
  head of Hut 3A 158
  in RAF 158
  tried to stop Dresden raid 159

Rote Drei, Die, see Lucy Ring
Royal Artillery (Maritime Regiment) 13
Ruland, Bernd
  witnesses spying at OKW 87
  Die Augen Moskaus (1973) 87
Rushworth, Edward 160-162
  lateral thinking 161
  marries Joyce Robinson 161
  transfer to Intelligence Corps 160
  member of TICOM 161
Rushworth, Mrs Joyce, see Robinson, Joyce

Schweik, The good soldier 95
  ghost of, in the camp 77
Seabury, Jean 36
Security 55
  lack of 107
  slogans 55
Shakespeare, William
  at BP 96-97
  foresees work at BP 97
Shenley Road Military Camp 77-81
  ablutions 93
  fire at 98
  heating in huts 108
  opened 77
  poem about 78
Shift system 108-109
Sigint 41
Sinclair, Hugh F. P. 162-163
  bought BP 162
  designated 'C' 163
  Director of Naval Intelligence 163
  head of GC&CS 163
SIXTA 52
Smoking 109
Special Liaison Units 63 186
Stalin 96
Stalingrad 96
Stephenson, Major 15
Strachey, Oliver 164-165
  Great War codebreaker 164
  work at GC&CS 164
Sugar, Alfred 9
  fire in camp 98
  died age 100 106
  training at Winchester 34-35
  The Nosey Parker 105
Switzerland
  Bureau Ha 86
  hotbed of spies 86

Taunt, Derek 165-167
  in Hut 6 166
  work in Qwatch 166
Tester, Ralph P. 167-168
  Head of Testery 168
  Lorenz cipher 168
Thirsk, Mrs Joan, see Watkins, Joan
Thirsk, James Wood ('Jimmy')
  interviews in London 17
  transfer to Intelligence Corps 19

  redundant at BP 90
  field security in Germany 90
Thomas, Edward 168-170
  joined RNVR 168
  work in Hut 4 169
Three Js 57
TICOM 161 168
Tiltman, John H. 170-172
  Japanese course, Bedford 171
  Great War service 170
  recruiting in Oxford 32
  veteran codebreaker 171
Traffic analysis, see Log reading
Transport 24 96
Travis, Edward 172-173
  Head of BP 172
  Director of GCHQ 173
Trevor-Roper, Hugh see Lord Dacre
Turing, Alan M. 173-177
Tutte, William 178-179
Twinn, Peter 179-180

U-Boats 110

V2
  incident in London 111
Vlasto, Alexis 180-182

Wallace, Helen
  foreword by 5
Wallwork, Mrs Jean, see Davies, Jean
Watkins, Joan 57
  on women at BP 114
  on Edward Rushworth 160
  return to university 90
Watkins, Vernon
  career before BP 70
  death in Seattle 71
  his books 70
  married Gwen Davies 71
Webster, Neil
  recruited 28
  lateral thinking 52
Welchman, Gordon 182-184
  value of Central Party 90
Winterbotham, Frederick W 9 184-186
  assists 'C' 63
  special liaison units 63
  The Ultra Secret (1974) 61
  Secret and Personal (1969) 63
Wynn-Williams, Charles 186-187